# PROCESS PHILOSOPHY
## AND
# POLITICAL IDEOLOGY

# PROCESS PHILOSOPHY
# AND
# POLITICAL IDEOLOGY

## The Social and Political Thought of
## Alfred North Whitehead and Charles Hartshorne

## RANDALL C. MORRIS

STATE UNIVERSITY OF NEW YORK PRESS

Published by
State University of New York Press, Albany

For information, address State University of New York
Press, State University Plaza, Albany, N.Y., 12246

Library of Congress Cataloging in Publication Data
Morris, Randall C., 1955–
    Process philosophy and political ideology: the social and
political thought of Alfred North Whitehead and Charles Hartshorne/
Randall C. Morris.
        p.    cm.
    Includes bibliographical references.
    ISBN 0-7914-0415-3. —ISBN 0-7914-0416-1 (pbk.)
    1. Process philosophy. 2. Political science. 3. Whitehead,
Alfred North, 1861–1947—Political and social views. 4. Hartshorne,
Charles, 1897-      —Political and social views. I. Title.
BD372.M67 1990
320.01—dc20                                                    89-49229
                                                                    CIP

10 9 8 7 6 5 4 3 2 1

*To Linda*

# Contents

# Acknowledgments

I am pleased to take this opportunity to express my gratitude to those many people who have helped to make the present volume possible. Most of the research that went into the writing of this book was undertaken while a graduate student at Oxford University. For his constant support and excellent supervision during those years, and for his continuing friendship since then, I am particularly grateful to Dr. Paul S. Fiddes, now Principal of Regent's Park College. I would also like to thank Professor John Cobb for encouraging me to pursue my interests in process thought and political theory, as well as for reading a draft of the manuscript. Although on occasion I criticize aspects of his work, the extent of my indebtedness to Professor Cobb far exceeds our points of difference. My friends and colleagues, Professor Pete Gunter and Professor Spencer Wertz, also deserve special mention for both reading portions of the manuscript and for patiently discussing with me many of the issues addressed in this volume. Their many valuable comments have certainly resulted in an improved manuscript. Of course, the final outcome of the book is my own responsibility, and whatever flaws remain are mine. Lastly, I wish to express my deepest appreciation to Linda for her unfailing support throughout the many, and oftentimes seemingly endless, years during which this work was in process. Without her assistance its completion would never have been possible.

Grateful acknowledgment is also made to the following publishers for permission to use the material listed:

*Process and Reality* by Alfred North Whitehead. Corrected Edition. Edited by David Ray Griffin and Donald W. Sherburne. Copyright 1978 by The Free Press, a Division of Macmillan

# Abbreviations

AI     Alfred North Whitehead, *Adventures of Ideas*. New York: Macmillan, 1933.

BH     Charles Hartshorne, *Beyond Humanism: Essays in the Philosophy of Nature*. Gloucester, Mass.: Peter Smith, 1975 (1937).

CAP     Charles Hartshorne, *Creativity and American Philosophy*. Albany: State University of New York Press, 1984.

CN     Alfred North Whitehead, *The Concept of Nature*. Cambridge: Cambridge University Press, 1964 (1920).

CSPM     Charles Hartshorne, *Creative Synthesis and Philosophic Method*. London: SCM Press, 1970.

D     Lucien Price, *Dialogues of Alfred North Whitehead*. London: Max Reinhardt, 1954.

DR     Charles Hartshorne, *The Divine Relativity: A Social Conception of God*. New Haven: Yale University Press, 1948.

ESP     Alfred North Whitehead, *Essays in Science and Philosophy*. New York: Philosophical Library, 1948.

FR     Alfred North Whitehead, *The Function of Reason*. Princeton: Princeton University Press, 1929.

IOGT     Charles Hartshorne, *Insights and Oversights of Great Thinkers: An Evaluation of Western Philosophy*. Albany: State University of New York Press, 1983.

LEW    Alfred North Whitehead, "Extract from the Speech of A. N. Whitehead, Esq., Sc.D., at the Annual Meeting of the Cambridge Women's Suffrage Association, Nov. 5, 1906." Reprinted as "Liberty and the Enfranchisement of Women," *Process Studies, 1977.*

LP    Charles Hartshorne, *The Logic of Perfection.* La Salle, Ill.: Open Court Publishing Company, 1962.

MT    Alfred North Whitehead, *Modes of Thought.* New York: Macmillan, 1938.

MVG    Charles Hartshorne, *Man's Vision of God and the Logic of Theism.* New York: Harper and Brothers Publishers, 1941.

NTT    Charles Hartshorne, *A Natural Theology for Our Time.* La Salle, Ill.: Open Court Publishing Company, 1967.

PR    Alfred North Whitehead, *Process and Reality.* Corrected edition. New York: The Free Press, 1978 (1929).

PSG    Charles Hartshorne and William L. Reese, *Philosophers Speak of God.* Chicago: The University of Chicago Press, 1953.

RM    Alfred North Whitehead, *Religion in the Making.* New York: Macmillan, 1926.

RSP    Charles Hartshorne, *Reality as Social Process.* Glencoe, Ill.: The Free Press, 1953.

S    Alfred North Whitehead, *Symbolism: Its Meaning and Effect.* Cambridge: Cambridge University Press, 1928.

SMW    Alfred North Whitehead, *Science and the Modern World.* New York: Macmillan, 2nd ed., 1926.

*part one*

# INTRODUCTION

# 1

## An Introduction:
## Process and Politics

*The true method of discovery is like the flight
of an aeroplane. It starts from the ground of
particular observation; it makes a flight in the
thin air of imaginative generalization; and it
again lands for renewed observation rendered
acute by rational interpretation.*
*Alfred North Whitehead,* Process and Reality

Anyone who follows the fortunes of process philosophy and theology
will be aware of the efforts that are now being made to relate the
metaphysical systems of Whitehead and Hartshorne to contemporary
social and political life. At the same time, one cannot help but be
cognizant of the degree to which this new-found interest in concrete
social issues contrasts with previous process scholarship. Prior to the
mid-seventies process philosophers and theologians, almost without
exception, expended their considerable intellectual resources on the
task of critically reflecting on cosmological and metaphysical questions. Having taken off with Whitehead and Hartshorne they had, to
borrow Whitehead's analogy, enjoyed an extended flight in the thin
air of metaphysical speculation. Although inordinantly delayed, this
flight has finally touched down for a growing number of theologians
and philosophers.

Many explanations for this delayed arrival are possible. David
Hall, one of the earliest philosophers to address contemporary social
problems from a process perspective, referred to the tendency among
philosophers in the present period to "remain content with . . . issues
which are relevant only to the profession itself."[1] The "eager
scholasticism"[2] typical of Whiteheadian scholarship can thus be
viewed as merely symptomatic of this general trend of the academy.
John Cobb, on the other hand, suggests that the neglect of political
theory on the part of theologians stems from the influence of

3

neo-orthodoxy and theological existentialism on the American theological scene, as well as a tendency among process theologians to appropriate the work of Reinhold Niebuhr rather than "develop the implications of the process tradition for social and political theory on an independent basis."[3] No doubt these and many other reasons contributed to the late arrival of process theologians on the political scene. However, having been propelled into action by the absence of significant interpretations of culture or perhaps in response to the challenge of other contemporary theological movements, an increasing body of literature relating process thought and public life is now being published.

Unfortunately, when one examines this literature one becomes acutely aware that a serious study of Whitehead and Hartshorne's *own* social and political thought has been neglected. What one does frequently find has been variously described as an attempt to "construct a unique political response coherent with the metaphysical structure,"[4] or to "develop a normative form of political organization"[5] in a process mode of thought, or in the words of Cobb quoted earlier, to "develop the implications of the process tradition for social and political theory."[6] In addition there are other neo-Whiteheadian scholars who employ process thought simply as an angle from which to approach political issues, rather than seeking to derive proposals "by strict entailment from Whitehead's philosophy."[7] Yet in all of these instances contemporary process scholars have failed to critically analyze Whitehead's and Hartshorne's social and political ideas and to reflect on the implications that those ideas might have for process metaphysics generally and for their own studies in particular.

This neglect is no doubt due in part to the fact that neither thinker produced a systematic political theory. Perhaps this is what Joseph Needham, one of the earliest critics of Whitehead's political thought, was seeking when he lamented: "One looks in vain in Whitehead's writings for some clear lead among the social tendencies of our times."[8] He continued saying that although Whitehead sketches features of economic individualism and its connection with seventeenth-century atomism, his thought remains "too abstract" and fails to "interlock with the concrete realities of political life."[9] In other words, Whitehead himself is being criticized for remaining aloft in a flight of imaginative generalization and not descending again into the concrete realities of life. Yet Whitehead's and Hartshorne's failure, if that indeed is what it is, to write systematic political theories should not blind us to the fact that they did produce a considerable volume of material concerning social and political issues. It just so happens, however, that what explicit comments, analogies, and allusions they do offer are strewn throughout their writings, making it less straightforward than might otherwise be the case to determine their own political commitments.

What follows is a thorough examination of the social and political beliefs of Whitehead and Hartshorne. Until recently, no one attempted this with regard to Hartshorne even in the most limited way.[10] Whitehead, however, has received some attention, perhaps the best known being the work of A. H. Johnson. Incorporated in Johnson's most extensive treatment of Whitehead's theory of civilization one finds brief recitations of the latter's views on social and political philosophy.[11] Although a few pages of critical comments are provided together with a superficial attempt to ground these views in the metaphysics, Johnson's work remains woefully inadequate not only in its methodology, but also in its execution and conclusions. In his immeasurably superior analysis of Whitehead's theory of culture Hall chastises Johnson for concentrating on the less speculative portions of Whitehead's writings and neglecting the "metaphysical underpinnings of these issues."[12] To a point Hall's criticism is well-taken. Unlike Hall, however, I do not disparage the task of providing an "orderly restatement" of Whitehead's social and political views.[13] On the contrary, I maintain that this is a necessary but neglected first level of argument for reasons which will become clear shortly. My fundamental objection to Johnson's work is that like everyone else he too has failed to give Whitehead's views historical context and depth by relating them to the wider social milieu in which and from which they emerged. This has resulted in a naive and uncritical repetition of ideas which remain disconnected not only from one another but from their social context as well. Consequently what we are left with is a partial and rather aseptic reconstruction of Whitehead's personal beliefs.

I believe that a careful exposition of the writings of Whitehead and Hartshorne will enable us to identify and reconstruct in considerable detail their underlying political beliefs. To this end we are guided at least in Whitehead's case by his autobiographical musings. "My political opinions were, and are, on the Liberal side, as against the Conservatives," he asserts. "I am now writing in terms of English party divisions. The Liberal party has now (1941) practically vanished; and in England my vote would be given for the moderate side of the Labour party" (ESP 14). This note is particularly revealing because Whitehead expressly identifies his political opinions as those of the Liberals, and not simply as being "liberal." That is, Whitehead himself relates his opinions to the concrete historical reality of British party political divisions. Moreover, with the demise of the Liberal party as a dominant political force in Britain those Liberals who were pushing for social reforms tended to join the Labour party.[14] R. B. Haldane, for example, a strong advocate of reform and an intimate friend of Whitehead's, left the Liberal party over the issue of educational reform to become the first Labour Lord Chancellor. That Whitehead, a Liberal, would now relate to the moderate wing of the Labour party suggests that he identified himself with the social reforming wing of the Liberal party.

This initial impression that Whitehead should be numbered among the Liberal reformers is supported by several other of his personal reflections, autobiographical details, and historical comments. In later life he reflected that the years from 1880 to 1910 were "[o]ne of the happiest times that I know of in the history of mankind" and that he experienced "a sense of purpose and progress in the world"; yet in the same breath he added that he was also aware that many things needed changing: "[B]ut we intended to change them and had set about doing so" (D 228). Whitehead's involvement in movements of social reform began perhaps as early as 1884 while a student at Cambridge.[15] Following a meeting at the Guildhall concerning the establishment of a settlement of university students among the poor in London, Trinity College, of which Whitehead was a member, organized its own Toynbee Association (named after the Oxford economist and Liberal reformer, Arnold Toynbee). Whitehead supported the reform efforts of Toynbee Hall by serving for more than two years beginning in 1889 as secretary of the General Committee of the Toynbee Association at Cambridge. The aim of Toynbee Hall and other settlements patterned after it was to provide a solution to the social problems of England. Toynbee Hall, according to Andrew Vincent and Raymond Plant,

> stood as an acknowledgement of the claims of all citizens to share in the good things of social life. These good things were culture, knowledge, beauty and cleanliness. In helping to lead and provide people with these good things, the settlements like Toynbee Hall hoped to mitigate class suspicion, to achieve greater social justice and to realize a more cohesive community.[16]

Although the practice of the Hall was at times overtly—and almost always covertly—patronizing, its aim to provide conditions for individual development and its emphasis on education accords well with Whitehead's own sentiments as recorded later in his writings on education.[17]

As a supporter of social reform Whitehead is probably best known for his advocacy of women's suffrage. On at least one occasion he addressed the annual meeting of the Cambridge Women's Suffrage Association, and he acted as chairman of the Cambridge branch of a national Men's League for Women's Suffrage, which was founded in 1907.[18] And it was not only on the issue of the enfranchisement of women that Whitehead found himself advocating a minority cause. While reminiscing at a symposium held in his honor he addressed the "younger members . . . who are of course in revolt against the previous age" and recalled:

> I have been struck with the fact that every cause I have in any way voted for in England has finally reached such triumphs as a cause can reach. I have never, never been at final variance with the bulk of my countrymen. I have sometimes and generally voted in a minority for a few years before the cause has triumphed. Most of my votes have been minority votes, but they have always ended in that final majority which settles the question. And thus I deduce that I can have no claim whatsoever to standing above, or beyond, or in any way outside of my age. I am exactly an ordinary example of the general tone of the Victorian Englishman, merely one of a group. (ESP 88)

Although a product of his age, Whitehead also perceived himself as part of the vanguard who with foresight led the majority in a revolt against the previous age resulting in the transformation of Britain's social and political landscape. In fact, although actively involved in a few issues, Whitehead's actual leadership role appears quite limited; even so, what is significant for our purposes is that he firmly aligned himself with the cause of social reform in his own day.

A successful inquiry into Whitehead's politics must take its cue from his own testimony to have been a "Liberal in revolt against liberalism." Such a description places Whitehead in the maelstrom of Liberal politics during his years at Cambridge and London. Recent investigations into political life and theory in Britain describe the three decades leading up to the First World War as a time of turmoil for the Liberal party.[19] A serious crisis of identity emerged following the passage of interventionist legislation by a Liberal government. Such legislation could not be reconciled with the traditional liberal ideology, which emphasized individual freedom and the principles of laissez faire. Led by men like Cobden, Bright, and Peel, and infused with the economic spirit of the Manchester school, the Liberal party historically arose in opposition to perceived governmental interference in the economic life of the nation. However, within a few decades of its birth it had become clear that the natural harmony of interests and social progress promised by the Manchester radicals were not forthcoming. The situation in 1882 was well described by Arnold Toynbee when he said

> The times are troubled, old political faiths are shaken, and the overwhelming exigencies of the moment leave but small breathing space for statesmen to examine their principles on which they found their practice. The result has been that startling legislative measures, dictated by necessity . . . have been defended by arguments in sharp contradiction to the ancient principles of those who have pressed these arguments into their service. I think this contradiction is undeniable. It is asserted in connexion with the support given by Radicals to recent Acts of Parliament not only by enraged political opponents but by adherents of the Radical and Liberal party who have refused to abandon their allegiance to their former principles. The gravest of these charges brought against Radicals is the charge of socialism; a system which in the past they strained every nerve to oppose.[20]

The consequences stemming from the failure of classical liberalism led many young radicals to support interventionist legislation to the horror of former friend and foe alike. The nature of liberalism itself became the subject of debate and eventually led to the reformulation of liberal ideology along "collectivist"[21] lines by the new liberals toward the end of the century.

Whitehead was neither unaware of nor impassive toward the divisions in the Liberal party. "The important internal division of the political liberals in England was not the prominent one between Radicals and Whigs," he writes. "It was the division between the pure liberals and the modified liberals" (AI 42–43). For Whitehead the distinguishing feature of the modified liberals was their repudiation of the "liberal doctrine of an atomistic society" (AI 43), which was at the heart of the new liberal collectivism. One can sense Whitehead's partiality for the "modified" or new liberals in his denunciation of pure liberalism. Only if one remembers that the "mere doctrines of freedom, individualism, and competition," which were the foundation of classical liberalism, "had produced a resurgence of something very like industrial slavery at the base of society" (AI 42), he asserts, can one understand nineteenth-century industrial politics. Whitehead was well aware that the failure of the pure liberal doctrine led to the introduction of "remedial industrial measures" to which the "great liberal leaders, Cobden, Bright, and even Cladstone, were either opposed, or were notably cold"(AI 42). In passing judgment on the Liberal party to which he belonged Whitehead concluded, with the aid of hindsight:

> Unfortunately for the liberal political party in England, its later leaders, Gladstone, Lord Hartington, Asquith, belonged to the pure liberal faction. If Campbell-Bannerman had been somewhat abler and, what is still more important, if he had lived, political history in England would have been different. As it was, in the last phase, English political liberalism under Asquith's leadership was engaged in direct opposition, or apathy, in respect to every reform which it was the task of a reforming political party to undertake—the Women's movement, Education, Industrial Reorganization. During the seventy years of its greatest triumphs, from 1830 onward, English liberalism was slowly decaying by its failure to acquire a coherent system of practicable ideals. (AI 43)

Although the Liberal party as a whole, being a house divided, was unable to put together a coherent system of practicable ideals, those who sought social reforms did produce a clearly identifiable political theory. As Whitehead was aware, the key feature of modern liberalism was its repudiation of an atomistic theory of the individual and society. While modern liberalism was in Whitehead's day a rather diffuse movement, what its proponents all shared was a common aim to reconcile individuality and sociability through a theory of human nature.[22] It was this that served as the foundation for the liberal reformers' political prescriptions. On the basis of Whitehead's personal reflections I maintain that there is ample justification for assuming that he was committed to the values and beliefs of the new liberals. This commitment is evident as early as his student days in Cambridge and, I shall argue, remained consistent throughout his life.

When we come to Hartshorne, however, his commitments are at once more difficult and easier to ascertain. They are more difficult because he does not expressly identify himself, as did Whitehead, with the activities of a particular political party.[23] Yet despite the absence of personal testimony, Hartshorne's political commitments are easier to identify than Whitehead's because Hartshorne has written more material with the express intention of addressing such issues. To take one example, in a review of Henry Simons's pamphlet *A Positive Program for Laissez Faire: Some Proposals for a Liberal-Economic Policy*, we find Hartshorne asserting very early in his career that "[a]lthough Professor Simons does not say so, I believe it could be shown that religious economics must be liberal economics."[24] This liberal economics, however, is not the negative laissez faire theory of classical liberalism, but one that enables people to compete on more equitable terms and provides for government programs to alleviate the worst effects of competition through tax reform—both key aims of the new liberal theorists. In other articles Hartshorne has also addressed the issues of democracy, equality, freedom, and individualism. An analysis of these writings will, I believe, substantiate my claim that he, like Whitehead, has been committed throughout his life to a modern liberal political ideology.

What follows thus aims to be, at least on one level, a study in the history of ideas; it is an attempt to reconstruct from the available data the political beliefs held by these two process philosophers. I propose to compare and contrast systematically their explicit references to social and political ideas with those advanced by the major modern liberal theorists around the turn of the century. Perhaps it might be objected that certain features of their political views, such as their organicism, could find equally cogent similarities with elements of classical Greek, medieval monarchist, and Marxist political theory as well as with modern liberalism. In other words, many would argue that establishing similarities is insufficient to demonstrate Whitehead's and Hartshorne's commitment to a particular ideology. In reply I would argue that the available personal testimony and biographical evidence supplies us with an adequate warrant for making an initial, in part tentative, identification of their beliefs. What is now required is a rigorous examination of their political comments and allusions. This will enable us to determine whether such an identification can be substantiated in detail. The thrust of my argument is that a strong *cumulative* case can be made for modern liberal theory, which cannot be made equally well for any other position. I endeavor to take the reader on an interpretive journey through the writings of Whitehead and Hartshorne and suggest that the most satisfactory explanation of the entire corpus of material, as opposed to particular isolated portions abstracted from this larger corpus, is that these philosophers were committed to a modern liberal ideology. I maintain that this proposed explanation is both simpler and more fundamental than possible alternative theses concerning their ideological commitments. The following study deals with the history of ideas and not with mathematics; therefore, we should expect a form of demonstration commensurate with this type of inquiry. A claim to have exposed Whitehead's and Hartshorne's ideological commitments can be deemed reasonable to the extent that we are provided with a coherent and unified interpretation of their political beliefs. I suggest that the value of the approach taken here, an approach that attempts to elucidate Whitehead's and Hartshorne's political ideas within the context of their wider social and intellectual environment, is that it reveals a unifying perspective that gives coherence to their scattered and seemingly disparate utterances.

The philosophers and theorists who will figure most prominently in the following exposition of Whitehead's and Hartshorne's writings are John Stuart Mill, Thomas Hill Green, and L. T. Hobhouse. From this list we can observe that very diverse ethical and metaphysical views—utilitarianism, idealism, and realism[25] respectively—have been pressed into service to underpin modern liberal theory. Yet despite this diversity they all share a consensus of beliefs concerning what "individuality" and "sociability" involve, and it is this shared conception of human nature that supplies the foundation for their further arguments for equality, liberty, and democracy.[26] Process philosophy, too, is concerned with a proper understanding of individuality and sociability, and this, not only as a feature of human nature, but of reality as a whole. What is more, an examination of the political ideas of Whitehead and Hartshorne reveals that they also, like the modern liberals, linked their organic theories of reality with a defense of the traditional liberal values of equality, liberty, democracy, and so forth. Process philosophy, in their hands, appears to be one more metaphysical theory by which a modern liberal political theory has been legitimized.

Although a variety of philosophical theories were employed in Britain to underpin modern liberalism, Idealism was particularly important. From about 1880 to roughly 1910 philosophical Idealism enjoyed considerable popularity among intellectuals. It reached its zenith at Oxford under the auspices of such notables as Thomas Hill Green, Edward Caird, F. H. Bradley, Arnold Toynbee, William Wallace, and David Ritchie. Yet while Oxford was the point at which the "Rhine flowed into the Isis,"[27] where British and German ideas met and mingled, the influence of Idealism was not confined to the university; it continued to flow down the Thames to London through its influence on MPs such as Haldane, Asquith, and Herbert Samuel and upon political and economic theorists such as Hobhouse and J. A. Hobson, many of whom were educated at Oxford. What Idealism provided has been aptly described as a "context of political discourse."[28] There is no clear causal relationship or correspondence between Idealism and political theory. Bradley and J. M. E. McTaggart, for example, were both Tories; indeed, McTaggart was apparently a materialist and political radical when he came up to Cambridge and only became a Tory after he discovered Hegel.[29] Bernard Bosanquet, another Oxford Idealist, was a strong critic of the collectivism of the new liberals; and yet, that same collectivism was steadfastly defended by liberal reformers with arguments derived from philosophical Idealism. Thus the connection between politics and Idealism is ambiguous; even so, Collini argues, rightly in my opinion, its reactionary impact was the exception: "English Idealism was a house of many mansions as far as political affiliation was concerned, but if it could be said to have had one overall political influence it would, historically, have to be called a radical one."[30]

What the new liberals found in Idealism was a set of categories that could assist them in their efforts to resurrect a liberal faith which, in Hobhouse's words, "had the air of a creed that is becoming fossilized as an extinct form."[31] Whereas liberalism adhered traditionally to an atomistic social philosophy, a negative theory of freedom, and a conception of the human person as an appropriator and consumer of utilities, the new liberals advanced an organic social philosophy, a positive theory of freedom, and a conception of the human person as an exerter and developer of his or her capacities. Many new liberals believed that this new political paradigm could ally itself with philosophical Idealism in its struggle with the individualist paradigm of classical liberalism. Hobhouse, for example, despite his antagonism to Idealist epistemology as well as his opposition to

Hegelianism's "bed-rock conservativism"[32] as exemplified by Bosanquet, accepted the validity of many Idealist insights, which he freely employed support of his own position. Indeed, Hobhouse perceived his own theory as being a development of many ideas first introduced into the British political arena by Green. In *The Rational Good*, for instance, Hobhouse expressly states that Green's idea of the common good "if pressed and defined, yields point by point the principle of harmony in development."[33] Hobhouse's political theory, like many of the radical liberals, "came to rest upon a recognizably Idealist metaphysics."[34]

The convergence of views that is evident between Idealism and new liberalism is interesting given the question of Whitehead's acquaintance with Hegel's philosophy and with Idealism in general.[35] Some of the leading Liberal reformers—Hobhouse, Haldane, and Toynbee—had a clear grasp of the way in which concepts and arguments derived from Idealism were being utilized to support the new liberal position. This was not true, however, of all the new liberals. "Others took hold of the theories more or less unconsciously as part of the context of discussion," claim Vincent and Plant.[36] Perhaps this might help to explain the Hegelian characteristics evident in Whitehead's later writings. It is common knowledge that Whitehead denied having any "first hand acquaintance" (ESP 88) of Hegel's work; indeed, he claims to have read but a single page of the latter's prodigious writings. Yet embedded within his well-known disclaimer concerning his lack of first-hand knowledge we find a very positive reference to Hegel: "[I]t is true that I was influenced by Hegel. I was an intimate friend of McTaggart almost from the very first day he came to the University, and saw him for a few minutes almost daily, and I had many a chat with Lord Haldane about his Hegelian point of view, and I have read books about Hegel"(ESP 88). Whitehead perceived Hegel's influence as stemming largely from his personal relationships with prominent Hegelians. These friendships began after coming to Cambridge in 1880—just as Idealism was coming into vogue among university philosophers and intellectuals— and would last throughout his life. McTaggart was Cambridge's leading Idealist philosopher and was, with Whitehead, a Fellow at Trinity College; though he was also an extreme Tory, many of Whitehead's other encounters with Idealism appear to have been through friends and movements aimed at social reform. The Toynbee Association, with which he was involved for several years, derived much of its theoretical support from the philosophy of Green. While at Cambridge he also developed an enduring friendship with Goldsworthy Dickenson, an Idealist who was interested in political philosophy and in promoting international peace.[37] And then there was Haldane, in whose house Whitehead claims to have read his single page of Hegel. Lord Haldane was both an eminent British politician and an outspoken new liberal who used Hegelianism as an intellectual foundation for his reform efforts. Indeed, Haldane regarded the architect of the progressive social policy of new liberalism to be none other than Green. When one considers that Whitehead's own thought matured and developed at a time when Idealism attained the peak of its influence on British life—in the universities where he worked, among the intellectual elite who were his friends, and in the movements for social and political reform to which was committed—it is entirely feasible that Whitehead took hold of Hegelian notions, as Vincent and Plant said, ''more or less unconsciously as part of the context of discussion.'' Perhaps we can postulate a ''political heritage'' as well as a ''poetic heritage'' when seeking to understand the influence of Idealism on Whitehead.[38]

Concerning the Hegelian character of Whitehead's work, George Lucas observed that ''the bulk of Whitehead's nonsystematic writings on history, culture and civilization suggest numerous comparisons with the generalized philosophy of culture which may be derived from Hegel's writings. The comparisons which might be advanced on such grounds, however, are easy to suggest but difficult to define or defend with precision.''[39] I suggest that if a connection between Whitehead and modern liberalism can be sustained, however, then given the clear relationship which existed between modern liberalism and Idealism in Britain, we are much better placed to elucidate the comparisons between Whitehead and Hegel on issues of history, culture, and civilization. The comparisons can be defined and defended with precision when one perceives that the similarities between them lie precisely in those areas where modern liberals frequently employed Hegelian concepts and arguments in order to substantiate their political theory. Consequently I would question Lucas' conclusion that ''the more superficial similarities which can be detected at such points proceed . . . as a result of the more basic metaphysical affinities exhibited between Whitehead and Hegel.''[40] On the contrary, perhaps Whitehead's basic affinities with modern liberalism resulted in superficial similarities with Hegelianism, which were in later life incorporated into his metaphysics.

This notion that the Idealist features of Whitehead's philosophy may in part derive from his adherence to a political theory that had freely made use of Hegelian arguments and concepts touches on a very important issue, namely, the relationship between Whitehead's and Hartshorne's political commitments and their metaphysical theories. Lucas's comment that the similarities between Hegel's and Whitehead's views on history and civilization "proceed" from the "more basic" metaphysical affinities exemplifies the penchant among process philosophers and theologians to discount the influence of Whitehead's *Sitz im Leben* on his metaphysical theory. That such an influence might exist, and that it might also have important implications for the present discussion concerning the relevance of process metaphysics to politics, has gone unnoticed. If A. H. Johnson is guilty of neglecting the metaphysical underpinnings of Whitehead's political theory, contemporary process thinkers are equally guilty of neglecting what might be termed the ideological underpinnings of Whitehead's and Hartshorne's metaphysical theories. Typically, Whitehead's and Hartshorne's political beliefs are dismissed as irrelevant or simply ignored by contemporary process thinkers concerned with concrete social issues. Instead, they begin with one or other of the metaphysical systems and then attempt to construct a political theory that coheres with it. By so doing they overlook the fact that these flights of metaphysical speculation, to return again to our original analogy, did not just appear out of thin air but took off from the ground of some particular historical reality. By focusing their attention on abstract metaphysical theories that have been uprooted from their historical contexts, process thinkers have overlooked the sociological conditioning of Whitehead's and Hartshorne's thoughts and with that the possible ideological functioning of their philosophies.

What follows aims to be not merely a careful analysis of Whitehead's and Hartshorne's social and political views; it also intends to provide an ideology-critique of their philosophies. To what degree do the principles of process metaphysics reflect the social locations of its founders? If we take seriously the hermeneutic of suspicion, is there evidence that Whitehead and Hartshorne's philosophical principles legitimate or rationalize the values and interests of modern liberals? Along with a reconstruction of their political commitments I am concerned to suggest ways in which such commitments may have received legitimation through their metaphysical

theories. I am interested, in other words, in determining the ideological significance of process philosophy.

Ideology is, to say the least, an elusive and equivocal concept.[41]
Although both the concept itself and the use of the term antedates
Marx, the wide currency that it now enjoys is largely owing to the
influence of his writings. For Marx ideology is a pejorative term; it is
a form of distorted consciousness, a false representation of reality.
This form of consciousness, however, does not arise arbitrarily; it
results from contradictions that exist in human social life. As Marx
wrote in the preface to *A Critique of Political Economy*, "[t]he mode of
production of material life conditions the social, political, and intellectual life process in general. It is not the consciousness of men that
determines their being, but, on the contrary, their social being that
determines their consciousness."[42] All forms of consciousness are
social products; however, the capitalist mode of production produces
contradictory social relations and, as a consequence, distorted repre-
sentations about them.[43] It is the nature of ideology to conceal social
contradictions and to do so in the interests of the dominant class.

From Lenin onward, however, ideology has also been used as a
positive concept by Marxists and non-Marxists alike. Karl Mannheim,
for example, seeks to supersede Marx by transforming the theory of
ideology into the sociology of knowledge. This transformation is
accomplished when one subjects all points of view to ideological
analysis.

> What was once the intellectual armament of a party is trans-
> formed into a method of research in social and intellectual
> history generally. To begin with, a given social group discovers
> the "situational determination" of its opponents' ideas. Subse-
> quently the recognition of this fact is elaborated into an all-
> inclusive principle according to which the thought of every
> group is seen as arising out of its life conditions. Thus, it
> becomes the task of the sociological history of thought to
> analyse without regard for party biases all the factors in the
> actually existing social situation which may influence thought.[44]

Thus the "thought of all parties in all epochs is of an ideological
character."[45] With Mannheim's general formulation of the total
conception of ideology the term "ideology" loses its deprecatory
connotations and comes to refer impartially to the element of social
determination in all historical thought-systems. Because of the nega-

tive connotations that adhere to the term ideology, Mannheim eventually proposes to avoid its use and to speak instead of the "perspective" of a thinker.[46]

With this transformation in the meaning of ideology the method of ideological investigation also changes. There are two approaches that Mannheim deems proper. The first approach, which is called the nonevaluative approach, "confines itself to discovering the relations between certain mental structures and the life-situations in which they exist." A nonevaluative study of ideology seeks to understand the narrowness and limitations of each point of view by demonstrating the relationship between the given ideology and the life-situation of the thinker. This is done without advancing further judgments as to the validity of the ideas in question. The second method of ideological investigation combines the former nonevaluative approach with an epistemologically oriented approach in an effort to determine "what constitutes reliable knowledge."[47] This leads Mannheim to offer his theory of "relationism." Since there are some "spheres of thought in which it is impossible to conceive of absolute truth existing independently of the values and position of the subject and unrelated to the social context," the task of discriminating between true and false historical knowledge centers on determining "which social standpoint *vis-a-vis* of history offers the best chance for reaching an optimum of truth."[48]

In my discussion of process philosophy and political ideology I will be using the term ideology as a positive rather than as a negative concept. To say of a body of thought that it is ideological is to emphasize two of its features: the *symbolic* and the *functional*.[49] To speak of ideology's symbolic character is to speak of its origin, its representational character.[50] An ideology is, as Mannheim would say, a perspective that reflects social existence; it is a product of its social location. The symbolic feature of ideas, including philosophical ideas, is a characteristic of human thought that Whitehead apparently was well aware of. "The few first-rate philosophic minds," he is reported to have said,

> need to be understood in relation to the times in which they
> lived and thought, and this is precisely what is not done. A
> philosopher of imposing stature doesn't think in a vacuum.
> Even his most abstract ideas are, to some extent, conditioned by
> what is or is not known in the time when he lives. What are the
> social habits around him, what are the emotional responses,

what do people consider important, what are the leading ideas
in religion and statesmanship? (D 225–26)

It is just such a contextual approach, a method of interpretation that
takes seriously the sociology of knowledge, which I will adopt in my
investigation of Whitehead's and Hartshorne's political beliefs.

The second feature of an ideology is that it is functional. As a
system of thought an ideology is not value-free; it is not socially
uncommitted. It is important to ascertain the social ends—typically
the class interests—that are aided and abetted by the cognitive
systems that we construct. An ideology-critique will therefore not
only elucidate the social origins of a given system of thought, but will
also attempt to analyze "how a theory or intellectual trend reflects the
interests, aspirations and characteristics of the social group which is
behind it and through which it finds expression."[51]

When I refer to the modern liberal ideology I am speaking of a
certain perspective on reality. A "more or less systematic set of ideas
about man's place in nature, in society, and in history,[52] that emerged
in Britain during the late nineteenth century and through which the
values and interests of its proponents found expression. It is this
ideology to which I believe Whitehead and Hartshorne were, to
varying degrees, personally committed. What is more, I contend that
this ideological commitment is reflected in their respective philosophies. While the metaphysical principles may not make overt political
recommendations, they have what might be termed an "ideological
significance."[53] The metaphysics supplies through its universal and
ostensibly neutral principles a foundation for a modern liberal ideology. "Despite their apparent abstention from values and norms,"
writes Hans Lenk about ideologies, "they are indeed dependent on
deep-rooted, if not hidden, commitments to values, norms and
evaluations or priorities/preferences. They serve as theoretically
disguised value-orientations."[54]

In saying that Whitehead and Hartshorne were personally
committed to a modern liberal ideology and that their presentation of
process philosophy has a particular ideological significance is not to
imply anything about the truth-value of either the ideology or the
metaphysics. This is because we are not employing the term ideology
as a negative, critical concept to signify the distorted ideas of a false
consciousness. Our interest is in investigating the origins and functions of certain ideas; but, as Williamson points out, "to describe the
origin and function of a belief is not yet to say anything, one way or

the other, about the truth, correctness, or validation of that belief."[55] This study seeks only to bring to consciousness the "theoretically disguised value-orientations" of process metaphysics; it is not, however, through its analysis claiming or even attempting either to negate or to endorse those value-orientations.

In making explicit the ideological significance of Whitehead's and Hartshorne's process philosophies this study further seeks to make a contribution, however slight, to the task of constructing a process political theology. John Cobb has recently summoned process theologians to reflect on the effects that social location has upon their theology. When we fail to recognize that "[w]hat and how we think is a product of who we are" then, he concludes, " . . . our work is likely to be unconsciously ideological, justifying our privileges."[56] However, I contend that process theologians must not only take seriously their own social location, but also the effects that social location had upon the philosophies of Whitehead and Hartshorne which they have appropriated. At this point the writings of Cobb are particularly instructive. Having called for self-criticism on the part of process theologians in the light of social location he goes on to assert that "[t]here is nothing in process categories that is inherently white, North American, or middle class."[57] Without the support of a detailed ideology-critique of Whitehead's and Hartshorne's writings I consider such a claim to be premature. The same hermeneutic of suspicion that Cobb says needs to be taken seriously by process theology[58] needs also to be applied to the works of Hartshorne and Whitehead. As I shall argue in the conclusion, failure to do so could result in an unconscious repetition of what is in effect an inherent ideological bias of the metaphysics.

What I am suggesting is that it is not sufficient for process theologians and philosophers to be critically aware of their own social location; the intellectual tradition in which they operate may itself possess an ideological significance that may be unwittingly inherited unless that tradition is also subjected to an ideology-critique. One purpose of the present study is to provide a critique of process philosophy through an examination of the writings of its founders. Of course, since this study is concerned with the origins of process philosophy one cannot on the basis of its findings alone make generalizations about the ideological significance of the work produced by any given contemporary representative of the tradition. The political thought of such scholars as Robert Neville, David Hall, Delwin Brown, Schubert Ogden, and John Cobb, to mention but a few, as well as their important and provocative contributions made on the topic of process thought and politics, would have to be examined in detail if one were to offer an ideology-critique of their works. This study does not intend to offer such a critique, nor does it intend to circumvent the detailed analysis necessary for that task by assuming that criticisms of Whitehead and Hartshorne necessarily apply to them. What I am providing are resources for an ideology-critique of process theology by bringing to consciousness the ideological genesis of the process tradition.

It is my hope that this study will stimulate philosophers and theologians who are interested in the area of process thought and politics to reflect anew on the issue of ideology. In examining the social and political ideas of Whitehead and Hartshorne and in raising the question of the importance of those ideas for the development of process philosophy, my aim is to point the way toward a neglected but promising field of inquiry. It is my hope that the following arguments will stimulate an interest in others to take up the challenge of such research.

*part two*

# THE METAPHYSICAL SYSTEMS

# 2

# Freedom and Causality
# in Whitehead's Philosophy

This study aims in part to provide an ideology-critique of Whitehead's and Hartshorne's metaphysics. If this goal is to be realized then it will be necessary to demonstrate how their metaphysical principles reflect their personal commitments to the values and norms of the modern liberal political ideology. To appreciate this connection between political ideology and process philosophy it is vital that the reader grasp certain basic principles of process thought. These principles can most easily be understood and most fully appreciated as part of a larger system; therefore, I propose in this and the subsequent chapter to introduce in a systematic fashion the fundamental tenets of Whitehead's and Hartshorne's metaphysics, emphasizing in particular those elements that are important for their social and political thought.[1] Following this introduction to the metaphysics, in Part Three of this study I will undertake the exposition and analysis of their social and political writings, being careful to illustrate how their ideological commitments have acquired support through their metaphysics.

Whitehead's is an atomic theory of actuality according to which the enduring objects that we perceive by our senses are themselves made up of smaller units. Whitehead calls these elementary particles "actual entities" and they are the fundamental building blocks in his cosmology; they are "the final real things of which the world is made up" (PR 18[27]). These atomic units, which are also called actual occasions and occasions of experience, are not static, unchanging subjects of change (PR 29[43]). Rather, an occasion of experience *is* a process: "[T]o be *actual* is to be a process. Anything which is not a process is an abstraction from process, not a full-fledged actuality."[2] Thus, according to Whitehead, "the actual world is a process, and . . . the process is the becoming of actual entities" (PR 22[33]).

Here we must be careful to distinguish between two types of process. First, there is the internal, or microscopic, process of concrescence. Concrescence is the means by which the many components of an actual occasion achieve a complex unity. The environment or "actual world" (PR 65[101]) of each occasion supplies it with data which are subsequently unified by the self-creative subject. When a final unity has been achieved concrescence ends; the occasion of experience has realized its "satisfaction." The satisfaction of the occasion is the "one complex fully determinate feeling which is the completed phase in the process" (PR 26[39]). In addition to the internal process of concrescence there is the external, or macroscopic, process of transition. The temporal process is the transition from "attained actuality to actuality in attainment" (PR 214[326]), that is, it is the process by which the past actual world contributes to the becoming of the present occasion.

These two modes of process correspond in turn to two forms of causation. Concrescence is that process in which the actual occasion "moves towards its final cause" (PR 210[320]). In its concrescence an actual entity is guided by an ideal of its own satisfaction. This is the actual entity's "subjective aim," which it presents to itself as the *telos* of its own self-creative process. It is the subjective aim that enables the actual entity to unify in a novel synthesis those objects given to it by its environment. Hence concrescence concerns the constitution of the individual entity via a teleological process. Transition, on the other hand, is the "vehicle of the efficient cause" which ensures that "the origination of the present [is] in conformity with the 'power' of the past" (PR 210[320]). This process concerns the influence that actual entities have upon one another. Whitehead concludes that "efficient causation expresses the transition from actual entity to actual entity; and final causation expresses the internal process whereby the actual entity becomes itself" (PR 150[228]). Thus, together, concrescence and transition express the full breadth of causality in Whitehead's philosophy of organism. I suggest that it is through an examination of Whitehead's theory of causation that we can best appreciate the importance of the relative concept, freedom, to process philosophy.

# I. TRANSITION: EFFICIENT CAUSATION

For Whitehead, the question of power is the search for a reason. How do we explain why an actual entity is what it is, why it attains the satisfaction that it does? Whitehead clearly specifies two reasons, namely, the environment, or actual world, from which it arises (efficient causation), and the entity's own subjective aim that guides its concrescence (final causation). Both of these reasons proceed from the nature of actual entities. The former reason stems from the objective character of the actual entity as a potential for other occasions of experience. The power of the actual entity, in the sense of its function as an efficient cause, is located in the way that entity's satisfaction can contribute to the becoming of future occasions. The latter reason stems from the subjective character of the actual occasion, its existence as an acting entity. Thus, power is in part to be explained by reference to the ontological principle "no actual entity, then no reason" (PR 19[28]). That which has real existence is that which has the power to affect another, or be affected by another. "[T]he essence of being," Whitehead writes, "is to be implicated in causal action on other beings" (AI 153).

The power of efficient causation concerns the way in which actual entities are objectified in the constitution of a subsequent actual entity. The reason why a particular entity is the way it is can only be comprehended when one understands how it is that an individual occasion includes other individual entities within itself. Whitehead seeks to explain this inclusion by positing a theory of essential relatedness between actual entities. Whitehead is adamant in his belief that "[a]ctuality is through and through togetherness . . . " (SMW 251). This togetherness can be accounted for only by recognizing the reality of internal relations. "Being 'internally related to' means 'making a difference to,' which involves being in some respect 'included' or 'immanent' in the percipient actuality."[3] In *Science and the Modern World* Whitehead expressly states that "internal relatedness is the reason why an event can be found only just where it is and how it is . . . . For each relationship enters into the essence of the event; so that, apart from that relationship, the event would not be itself. This is what is meant by the very notion of internal relations" (SMW 180). The given world of actual entities thus makes an essential difference to the new concrescence; those actualities are immanent in, and hence internally related to, the present actual occasion.[4]

The notion that every occasion of experience is internally related to its social environment is a fundamental axiom of Whitehead's philosophy, one that carries with it a rejection of the substance-quality doctrine of actuality. There are two elements in the traditional doctrine about substance that process philosophy rejects. First, there is the concept of "vacuous actuality" by which Whitehead means the notion that there exists a "substratum with vacuously inherent qualities" (AI 281; see FR 24). The idea that underlying the material objects perceived by sense perception is some stuff or primary substance that is passively informed by certain qualities is rejected both on the grounds that it conflicts with ordinary experience (PR 75[116]) and because it is unacceptable as an ultimate concept in physics (PR 78–79[121–22]). The second element of the traditional doctrine of substance rejected by Whitehead is the notion that actualities exist in complete independence of one another. The substance-quality conception of reality "entirely leaves out of account the interconnections between real things. Each substantial thing is thus conceived as complete in itself, without any reference to any other substantial thing" (AI 169). A substance-quality conception of reality, if it remains consistent, invariably leads to the denial of all internal relations between actualities: "substantial thing cannot call unto substantial thing" (AI 170).

Thus far we have seen that in Whitehead's organic philosophy the notion of substance has been transformed into that of actual entity, and the concept of power has been transformed into the principle that "the reasons for things are always to be found in the composite nature of definite actual entities . . . " (PR 19[28]). An actual entity is not explicable in terms of "stuff" but is a unifying process that includes past actual entities as data. To discover how it is that one actuality can be internally related to, and hence conditioned by, another we must examine Whitehead's theory of prehensions. Prehension is a technical term chosen by Whitehead to refer to the way in which an actual occasion can include, as part of its own essence, other entities without implying either consciousness or representative perception (AI 300). An actual entity is essentially a "concrescence of prehensions" (PR 23[35]); it is "a process of 'feeling' the many data, so as to absorb them into the unity of one individual 'satisfaction' " (PR 40[65]). The basis of experience is thus emotional. There is a transference of feeling from one actual entity to another as a feeling within the object is reproduced in the new subject.

There are two basic types of prehensions: physical and conceptual.[5] When the datum of the prehension is an actual entity the feeling is termed physical; when the datum is an eternal object the prehension is called a conceptual feeling. An eternal object is a "pure potential" by which Whitehead means an entity "whose conceptual recognition does not involve a necessary reference to any definite actual entities of the temporal world . . . ."[6] Unlike actual entities, which are temporal, determinate, and concrete, eternal objects are timeless, indeterminate, and abstract.[7]

Eternal objects are frequently equated by Whitehead with the platonic forms (PR 43–44[69–70], 46[73]). However, unlike Plato's Ideas, eternal objects are neither fully real nor do they exist in a separate realm.[8] According to the ontological principle, everything, including the general potentiality of the universe, must be somewhere, that is, some actual entity, and this "somewhere" is the "primordial nature" of God.[9] The primordial nature of God is the nontemporal envisagement of all eternal objects whereby they achieve an order and a relevance to the actual world. In other words, in God's primordial nature the eternal objects are conceptually prehended and ordered so that they become relevant to the creative process. "This ideal realization of potentialities in a primordial actual entity," writes Whitehead,

> constitutes the metaphysical stability whereby the actual process exemplifies general principles of metaphysics, and attains the ends proper to specific types of emergent order. By reason of the actuality of this primordial valuation of pure potentials, each eternal object has a definite, effective relevance to each concrescent process. (PR 40[64])

We now possess the most important ingredients of Whitehead's theory of efficient causation. Whitehead's is a social or organic theory of reality according to which each new individual is conditioned by its environment. Efficient causation is the means by which the environment exerts its power over the subject. Each new occasion of experience is initially constituted by its prehensions of the world. In the process of transition between actual entities there is a "flow of feeling" (PR 237[362–63]) whereby one of the component feelings of the unified satisfaction of the preceding actual entity is reproduced by those subsequent occasions of experience that prehend it. In this way there is always an initial conformation of feeling in the primary phase of concrescence; the new subject's physical feelings reproduce or reenact the feeling that the previous entity, the efficient cause, passes on to it. Thus, for Whitehead, the "primary phase of simple physical feelings constitutes the machinery by reason of which the creativity transcends the world already actual, and yet remains conditioned by that actual world in its new impersonation" (PR 237[363]).

A partial answer to the question of power, therefore, is the actual world as given to the percipient occasion. The actual entities that have perished are held to provide the "reason" for efficient causation because every actual entity *must* enter into the concrescence of a subsequent subject through some simple causal feeling. In the prehension of these past entities there is a necessary conformation of feeling thereby conditioning the freedom of the new subject. Causal efficacy, as described by Whitehead, is "the hand of the settled past in the formation of the present" (S 59). Each actual entity, having reached satisfaction, contributes a determinate condition to the future.

Whitehead's doctrine of efficient causation provides us not only with a partial answer to the question of power, but also with a partial answer to the question of freedom. The essential interrelatedness of actual entities and the doctrine of initial conformation of feelings entails a repudiation of the notion of "absolute" or "abstract" freedom. Whitehead explicitly states that "there is no such fact as absolute freedom; every actual entity possesses only such freedom as is inherent in the primary phase 'given' by its standpoint of relativity to its actual universe. Freedom, givenness, potentiality, are notions which presuppose each other and limit each other" (PR 133[202]).

Freedom is always within limits and those limits are set by the antecedent entities making up the subject's actual world. Concerning the implications of the social nature of the actual occasion he writes:

> First, the outlines of its own character are determined by the data which its environment provides for its process of feeling. Secondly, these data are not extrinsic to the entity; they constitute that display of the universe which is inherent in the entity. Thus the data upon which the subject passes judgment are themselves components conditioning the character of the judging subject. It follows that any general presupposition as to the character of the experiencing subject also implies a general presupposition as to the social environment providing the display for that subject. In other words, a

species of subject requires a species of data as its preliminary phase of concrescence. (PR 203[309])

The past actual world of an occasion of experience limits that occasion's freedom for self-realization. In as much as the actual entities comprising an occasion's actual world must be physically prehended, and since there are a limited number of potential ways of synthesizing this data, the real potentiality of the present subject, the scope within which it can exercise its freedom is settled for it (see PR 220[336]). Whitehead writes,

> The character of an actual entity is finally governed by its datum; whatever be the freedom of feeling arising in the concrescence, there can be no transgression of the limitations of capacity inherent in the datum. The datum both limits and supplies. It follows from this doctrine that the character of an organism depends on that of its environment (PR 110[168]).

A person's character is not wholly of his or her own making; there is no absolute freedom in this sense. On the contrary, perception in the mode of causal efficacy is the "given uncontrolled basis upon which our character weaves itself" (PR 178[271]). The significance of this for social theory is clear: "[I]f we want to be a certain type of person, or persons with certain types of experiences," states Russell Kleinbach, "this will require a certain type of social environment to be the relevant past environment of those experiences."[10]

Simple physical feelings are Whitehead's mechanism of efficient causation whereby the past conditions the present. However this remains an incomplete analysis of both power and freedom in Whitehead's process philosophy. True it excludes absolute freedom as a possible understanding of the essence of freedom; but it does nothing to exclude determinism as a possible understanding of causation. Consequently, if Whitehead had nothing more to say about power and freedom than what we have outlined above, *his theory of reality would be compatible with a purely negative conception of political freedom like that adopted by Thomas Hobbes*. According to the mechanistic materialism of Hobbes, freedom consists in the absence of impediments to the enactment of one's will; however, the activity that is willed is not itself free but determined. As D. D. Raphael points out in his discussion of Hobbes, "To say that a man is free to do what he chooses is not to say that he is free to choose."[11] To understand how Whitehead's theory of reality excludes determinism, and thereby supports a theory of political freedom different from that of Hobbes, we must turn to his theory of final causation.

## II. CONCRESCENCE: FINAL CAUSATION

Our examination of power in the form of causal efficacy led to an emphasis on the primary phase of concrescence. This is the conformal phase, dominated by simple physical feelings. The multitude of initial feelings that arise in this phase now need to be unified in a determinate satisfaction. How is this to be accomplished? According to Whitehead, "[t]he concrescence of each individual actual entity is internally determined and is externally free" (PR 27[41]). By this he means that although the decision of the whole arises out of the determination of the parts, there is always a remainder to be decided by the subject itself (PR 27–28[41]). The synthesis is not determined by the data.

The process by which an occasion moves from its initial stage of conformation to its final satisfaction is made possible by the occasion's mental pole: "self-determination is always imaginative in its origin" (PR 245[374]). Hence while the occasion "arises as an effect facing its past," ultimately, owing to the functioning of the mental pole, it " . . . ends as a cause facing its future. In between there lies the teleology of the Universe" (AI 249). It is the mental pole that introduces the subject as "a determinant of its own concrescence" (PR 248[380]). The determinate bond that an occasion of experience has with each element in its actual world conditions that occasion. However, that conditioning is not complete; the past does not determine the satisfaction of the new subject. With regard to the second element of its character, its mental pole, the occasion is *causa sui* by which Whitehead means that "the process of concrescence is its own reason for the decision in respect to the qualitative clothing of feelings" (PR 88[135]). This claim is based on the ontological principle. The reason for efficient causation is the past actual world; the reason for final causation is the present concrescent subject. "[T]he causal antecedents of an entity are *necessary* to explain its concrescence, but not *sufficient* to determine the outcome of its synthesis."[12] Because the causal antecedents always leave room for individual decision, each actual entity is itself finally responsible for what it becomes. It is this ability to create oneself in accordance with an ideal given to oneself that is the essence of freedom. "The freedom inherent in the universe is constituted by this element of self-causation" (PR 88[135]). Thus freedom is itself a form of power; final causation is the freedom of self-determination, the power to create oneself. It is by reason of this freedom that all actual entities share with God the characteristic of transcendence. Every actual entity transcends all other actual entities, including God (PR 222[339]).

The process of self-creativity is governed by the subject's "own ideal of itself" (PR 248[380]), which Whitehead calls its subjective aim. The initial stage of the subjective aim is "an endowment which the subject inherits from the inevitable ordering of things, conceptually realized in the nature of God" (PR 244 [373]). In other words, the subjective aim originates with the actual entity's prehension of God's primordial nature: "His particular relevance to each creative act, as it arises from its own conditioned standpoint in the world, constitutes him the initial 'object of desire' establishing the initial phase of each subjective aim" (PR 344[522]). God is thus, for Whitehead, the "aboriginal condition" (PR 225[344]) that qualifies creativity by supplying each temporal occasion with "that initial aim from which its self-causation starts" (PR 244[373]). God and the world conspire together to create each new occasion of experience. The actual world limits the occasion to a certain range of real possibility, while God provides it with an initial aim that "is the best for that *impasse*" (PR 244[373]).

If the actual world determines the realm of real potentiality for a subject, and if God provides it with an initial aim, wherein lies the freedom of the subject?[13] If God is the source of the subjective aim, and if that aim is the locus of finite freedom, then how can Whitehead avoid the charge of radical finalism? Is not God in the end responsible for the outcome of the creative process? In reply to these questions we must note a distinction that Whitehead makes between the subjective aim's initial phase (the "initial aim") and its later phases. Each temporal entity "derives from God its basic conceptual aim, relevant to its actual world, *yet with determinations awaiting its own decisions*" (PR 224[343]; emphasis added). The initial aim provides the subject with a gradation of possible aims for realization; the subject then admits a "selection" from the objective lure into subjective efficiency, which then functions as the subjective "ideal of itself," guiding the process of concrescence (PR 87[133]). Throughout this process the subjective aim continues to undergo development and specification: "The lure for feeling develops with the concrescent phases of the subject in question" (PR 189[287]). What begins with "conditioned alternatives" (PR 224[342]) is reduced to coherence through successive decisions by the actual occasion; in this way, the subject is "the autonomous master" (PR 245[374]) of its own self-creation.[14] "This self-determination of its own aim," concludes Cobb, "is the final locus of freedom within the limits of causal force as determined by the settled past and the principle of order inherent in its initial aim."[15]

If God presents as the initial aim a range of possibilities for realization, then the freedom of the actual occasion would appear to lie in its specification of this range so as to produce a unified satisfaction. But if the subjective aim is the occasion's principle of guidance, what guides the development of that principle? What reason is there for the subject's selection of one aim over another? Whitehead resorts to claiming that the subjective aim is a limiting case of the ontological principle. It exemplifies the principle in that the subject "completes itself during the process of concrescence by a self-criticism of its own incomplete phases" (PR 244[373]). However, it limits the ontological principle "by its own autonomy" (PR 244[373]). The subject's decision is ultimately autonomous. This "autonomous energy" is the creativity of the universe in which the freedom of each entity is finally grounded.[16] In *Adventures of Ideas*, Whitehead speaks of the final autonomy of the process:

> This process of the synthesis of subjective forms derived conformally is not settled by the antecedent fact of the data. For these data in their own separate natures do not carry any regulative principle for their synthesis. The regulative principle is derived from the novel unity which is imposed on them by the novel creature in process of constitution. Thus the immediate occasion from the *spontaneity of its own essence* must supply the missing determination for the synthesis of subjective form. (AI 328; emphasis added.)

The freedom of the actual entity would appear to reside in its ability to modify its initial aim, to make some specific aim its own. However, since the initial aim includes a specific ideal which is God's ideal for that occasion, the data and valuation of which the occasion initially conforms to, must we not conclude that any modification is in fact degradation? Cobb notes this problem and assumes that Whitehead solves it by his idea of graded relevance. Hence while "[s]ome particular possibility must be ideal, given the situation," there are closely related possibilities that are "appropriate to the situation, although deviating from the ideal."[17] Rather than being a solution, this is precisely the problem. While free to modify the initial aim, any such modification will result in a degradation of the ideal. Our freedom seems to reside in our decision to ratify or to deviate from an ideal imposed from without. This could be avoided by denying that God specifies one possibility as the ideal toward which the occasion is lured. God would then be depicted as generally luring an occasion toward an exhaustive hierarchy of possibilities for realization. But this renders vacuous the meaning of God's persuasive power for in luring an entity toward everything possible God would in fact be luring it toward nothing. To preserve God's activity in the world we would then have to conceive of it solely in terms of efficient causation. Or perhaps we could think of God as luring an occasion, not toward some particular ideal possibility, but toward an indeterminate ideal, a "type" of satisfaction. This would fit well with the notion that the initial aim undergoes modifications: God's ideal aim for an occasion, while initially indefinite, progressively becomes more distinct. However this interpretation falls foul of Whitehead's insistence upon fully definite eternal objects.[18]

Although Whitehead's analysis of the process of concrescence is not without its ambiguities, what he desires to say is relatively clear. While the past influences and limits the freedom of subsequent occasions, the final determination of each concrescence lies with the creativity of the subject itself. The past actual world both "limits and supplies"(PR 110[168]); it determines the range of possibilities open for realization by the subject. Yet the subject remains free to decide the precise character of its own self-development in accordance with its subjective aim. The subjective aim is an immanent teleological principle that guides the synthesis of the data into an intense and harmonious satisfaction. I suggest that in presenting freedom in terms of self-development and the realization of an ideal, Whitehead provides us with a "positive" conception of freedom. In its fullest sense freedom is not merely the absence of coercive restraints. Freedom so understood would be a merely negative conception. Properly understood freedom is a positive power of self-realization, the ability to develop fully one's own innate capacities. Understood thus, the ideal aim is that possibility that enables the individual to realize most fully his or her potentialities. Hence, to make God's ideal aim one's own subjective aim is to be "free in the service of God," to be most fully oneself.[19] To choose a different aim is not only a deviation from the ideal; it is also a diminution of true freedom. True, one is free in the negative sense of being capable of doing this rather than that; however, if freedom is defined actively as the development of one's capacities, then full freedom will correspond with full development. The distinction between negative and positive freedom and its implications for politics and society will be discussed more fully in Part Three.

## III. GOD AND THE WORLD

In pursuing our aim of introducing the main features of Whitehead's philosophy we have had occasion to refer more than once to God's activity in the world. From the time of his earliest excursion into metaphysics Whitehead recognized the need for some principle by which he could explain order in the universe. In *Science and the Modern World* the ultimate principle is termed "substantial activity," eternal objects and actual entities being attributes of this "one substance." Whitehead argues that a further element in the metaphysical situation is required in order to explain (a) the fact that there is a process of actual occasions, and (b) the fact that these occasions are the emergence of values. This further element is termed the "Principle of Concretion" or God (SMW 250). At this stage in Whitehead's thought God functions as a principle of limitation. God is that attribute of the substantial activity that explains why the particular course of events, which could have been different, is that course (SMW 255). Neither the substantial activity nor the eternal objects can supply a reason for the logical and causal relations that pertain; in themselves they are neutral with respect to the course of events. If the eternal objects are to be relevant to actual entities, then they require a primordial conceptual ordering. God *is* this ordering.

This conception of God as the principle of limitation in virtue of which there is order in the world is developed further in *Religion in the Making*. The order of the world is no accident, but exists "by reason of this truth: that the universe exhibits a creativity with infinite freedom, and a realm of forms with infinite possibilities; but that this creativity and these forms are together impotent to achieve actuality apart from the completed ideal harmony, which is God" (RM 119–20). Whereas God was conceived of as a nonconcrete attribute of the substantial activity in *Science and the Modern World*, God is now presented as "a definite entity, already actual among the formative elements, as an antecedent ground for the entry of the ideal forms into the definite process of the temporal world" (RM 152). Whitehead is progressing toward that ontological principle that stipulates that every condition to which an actual occasion must conform in its concrescence has its reason in some actual entity.

Although God is an actual entity, he is an actual entity of a peculiar sort. First, the deity is a nontemporal actuality. God is the "ground antecedent to transition" and as such must "include all possibilities of physical value conceptually, thereby holding the ideal forms apart in equal, conceptual realization of knowledge" (RM 153). God envisages and orders the eternal objects so as to determine every possibility of value. Second, I believe that Whitehead's descriptions of God as a "*conceptual* fusion" (RM 157; emphasis added) into one perceptivity, as the "one systematic, complete fact" (RM 154), and as the "completed *ideal* harmony" (RM 120; emphasis added) imply that at this stage of his thought God is not yet a dipolar actuality. God has no "consequent" nature: "This ideal world of conceptual harmonization is merely a description of God himself. Thus the nature of God is the complete conceptual realization of the realm of ideal forms. The kingdom of heaven is God" (RM 154). Like Plato's Demiurge, who is probably a pictorial representation of the Reason that operates in the world, God is "the realization of the ideal conceptual harmony by reason of which there is an actual process in the total universe—an evolving world which is actual because there is order" (RM 156).[20] God is a definite entity, already actual and therefore an antecedent ground of the temporal world. Whitehead continues saying: "But such a complete aboriginal actuality must differ from actuality in process of realization in respect to the blind occasions of perceptivity which issue from process and require process. These occasions build up the physical world which is essentially in transition" (RM 152-53). In other words, God is not an occasion in the physical world, but a "purely spiritual" (RM 111) being; God is not in process of realization, but is complete and above change (RM 98). In the divine vision of eternal objects God determines every possibility of value and "his knowledge of the relationships of particular modes of value is not added to, or disturbed, by the realization in the actual world of what is already conceptually realized in his ideal world" (RM 154). History is the incarnation of God's ideal world; it is not yet the vehicle by which God himself finds completion.[21]

Whitehead did not deviate in *Process and Reality* from his earlier emphasis upon the metaphysical necessity of some principle of order.

Just as we read in SMW 255–57 that God is the ground of rationality that limits the course of history, so in PR 46(74) we read that "[n]o reason, internal to history, can be assigned why that flux of forms, rather than another flux, should have been illustrated." What is new is not that the world "lives by its incarnation of God in itself" (RM 156), but that *God's own life* finds completion through the world. Whitehead's conception of God has developed in a highly significant way. In addition to the primordial evaluation of eternal objects, that is God's primordial nature, God is also said to have a consequent nature. God's nature is no longer simply that of a complete, ideal realization of the eternal objects. God also is now dipolar and stands in need of completion. God originates in the conceptual valuation of eternal objects and is completed by his consequent, physical experience of the world. As primordial God is the creator of the world; as consequent God is the *telos* of history: "He is the beginning and the end" (PR 345([523]). Indeed, perhaps we could even say that in *Process and Reality* God is for the first time presented as truly living, and not simply as the unchanging principle of order. Such a description is now only applicable to God's primordial nature in abstraction which is held to be "free, complete, primordial, eternal, actually deficient, and unconscious." God's consequent nature, on the other hand, is "determined, incomplete, consequent, 'everlasting,' fully actual, and conscious" (PR 345[524]).

I believe that aspects of God's primordial nature, which is God's only nature in *Religion in the Making*, are subsequently attributed to the consequent nature in *Process and Reality* where they undergo a transformation of meaning. Take, for example, the idea of the "kingdom of heaven." The kingdom of heaven and the "ideal world of conceptual harmonization" are in Whitehead's early work synonymous, and they are both identified with God (RM 154). In the kingdom of heaven, so understood, there occurs a *primordial transmutation* of evil. God as primordial possesses a knowledge of evil, but God also has an "ideal vision of each actual evil so met with a novel consequent as to issue in the restoration of goodness"(RM 155). This vision enters the world by means of God's immanence and by reason of its relevance to the course of events. No fact, of pain or of pleasure, is a "total loss" because, together with God's novel ideal, it is "woven immortally into the rhythm of *mortal things*" (RM 155; emphasis added). It is saved because it is incorporated into the becoming of subsequent occasions and serves as a means, a "stepping-stone," for God to introduce ideals into the process of history. In his latter work the values realized in history contribute to the consequent nature of God; they contribute their value, evil as well as good, to the divine life itself. The kingdom of heaven is not the "ideal" world of conceptual harmonization, but the actuality of God's own experience of the world. It is in the divine life rather than in the "rhythm of mortal things" that finite values are transmuted and preserved.[22]

Given that God's consequent nature was a secondary development of Whitehead's metaphysical system it is not surprising that some difficulties arose concerning the interrelation of these two aspects of God's being. Instead of treating the two natures of God as abstractions in need of some overarching unity, I believe that Whitehead's language is misleading and that the consequent nature is better understood as the unity of God's conceptual vision and physical feelings. This interpretation, as opposed to that which takes the primordial and consequent natures to parallel the mental and physical poles of other actual entities, relies on a more literal reading of Whitehead's references to the consequent nature.[23] For example, he writes: "The consequent nature of God is conscious; and it is the realization of the actual world in the unity of his nature, and through the transformation of his wisdom. The primordial nature is conceptual, the consequent nature is the weaving of God's physical feelings upon his primordial concepts" (PR 345[524]). It would be an error to identify the consequent nature with God's physical feelings which stand in need of unification with the conceptual vision of the primordial nature. Rather, God's consequent nature *is* the *"unity"* of that conceptual vision and God's physical feelings of the world; it *is* the *"transformation,"* and not mere conformal (physical) feeling, of the actual world through divine *"wisdom;"* it *is* the *"weaving,"* and not simply the reception, of the physical feelings upon God's primordial concepts.

God's physical feelings of the world should not be equated with the consequent nature for this would require that we look for a unification of the primordial and consequent natures on a higher level. A close reading of Whitehead's statements about the consequent nature leads me to believe that he saw it as the *synthesis* of the infinitude of conceptual possibilities and the world of actuality. This explains why he never spoke of the consequent nature as an abstraction of God. Repeatedly the primordial nature is said to be an abstraction: the primordial nature is "God in abstraction, alone with himself" (PR 34[50]). Whitehead says that we can "consider God in the abstraction of a primordial actuality . . . '' (PR 344[522]). Similarly, the primordial nature is actually deficient; the consequent nature, on the other hand, is "fully actual" (PR 345[524]). A few pages later he adds: "The consequent nature of God is the fulfillment of his experience by his reception of the multiple freedom of actuality into the harmony of his own actualization. *It is God as really actual,* completing the deficiency of his mere conceptual actuality" (PR 349[530]; emphasis added). Thus the language that Whitehead uses at times to speak about the consequent nature suggests that he had in mind the fullness of God's being, inclusive of the primordial nature and the world, God as a complete, fully actual entity, and not simply an abstraction of God.

Further support can be gathered from Whitehead's two summary statements of the creative process. The first comes from PR 346(525): "The universe includes a threefold creative act composed of (i) the one infinite conceptual realization, (ii) the multiple solidarity of free physical realizations in the temporal world, (iii) the ultimate unity of the multiplicity of actual fact with the primordial conceptual fact." The first and second moments are clear references to the primordial nature of God and the world of finite actual entities. I believe that the third moment is what Whitehead calls God's consequent nature—it is the "ultimate *unity*" of the primordial nature and the world.

The second summary is found on the closing pages of *Process and Reality.* Here Whitehead describes the phases in which the universe accomplishes its actuality:

> There is first the phase of conceptual origination, deficient in actuality, but infinite in its adjustment of valuation. Secondly, there is the temporal phase of physical origination, with its multiplicity of actualities. In this phase full actuality is attained; but there is deficiency in the solidarity of individuals with each other. This phase derives its determinate conditions from the first phase. Thirdly, there is the phase of perfected actuality, in which the many are one everlastingly, without the qualification of any loss either of individual identity or of completeness of unity. In everlastingness, immediacy is reconciled with objective immortality. This phase derives the conditions of its being from the two antecedent phases (PR 350–51[532]).

Again we find the same triune pattern. The primordial nature constitutes the first moment; it is deficient in actuality. The second moment is fully actual, but owing to its finitude it expresses the eternal objects merely as a multiplicity. The third moment, given the context, must be a reference to the consequent nature in which the unity of the primordial nature and the multiplicity of finite actualities achieves a synthesis. "In this later phase, the many actualities are one actuality, and the one actuality is many actualities" (PR 349[530]). Universality (primordial nature) and particularity (finite world) have been synthesized in the divine individual (consequent nature).[24]

## IV. SOCIETIES: FREEDOM AND CAUSATION ON THE MACROSCOPIC LEVEL

In Whitehead's mature metaphysics God is both the beginning and end of history. The ultimate creative purpose that guides the divine activity in history is the realization by each actual entity of "some maximum depth of intensity of feeling, subject to the conditions of its concrescence" (PR 249[381]). As we saw earlier, the social nature of reality is such that the character of an actual entity is dependent upon environmental conditions; therefore, if the deity is to realize its creative purpose then there must evolve an environment conducive to the achievement of high levels of satisfaction. Such an environment, according to Whitehead, is one which exhibits a balance of order and novelty. If there is a lack of coordination among the factors that make up the environment the result is "triviality" (PR 111[170]). Too much disorder leads to mutually inhibiting experiences and, consequently, satisfactions of slight intensity; lacking a principle for harmonizing the component feelings, the discordant elements cancel one another out thereby impoverishing the final satisfaction. At the same time, an excess of order will also result in low-grade satisfactions. In such instances there is "vagueness" owing to an excess of identification among the data. As a result, "the differences between the actual entities so prehended are faint chaotic factors in the environment" (PR 112[171]) and are consequently dismissed as irrelevant. Thus, if God's aim at intensity of feeling is to be realized, an excess of either order or disorder among those elements given for prehension must be avoided.

This need for an environment in which order and disorder achieve a productive balance is met by the grouping of actual entities into larger, organized nexūs and "societies." Whitehead distinguishes between several different grades of social order. The simplest form of society, the "personal" society, is purely temporal and continuous. No two occasions of a personal society exist at the same time, but rather follow one another sequentially like frames of a movie. If we are considering a human being as an enduring percipient then that individual is such a serially ordered society. The ordinary physical objects or enduring organisms with which science is concerned are societies analyzable into numerous strands of actual entities. These objects, such as tables and chairs, rather than the actual entities themselves, are the "permanent entities which enjoy adventures of change throughout time and space" (PR 35[52]). Societies made up of many strands of personal order, all unified by a defining characteristic, are called "corpuscular" societies (PR 35[52]). They tend to be highly stable and often endure for great lengths of time; however, they generally produce low-grade satisfactions. The occasions constituting that society experience "intense narrowness" on account of the massiveness of the shared order inherited from the society. Whatever contrasts there are tend to be reduced to irrelevance. The mental functioning of the occasion is consequently negligible, basically being confined to conceptual reproduction and unoriginative repetition. Thus order tends to reproduce itself; without novelty arising through mental development power becomes repetitive, preserving the status quo. When there is minimal mental activity, there is correspondingly little creative novelty: "Mental experience is the organ of novelty, the urge beyond. It seeks to vivify the massive physical fact, which is repetitive, with the novelties which beckon" (FR 26–27; see AI 249). Apart from the activity of the mental pole there would be endless reproduction of the past in the present without creative advance. In other words, the power of final causation (purpose), without the introduction of novelty, tends to preserve the power experienced in efficient causation. Order tends to impose itself on an actual occasion, promoting stability, and therefore in some sense enhancing the power of efficient causation to determine the nature of subsequent occasions.

There is a third type of society which Whitehead calls "structured societies." These societies, such as living cells, human beings, and ultimately the universe itself, are all composed of "subordinate societies and nexūs with a definite pattern of structural inter-relations . . . " (PR 99[151]). Because of the ordered complexity of the contrasts that it can provide, a structured society permits the emergence of a special class of occasions whose members experience particularly intense satisfactions. such occasions are said to be "living." A living occasion is one that is not "*bound* by a single line of physical ancestry" (PR 104[159]; emphasis added); it is missing the "*shackle* of reiteration of the past" (PR 105[161]; emphasis added). In other words, a living occasion is one in which final causation predominates rather than social tradition (efficient causation). Life, writes Whitehead, is "a bid for freedom on the part of organisms, a bid for a certain independence of individuality with self-interests and activities not to be construed purely in terms of environmental obligations" (S 76). Consequently, living occasions that constitute entirely living nexūs are not social; they are socially deficient (PR 105[161]).

A living occasion emerges from an environmental situation conducive to novelty. The environment provokes novelty rather than reiteration. Intensity of feeling is thus best achieved through the introduction of novelty into a stable social matrix. Such a complex society is absolutely necessary as Kraus notes:

> Without a highly structured environment to pattern its data and assimilate its reactions, [a living occasion] is merely a moment of valueless, anarchic disorder, resembling a revolutionary so radical as to eschew any contact or communication with the society he revolts against, thereby forfeiting both the platform and the fruits of his revolt.[25]

The complex order not only provides a basis for promoting intense experience, it also enables the relevant novelty that is realized to be given as data to the structured society thereby assisting that society to adjust to novel situations. Such an adaptation of the society to its environment is one way in which nature seeks to unite intensity with survival.

The mental originality of the living occasions receives a character and a depth, that is, its originality is "canalized" and "intensified," through its assimilation into the society (PR 107[163]). This is important for our understanding of freedom and causality as operative in a social environment. The greatest freedom is to be found among those occasions comprising a living nexus. But these occasions are themselves the product of social order, not in an absolute sense, but in the sense that the order of the environment is such as to promote "a bid for freedom." But radical freedom, apart from canalization, would be destructive of the very social order that gave rise to it. Intensity of experience is promoted by *limitations* as well as by freedom: it requires freedom within limits. Reiteration through canalization provides continuity and the intensity which comes from massiveness. Consequently, even as life emerges from society, so also it "turns back into society . . . " (PR 107[163]). Just as order provokes the freedom of life, so the *telos* of freedom, the aim of life, should be the intensification of experience within a society.

What significance do these metaphysical principles have for understanding human social structures? I am of the opinion that the principles that relate to the emergence, preservation, and destruction of social order generally are also exemplified within human societies. Such a claim can be supported by specific comments drawn from Whitehead's later writings. For example, we read that

> [t]he Universe achieves its value by reason of its co-ordination into societies of societies, and into societies of societies of societies. Thus an army is a society of regiments, and regiments are societies of men, and men are societies of cells, and of blood, and of bones, together with the dominant society of personal human experience, and cells are societies of smaller physical entities such as protons, and so on, and so on. (AI 264)

It is plainly evident from this passage in *Adventures of Ideas* that Whitehead intends no distinction to be made between the use of the term society when applied to regiments in an army and when applied to the human individuals that together make up those regiments. Both are examples of "societies" in Whitehead's technical sense of the term. Again in *Symbolism* we find further evidence that Whitehead imagines his concept of society to apply equally to human social arrangements and to subhuman group interrelations:

> Communities with geographical unity constitute the primary type of communities which we find in the world. Indeed the lower we go in the scale of being, the more necessary is geographical unity for that close interaction of individuals which constitutes society. Societies of the higher animals, of insects, of molecules, all possess geographical unity. A rock is nothing else than a society of molecules, indulging in every species of activity open to molecules. I draw attention to this lowly form of society

in order to dispel the notion that social life is a peculiarity of the higher organisms. The contrary is the case. (S 76)

It would appear that when discussing social order, Whitehead does not speak of human societies as merely metaphorically exemplifying the principles by which actual entities constitute societies. A nation *is* a society, just as much as a human body, a rock, or even a society of insects is a "society." Indeed, human social structures, like a human body, are complex structured societies inclusive of numerous subsocieties and nexūs.

Not only does Whitehead consider human societies to exhibit the same principles as societies of occasions, I believe that he often writes as though an analogy exists between human individuals as members of a society and the interaction of actual occasions.[26] In other words, human beings, while not of the same ontological status as actual occasions, appear to operate like actual entities in their mutual interaction. Concerning the relationship between the two orders of reality in Whitehead's thought, the microscopic and the macroscopic, George Allan asks:

> Can a theory of momentary events provide any clue to an understanding of realities that emerge, change, thrive and suffer decline, endure for millennia? Whitehead's insistence upon the organismic connectedness of things is "certainly conducive to answering this question by means of analogy and metaphor, mapping in isomorphic fashion characteristics of the actual occasion onto the macrocosmic objects of human experience. But is it legitimate to treat the actual occasion as a model for interpreting the nature of a human life-course, the structure of an institution, the dynamics of a nation-state?[27]

I believe that a strong case can be made for an affirmative answer to these questions. When discussing the social nature of an actual entity Whitehead expressly states that "the philosophy of organism appears as an enlargement of the premise in ethical discussions: that man is a social animal. *Analogously, every actual occasion is social*, so that when we have presumed the existence of any persistent type of actual occasions, we have thereby made presumptions as to types of societies comprised in its environment" (PR 204 [310–11]; emphasis added). This passage is particularly revealing as it implies not only that an analogy exists between a human individual and an actual occasion, but also that the primary analogate is the nature of the human person. In other words, certain aspects at least of his metaphysical theory are generalizations derived from his conceptions of human nature and society—a conclusion that is not insignificant given our interest in providing an ideology-critique of Whitehead's philosophy! If the actual entity provides an analogue for the human social order it is precisely because the human social order (as concretely experienced and theoretically interpreted by Whitehead) was the primary analogate for his conception of the actual entity.

Nor is it only with regard to the social nature of the actual entity that an analogy with human nature and society can be detected. Another clear example is his use of concepts derived from the sphere of human social relations when describing the principle of efficient causation. "Explanation by 'tradition,' " he says, "is merely another phraseology for explanation by 'efficient cause' " (PR 104[159]). And in the same context we are told that "[l]ife is a bid for freedom: an enduring entity binds any one of its occasions to the line of its ancestry" (PR 104[159]). Other terms used elsewhere by Whitehead include "inheritance," "custom," "instinct," and "prejudice." Victor Lowe is led to conclude that "Whitehead's central doctrine of causal inheritance seems to . . . have sprung chiefly from his reflections on the characteristics of human society. The reflections are of the sort made, on a smaller scale, by Burke in his conception of "prejudice."[28]

Finally, that Whitehead perceived an analogy to exist between the way individuals interact in a human society and in a society of actual occasions is evident from his method of argumentation. Compare, for example, his discussion of the laws of nature and the laws that govern human societies. Every society requires an environment; there is no society in isolation (PR 90[138]). The universe is to be conceived as exhibiting layers of social order in which the wider and more general societies provide the necessary character presupposed by the more specialized societies. The rise and continued existence of any specialized society is dependent upon the favorable background of a larger environment. This background constitutes the "system of 'laws' determining reproduction in some portion of the universe . . . " (PR 91[139]). However it must be understood that such laws are not inviolable, as though they were imposed by divine decree. In an important passage Whitehead writes:

The causal laws which dominate a social environment are the product of the defining characteristic of that society. But the society is only efficient through its individual members. Thus in a society, the members can only exist by reason of the laws which dominate the society, and the laws only come into being by reason of the analogous characters of the members of the society. (PR 90–91[139])

Social laws express the characteristic interrelationships between the individuals that constitute that society. "[T]he order of nature," claims Whitehead, "expresses the characters of the real things which jointly compose the existences to be found in nature" (AI 142).

These principles are equally evident in human social arrangements. Human nature is a social product and to understand the essence of human beings requires knowing their mutual relations to each other (AI 142). Our social structures provide us with a wider environment in which each of us, as a more specialized society, realizes his or her potentialities. It is our wider environment that provides us with whatever real potentialities we have: it both enables and limits. There is no absolute freedom to become any sort of person we want to be. Our freedom is limited by our social environment which must at least be permissive of the self-sustenance of that type of individual. At the same time, it is because we are the individuals we are that our social "laws" are what they are. These laws are the product of human interaction and are as such modifiable. "The ideals cherished in the souls of men enter into the character of their actions. These inter-actions within society modify the social laws by modifying the occasions to which those laws apply. Impracticable ideals are a programme for reform" (AI 52). There is thus a reciprocal relationship between society and its constituent members. Human social arrangements tend to produce certain types of individuals, and those types of individuals tend to produce certain types of societies.

## V. CONCLUSION

In our initial introduction to Whitehead's philosophy a number of significant conclusions have been reached which will prove important when we come to analyze his social and political thought. First, it has been observed that both extremes of absolute determinism and absolute freedom have been metaphysically excluded. A strict determinism would hold that each new actual entity can be fully explained solely in terms of its antecedent causes, that is, its actual world. But Whitehead insists that every actual entity transcends all other actual entities by reason of its novel synthesis of the data given to it in its primary phase. Hence Whitehead says that " 'decided' conditions are never such as to banish freedom. They only qualify it. There is always a contingency left open for immediate decision" (PR 284[435]). Second, we have seen that Whitehead's concept of freedom is not a purely negative one but includes some positive elements. This is grounded in his assertion that freedom is located within the process of concrescence whereby the individual aims to realize an ideal of self-development. As we shall see later, this ideal is itself a social and not a purely private ideal. Third, in outlining God's role within the cosmological scheme we observed that in Whitehead's mature metaphysics this includes not only the presentation of an ideal aim to an actual occasion, but also the summation of the creative advance in the divine life. Finally, it is apparent that when it comes to the macroscopic world of enduring objects *human* societies should be regarded as fully expressing the principles governing social organization and that human persons are individuals who can be treated as analogous to actual entities. These issues will all resurface in our discussion of Whitehead's social thought. Before turning to that, however, we must first provide a parallel introduction to the thought of Charles Hartshorne.

# 3

## Freedom and Causality in Hartshorne's Process Philosophy

Having presented Whitehead's metaphysical system in the previous chapter, we must now go on to outline the central features of Hartshorne's philosophy. Our investigation will be once again conducted from the perspective of freedom and causation. In one of his earliest writings Hartshorne argued that all causality is to be explained through the notion of "organic sympathy" (BH 195). What is more, organic sympathy is held to be the solution to the further problems of the nature of time, the subject-object relation, the mind-body relation, and the nature of individuality. Because of its significance, I will begin with a discussion of the basic elements of the theory of organic sympathy before moving on to the issues of determinism and divine activity in the world.

## I. ORGANIC SYMPATHY AND CAUSAL CONNECTIONS

Like Whitehead, Hartshorne advocates a pluralistic ontology in which the fundamental building blocks of the universe are relatively discrete unit-events of becoming. By "event" Hartshorne means "a minimal temporal unit" (CSPM 173) of some actual process. Such events are substances in the sense that each is a unitary subject of many predicates; but they are not substances in the Aristotelian sense of a self-identical subject that undergoes accidental changes. "The only 'stuff' of change," he writes, "is finally just process itself and its unit is an event, not a bit of persisting substance" (LP 222). These events, and not the macroscopic individuals apprehended by sense perception, are the truly concrete subjects, the "basic descripta" (CSPM 173) of Hartshorne's philosophy.

As was the case with Whitehead, the temporal-causal structure is the consequence of the interaction of these unit-events. How is this interaction to be understood? Hartshorne does not take issue with Hume's dictum that sense perception alone cannot disclose any causal connectedness. In the natural world all we ever perceive is the continual, and at times repetitive, succession of events. We do not directly observe causal relations. But Hartshorne rejects the sceptical Humean conclusion that what are commonly termed causal relations are mere constant conjunctions. At this juncture Hartshorne appeals to memory, which he claims provides experiential evidence in support of a theory of real causal connectedness. Memory and not perception is the paradigm of experiencing (CSPM 75). In our experience of memory we find the key to understanding the influence of the past upon the present. "Memory *is* influence," asserts Hartshorne.[1] Not only is memory the presentation of the past in the present, it is also the modification of the present by the past.[2] The process of becoming is a creative synthesis in which novel wholes are created with nonnovel parts—the many become one and are increased by one. Past experiences, which are "remembered" by the present unit-event, impose restrictions upon the new subject. "Memory preserves something of the ideas, emotional qualities, and valuations in prior experience, and the whole of the remembering experience, as one experience, must achieve its integration of feeling and value because, or in spite of, what memory imports into it."[3] Obviously, if memory is to function as an explanation of causal connectedness then its meaning must be expanded so as to be applicable to all types of experience. In *Beyond Humanism* Hartshorne offers us a "generalized comparative psychology" in which various psychological concepts such as memory and feeling are made "cosmic variables" (BH 116–23). Such variables have an infinite range of values and are therefore applicable to all individuals regardless of their simplicity or their complexity. This is Hartshorne's doctrine of panpsychism. The dualism of mind and matter is rejected and replaced by a metaphysical theory according to which mentality characterizes all levels of reality. There is no such thing as mere matter which exhibits a zero-level of mentality.

Psychicalism, not materialism, unlocks the secrets of causal connectedness. As with Whitehead, who claims that every actual entity is characterized by both a mental and a physical pole, so Hartshorne argues that nature does not exhibit a dualism of mind and matter, but rather of various levels of mentality or experiencing. This approach avoids the problem of explaining how two different sub-stances, material substance and thinking substance, interact. Thus, for example, the events that constitute one's soul prehend the cells that comprise one's body, and vice versa. This is the concept of organic sympathy; a subject "feels the feelings" of other entities which are its objects.

All experience is the experience of something. Moreover, this experience must be of something other than the subject of the experience itself. "To be aware of something is *ipso facto* to be influenced by it. . . . Thus, to explain how something influences an experience, we have only to explain how this something comes to be an object or content of the experience" (LP 227). We see then that the social character of feeling is the meaning of the subject-object relation and that this in turn is inseparable from the cause-effect relation (BH 175). Hartshorne is presenting us with a causal theory of perception. A subject is caused by the objects that it experiences. This experience is a sympathetic participation in the feelings of other individuals. According to Hartshorne's "revolutionary theory of power or influence . . . nothing influences experience except the things that are experienced" (LP 230). A subject is just what it is because of the nature of the objective data experienced by the novel event. Alter the objects of experience and one alters the subject of experience.

## II. RELATIVE INDETERMINISM

The experience *of* something is an essential relation. The subject is internally related to the object and therefore constituted by it. At the same time, the object is externally related to the subject. The causal relationship, therefore, exemplifies an asymmetrical character. That which is absolute is that which is independent of relations. A term is independent of those relations that are external to it. Following G. E. Moore, Hartshorne says that in the relation X R Y, X is externally related to Y when it would have had the same nature apart from its relation to Y. The absolute term is the independent and externally related cause; the relative term, on the other hand, is the dependent and internally related effect. It is the concrete whole which includes its externally related terms as abstract aspects; the relation is possessed by that term to which the relation is internal. "[T]he relations of abstractions are made possible by the fact that both universals and particulars are embraced in, or are internal to, concrete experiences, or individual events, as wholes" (MVG 238). Thus Hartshorne argues that the temporal-causal process is cumulative in nature: "[I]t is the generic character of process to enrich the sum of determinateness" (DR 96–97). The later term includes the former, the subject includes the object, the effect includes the cause. The experience-of-X includes X together with an additional definiteness of feeling regarding X and therefore it is richer in content than X.

An effect is internally related to its cause; therefore, there are real necessary connections between events. Real necessary connections are not such as to make any particular event necessary, "but only that a certain *kind* of event (relatively, but not absolutely, particularized) shall not remain a null class . . . ."[4] This is the idea of relative indeterminism which Hartshorne opposed to the classical notion of strict determinism. Every event undoubtedly has a cause, and this cause determines to some extent its effect. But what is the extent of this determination? Hartshorne virulently opposes the definition of a cause as "a condition, or set of conditions, from which only one outcome is possible, or from which, in principle or ideally, the outcome is wholly predictable" (LP 163). To say that something is possible, for absolute determinism, is simply to say that we are ignorant about some details of what is actual. If we were not deficient in our knowledge of actuality we would not be in ignorance about the future. Perfect prediction would be possible. To an ideal knower the future would withhold no secrets. Yet in what sense then is it future, and in what sense would one's knowledge of the future be prediction? "If a prediction is to be true when made," writes Hartshorne, "the truth relation must *then* obtain, and its relation cannot then be lacking either."[5] How does one avoid collapsing possibility into actuality? "If it is only ignorance of causes which prevents us from mentally seeing the effect in advance, then the entire character of 'coming events' is real beforehand. Before events happen, they lack nothing except a totally transparent, featureless something called 'actual occurrence' " (LP 165; see MVG 246). Only by claiming that an effect lacks "actuality" can a determinist avoid the collapse of possibility into actuality and of the future into the present. But here one encounters an obvious problem: how does one account for the acquisition of "actuality" by the effect? If it is provided by the cause, then the effect is totally contained within it and the distinction between cause and effect is abolished. If, on the other hand, it is not provided by the cause, then the determinist thesis that an effect is completely deducible from its cause is repudiated.

Absolute determinism holds that events in their full particularity are determined by their antecedent causes. Hartshorne denies that there is in a cause "any relation whatever to . . . *particular* future effects" (DR 68). Particulars cannot be related prospectively to particulars because whatever "has relation to X has X, for X is a constituent of relation-to-X. Now if the cause has the effect, by virtue of having relation to it, then in the cause the effect *already is,* and the whole time process is the illusion of new events, whereas all events were precontained in their predecessors. This reduces the idea of time to an absurdity" (DR 69).

Hartshorne specifically says that the problem of causality is an aspect of the problem of time.[6] Time is an asymmetrical relation in which the past (cause) is internal to the present (effect) while the present is external to the past. If causes fully contain their subsequent effects then they are logically inseparable from one another. Everything would then be implied by everything else thus eliminating the temporal-causal order.

Causal relations are not logical necessities that connect an event with its successor in its full particularity; rather, conditions logically imply only a class of "really possible" (LP 173) outcomes. That which can happen is not a single, particular event but a range of possibilities, and it is this range of possibilities that is determined by the past. A cause is that which "distinguishes from the logically possible . . . that which is *really* possible in a given actual situation" (RSP 88). A cause only requires that there be *some* effect within certain *limits* of variation. But what is finally actualized did not exist as an antecedent possibility; it was the chance creation of that event. The actually possible is narrower than the logically possible; however, it is not as limited as the actual itself. To be actual is to be a determinate reality; actuality *is* determinateness. To be possible, on the other hand, is to be determinable.

Actualization is the process by which possibilities are excluded and definiteness is attained. It is more than the simple addition of a vacuous something called actuality to an otherwise fully determinate possibility. It is a qualitative enhancement. Becoming actual and becoming particular are the same thing. "[M]erely possible qualities are lacking in individual definiteness. There are no possible individuals, but only possible kinds of individuals . . . . [P]ossibility is in principle general rather than particular, determinable rather than determinate" (NTT 73). Clearly, Hartshorne rejects Whitehead's belief that pure possibilities are fully particularized eternal objects ordered by the primordial nature of God.[7] Hartshorne argues that possibility consists in an infinite continuum without definite parts (CSPM 66).[8] All specific qualities are emergent; only the metaphysical universals, which are always envisaged and somehow applied by God, are eternal.[9] Furthermore, even when a particular quality has emerged, for instance, a shade of blue, that very same quality cannot be repeated. "Something very like this blue can occur over and over, but not precisely *this* blue. Particular qualities in their absolute definiteness are irreducibly relational and historical" (CSPM 64). Hartshorne feels that Whitehead's theory of eternal objects leaves the impression that the historical process is in some ways a duplicate reality.[10] The abolition of eternal objects would in his opinion make room for genuine creativity on the part of finite historical agents.[11]

Hartshorne is offering us a theory of relative indeterminism. All events are caused, but no event in its full particularity is determined by its causes. There always remains an element of indefiniteness which awaits final determination by the subject itself. Thus all events are both caused *and* occur by chance. Causality is the restriction of logical possibility; it is the determination of real possibility. Within this range of real possibility there will be factors common to the entire set. These abstract features will therefore inevitably be realized by the event. They are what Hartshorne terms conditional necessities. Unconditional necessities are those factors that are common to *all* possibilities whatever. Chance, on the other hand, is defined as the "particularity of the particular" or its "self-creativity" (RSP 87). This is the entity's "undeducibility" from the past.

> The causes of an event furnish its possibility . . . but not its actuality. Actuality is more than any mere possibility . . . and this "more" cannot come from the thing's real possibility which is the cause; it cannot *come from* anything, it has to *become*, and this is an act, not of the cause, but of the event itself. Thus "creation" with respect to events is inevitably, in part, self-creation.[12]

Each unit event is the creative synthesis of the data that it prehends. It is a unitary experience in which the many parts are fused together into a novel whole. It is this synthesis that distinguishes the effect from its causes. The whole is greater than its parts. This synthesis is the free creation of the subject. "[T]he very meaning of freedom is the transition from the experienced antecedent many to the new unit experience of that many, the many being the previous acts of freedom" (CSPM 7). Creation is the freedom of self-determination.

Freedom is an ultimate principle, a final explanatory concept (BH 30). Although there are higher and lower forms of freedom, there is never the complete absence of freedom. Causality, and therefore freedom, is a matter of degree. "[T]he zero of freedom can only be the zero of experiencing, and even of reality" (CSPM 6). There is no experience that is not the experience of freedom. On the lowest levels of experience the range of possibilities open for determination may be minute; consequently, there is little freedom and prediction becomes highly accurate. As one moves up the scale of experience the possibility of accurate prediction diminishes as the degree of freedom is enhanced (BH 215).

This implies that God is the one who experiences the eminent degree of freedom. Since the essential nature of God is compatible with any possible world God is eminently free. An infinity of possibilities for realization are open to deity because there is no concrete experience that can threaten the divine existence.

It obviously follows from Hartshorne's claim that freedom is a matter of degree, that absolute, or abstract, freedom is as much a myth as is the belief in the total absence of freedom. Restrictions are imposed on the freedom of every individual by the free decisions of other individuals. "Causality is crystalized freedom," asserts Hartshorne, "freedom is causality in the making. There is always freedom, for there is always novelty. There is always causality, for always freedom has already been exercised, and a decision once made can only be accepted, it cannot be remade" (LP 233). It is God's freedom that, as we shall see, sets cosmic limits to the world's freedom; but within these limits finite agents determine one another's destiny by their free choices. Moreover, the world in some sense "creates" God as well, for God as concrete subject has the world as his object; therefore, the world is partial cause of God's concrete being. Thus even God's maximal freedom is not absolute, for while the abstract nature of God is compatible with any world whatsoever, God's concrete experience is limited by the actual world that is prehended.

## III. GOD AND THE WORLD

Thus far we have attempted to outline some of the essential features of Hartshorne's metaphysics as they relate to his theory of relative indeterminism. We shall now continue this examination but from a new perspective, namely, from Hartshorne's concept of dipolar theism. We will begin, as we did with Whitehead, with an analysis of his dipolar concept of God and then turn to the question of how God can be said to act in the world.

### 1. The Dipolar Nature of God

Hartshorne agrees with Whitehead that God is dipolar; however, whereas for Whitehead the two poles are the primordial and consequent natures, for Hartshorne they are God's abstract essence and concrete states. These two conceptions of dipolarity are not identical despite Hartshorne's frequent statements to the contrary.[13] Hartshorne believes that Whitehead was "rather seriously confused" in those places where he implies that God is a singular actual entity. "If the many in becoming prehended into a novel unity is thereby 'increased by one,' then in the case of God there is a new entity with each of His unified prehensive acts."[14] Consequently, if the metaphysical principles are not to be violated, Hartshorne concludes that God must be a society of actual entities. Thus while each divine occasion is analogous to finite occasions with its physical and mental poles, the dipolarity of God as an individual is analogous to the distinction between an individual's enduring character and the concrete states of that person's existence in which this character is instantiated.

In his abstract nature God is said to be absolute. The absolute is that which is independent of relations. Thus God in his abstract nature is externally related to everything else; God is the "object-for-all-subjects," the abstract constituent of all things (DR 70). The divine essence is not accidental, but necessary, and God will continue to exist with deity's essential characteristics regardless of what happens, since God cannot lose the unlimited ability to receive any cosmic datum whatever into the divine consciousness. "Because the defining character of his self-identity is utterly neutral to such alternatives, the concrete embodiment can be wholly expressive of and variable with relations. The character can be expressed in any relational pattern, hence God can contain any relational pattern and still be himself" (DR 81). This is in part what Hartshorne means by "individual." An individual exhibits self-identity through time in as much as certain abstract qualities remain the same despite changes in its environment. In this sense "individuality" means "independence from others." In its essential individuality the deity is the most neutral being, possessing an infinity of possibility owing to the utter abstractness of God's individual character. Hartshorne speaks of this independence of God as admirable (DR 44–45). It is a requirement of the religious conception of God that such characteristics as holiness and love be eminently and invariably exhibited by God and therefore independent of what the world does.

There is another sense of individuality in addition to the one just described. In God, as in all concrete realities, there are two grades of individuality: "the abstract or outline individuality which the thing has indifferently at diverse times of its history, and the fullness of individuality which the thing has in a given present, as containing its history up to date and in outline foreshadowing its future" (MVG 249). This "individual" is not an abstract essence, but a concrete reality. The abstract relational form of God "is only the form of adequate or supreme personality as such. Personality is not itself a person . . . " (DR 143). As a concrete reality God is a person; and it is only as a concrete person that God can think, will, or act. Furthermore, Hartshorne says that the "genetic identity of the divine personality is not a simple unity," although God's abstract essence is said to be "simple," but "an integration of a very real multiplicity of states and of lives sympathetically participated in" (NTT 104). Thus, whereas the abstract nature of God is independent of the world, God's concrete nature is dependent on it.

God is supremely relative as well as supremely nonrelative. In opposition to classical theism, Hartshorne argues that relativity as well as absoluteness are to be attributed to the divine being. This is because there are two aspects of perfection, one absolute and the other relative. Perfection is an excellence such that its possessor surpasses all other conceivable beings. That which is perfect in the Platonic-Aristotelian tradition excludes change and the possibility of being excelled by another. This notion of absolute perfection under-lies Anselm's understanding of God as "that than which nothing greater can be conceived." Hartshorne found absolute perfection to be an appropriate description of God's *essence* because of its fully abstract nature (DR 76). Yet the belief that the idea of an absolute maximum provides one with an exhaustive definition of perfection is warranted only on the assumption that what is unsurpassable by another must also be unsurpassable by itself. Hartshorne argues that we should define the word perfect, not as that which in no respect could conceivably be greater, but as that individual being "than which no *other individual* being could *conceivably* be greater, but which *itself*, in another 'state,' could become greater . . . [T]he perfect is the 'self-surpassing surpasser of all.' " (DR 20). This is the second aspect of perfection, that is, relative perfection, and it comprises Hartshorne's doctrine of "surrelativism." Deity is not self-surpassing in every way, for God's abstract essence is absolutely perfect. In God's concrete nature, however, the deity sure passes even itself as a new totality is constituted at each new moment.

The concrete nature is properly understood as inclusive of the absolute aspect of God's being. The absolute nature of God is, as we have seen, externally related to all things whereas God's concrete nature is internally related to all things. As absolute, God is the object-for-all-subjects; as concrete God is the subject-for-all-objects. Consequently, the absolute cannot be all-inclusive; however, it can be included in the concrete. The absoluteness and the all-inclusiveness required by the religious concept of deity can both be retained only by restricting the former to an abstract dimension of God's being. The absolute is, according to Hartshorne, "a divine object in the divine subject and for the divine subject" (DR 87). Thus there is an asymmetrical relationship between the two poles of God's being. The abstract nature is externally related to the concrete nature, while the concrete nature is internally related to the abstract nature.

To understand God's eminent relativity to the world we must recall our earlier discussion of the subject-object relationship. In his concrete nature God is the all-inclusive subject. The universe, which is the objective term of the relationship, is literally contained within the divine experience. God includes the world through the divine knowledge of the world. To say that God is supremely relative is thus identical to saying that God is omniscient, for "such relativity means that every difference makes a difference *in* the all-relative one, that for every diversity anywhere there is a diversity of relationships *in* him. Only the conception of an intuition whose datum is the universe gives any positive meaning to such an idea" (DR 77).

Hartshorne agrees with the Thomists that in the cognitive relation it is the knower who is internally related to the known and therefore qualified by the object of its knowledge. What he objects to is the reversal of this cognitive relation when the subject is God. On the contrary, "it is precisely the ideal case of knowledge, knowledge absolute in certainty and complete adequacy to the known, that must in some other aspects be literally and unrestrictedly relative" (DR 9). God's knowledge must be one thing if there is this world and another thing if there is *that* world. Divine knowledge is equal to its object whereas finite knowledge is able to misconceive reality precisely because it is not completely relative to the universe.

Before proceeding to the question of divine activity in the world, there are a couple of issues concerning God's knowledge of the world that should be raised. These problems revolve around Hartshorne's fundamental claim that reality is the content of divine knowledge (CSPM 286).[15] First, Griffin questions how this fits with the claim that contemporary entities do not prehend one another.[16] Although for many years Hartshorne maintained the doctrine of "complete inter-dependence between contemporaries," he later came to "deny interaction between God, as in a certain state, and any other individual in a strictly simultaneous state" (CSPM 115). But if, as Hartshorne now wants to say, "experiencing is never simultaneous with its concrete objects but always subsequent" (CSPM 109), if the present is "nascent" rather than "definite," constituting an "ever-changing class of 'latest subjects' " (CSPM 110) that are unavailable for prehension, then how can the divine knowledge be said to define reality? Such nascent subjects are certainly real even if they lack full actuality. Moreover, if there is always a class of "latest subjects" that have not been objectified, then Griffin rightly concludes that "God and the world" has a different referent than "the world in God," notwithstanding Hartshorne's claim to the contrary (CSPM 110). [17] In what sense, then, can God be said to be the all-inclusive whole given Hartshorne's correlation of God's omniscience and his inclusiveness?

There is a further difficulty raised by Hartshorne's related claim that the object of knowledge is contained within the subject. God's omniscience guarantees that every value realized in the world is taken up and given a permanent place in the divine life. There is nothing "lost" in the perishing of actual occasions. As Sessions says, "If God did not include in His experience all that a thing is—if something, such as 'subjective immediacy,' were inevitably 'lost' to His experience—then in Hartshorne's view what is omitted could not be real."[16] In his article, "The Social Theory of Feelings," Hartshorne explains this in terms of the privacy of feelings. There he argues that it is "logically absurd" to suggest that A feels B's pain "as B feels it." This is because how B feels it represents "the total momentary standpoint of B, and if it also equally represented the total momentary standpoint of A, then A and B would be the same subject."[19] A could feel B's pain as B's, but apart from God this involves an abstractive deficiency. However, divine omniscience enables God "to have another's standpoint in its fullness" as datum for God's own standpoint.[20] Using Whitehead's terminology, Hartshorne concludes that "God's subjective forms . . . are the only ones able to enjoy as their data or objective forms the subjective forms of other individuals in their full value."[21]

The problem, as Peters has pointed out, is that the full particularity of an individual does not seem available to *any* knower.[22] If we are afraid of the future is God also fearful? Our feelings of fear represent our total momentary standpoints. But can God have the same momentary standpoint as another individual? Certainly it is not the *same* standpoint for then God would be indistinguishable from that individual. But without it being the identical standpoint, can God have it in its "fullness," for its fullness would seem to require its finiteness? The fear that I experience would not be the same experience if I had a different standpoint. God cannot experience *my experience* of fear without having my standpoint and only my standpoint. Is there not, then, something lost even in God's feeling of another's feeling?[23] Peters suggests that there is a necessary distinction between an event and the facts about it. This is the distinction between "definiteness (definite truth) and concrete entities themselves . . . . Correlatively, there is the distinction between X-as-known and X-as-existing."[24] What is lost, what cannot be experienced even though the ideal knower can know all the facts (truth) about it, is the experience of X-as-existing.[25]

Hartshorne's claim that divine knowledge defines reality is therefore not without its difficulties. This is important because of the significance that the idea of God as supremely relative has for his social and political theory. What could be in jeopardy is the claim that a dipolar concept of God supplies us with a better guide for determining the common good than other criteria, for example, the good of humanity. We will return to this question when we come to analyze Whitehead's and Hartshorne's political ideas in the following chapters.

## 2. God as Causal Agent

Turning now to Hartshorne's understanding of divine activity, we note that he raises several objections to classical theism's traditional definition of omnipotence as absolute power. Most obviously, to attribute to God the power to determine everything that happens is to deprive finite creatures of their freedom. Whatever state of affairs is actualized is wholly of God's choosing for God has the power to bring about infallibly any logically possible world (CSPM 137). It necessarily follows that God alone is responsible for all that is evil in the world. Second, the very idea of "all power" is nonsensical. Unsurpassable power is one thing, but "to identify this unsurpassability of power with its sheer monopoly, a control by which all concrete details of existence are determined, leaving the creatures with nothing to determine for themselves, no genuine options of their own, is to burden the divine worshipfulness with a logical paradox of our own making" (NTT 119). Power requires something to work on and this necessitates that there be other centers of power. "To be is to have some power because it is the actualization of some potentiality. Actualization is to some extent self-creation."[26] Third, the description of God as sheer power or activity is a representation of the tyrant conception of deity.[27]

In keeping with his doctrine of surrelativism, Hartshorne claims that God's power must be unsurpassably great. Omnipotence means power such that none could conceivably be greater. It is in this sense that God can be said to have "perfect" power. Religious faith imputes to God "power adequate to cosmic need" (DR 134). Such power is not the ability to determine completely what will happen in the world. This would not be in keeping with the metaphysical claim that freedom and causality are cosmic variables applicable to some degree to every entity. God's power is the greatest power, as opposed to being the only power.[28]

As we saw above, power is social influence. Causal conditions do not determine the effect in its full particularity, but only require that there be some effect of a more or less general description. A cause limits the possibilities open for realization by the new entity. In keeping with this God is understood to be the supreme case of social influence. As such God is no more able to ascertain beforehand what God is causing than we are (CSPM 127). God is only able to set limits to the possible actions of local agents within the world. "The subordination of all to one power . . . means . . . that all things are self-determining (and mutually determining) *within limits*, and it is the setting of these limits which constitutes the divine ordering of the world."[29] Such conditions represent the optimal risk-opportunity ratio avoiding both the extremes of too much and too little freedom.

In a very interesting passage in *The Logic of Perfection* Hartshorne provides a political analogy to the exercise of divine power in the world:

> Statesmen know that beyond a certain point interference with the lives of citizens does more harm than good, and this not solely because of the weakness or stupidity of statesmen but also because of the meaning of good as self-activity. This is part of the reason for the ideal of democracy, that people need first of all to be themselves, and this self-hood no tyrant, human or superhuman, however benevolent, can impose upon them. (LP 204)

The argument used here is common among modern liberal political theorists such as Mill, Hobhouse, and Green. Human nature is not a static, given reality as the classical liberals believed but is capable of development. Freedom is therefore held to be necessary if a person's capacities are to be fully realized. This suggestion, that political freedom is to be modeled after the divine action, that is, the establishment of optimal limits whereby human capacities can be created, will be discussed when we come to look at the issues of coercion and state intervention.

Because there are numerous centers of freedom and creativity, the world contains an unavoidable element of chaos and tragedy. "Risk of evil and opportunity for good are two aspects of just one thing, multiple freedom . . . " (NTT 81). The universality of freedom lies behind the recalcitrance of the world which prohibits the cosmic designer from imposing a final order on it. However the fact that there is not pure chaos is only explained by "the primary inspiration of deity upon all. . . . " Hartshorne continues saying, "God is the orderer of the world . . . making the best use possible of the irrepressible part-chaos of free acts."[30] It is only the providential activity of God as the supreme power that limits the anarchy otherwise endemic to a situation in which there is multiple creativity. Divine providence is not the elimination, but rather the limitation, of chance. It does not determine what will happen, but is a "golden mean" that limits what can happen.

The implication of this, which Hartshorne himself notes, is that God does not intervene in particular situations to send us particular evils; rather, God "establishes an order in which creatures can send each other particular goods and evils" (NTT 120). As in Kafka's *The*

*Castle,* where the actions are taken by the bureaucrats rather than by the unapproachable owner of the castle, so the universe is a bureaucracy in which we are all members setting each others' destiny by our actions. In *Creative Synthesis and Philosophic Method* this point is elaborated further. Universal creationism means that "creatures determine worldly particulars, good or evil. God wills good *as such.* Good and not evil is his aim everywhere; but the *particularization of this aim at good in the world is left to creatures"* (CSPM 240; emphasis added). God's concern is not with particular goods in the world, but with good "as such," that is, the universal good. This universal good is identical to that good which is the divine experience. "The particular goods which God himself determines are not in the world, but as Niebuhr says, 'beyond history.' They are the particular responses which God makes to the creaturely decisions, the way in which he makes optimal use of them as data in his own consciousness" (CSPM 240).

I believe that Hartshorne's suggestion that God's experience is "beyond history" is at best misleading, at worst inconsistent. It is precisely the concrete nature of God that is eminently historical.[31] Perhaps it would be better to say that the divine experience is not localized or "in the world," but universal in scope. This helps explain why it is that God does not act locally. According to the principle of relativity, it belongs to the nature of a being that it is a potential for every becoming. There is no effect that is not also a cause. A finite effect becomes a finite cause; an infinite effect becomes an infinite cause. According to Hartshorne's process philosophy, "God's creativity is his higher form of emergent experiential synthesis, or response to stimuli. He influences us supremely because he is supremely open to our influence" (CSPM 12). Thus, it is precisely because the divine experience of the world is universal that God's activity in the world is cosmological rather than local.

This relationship between God as supremely relative and God as supreme power is found again in Hartshorne's discussion of "direct power" and the depiction of God as love. The distinction between direct and indirect power is one that Hartshorne has made throughout his career. In *Beyond Humanism* he wrote that any world state would most certainly be

> relatively abstract and brutal and blind in relation to the intimate life of the personality, and that its indirect sources of power over persons (guns, radio stations, fixing of salaries, hiring and

firing) will be on a much more godlike scale than its direct power to move the individual through understanding and love. (BH 34)

Political power is indirect. The only direct power one has over others is that which one has over the members of one's own body. The mind-body relation is the analogy that Hartshorne uses to explain how God exerts power in the world and in what sense God is love. These two features are not distinct. "Only in the mind-body relation is power also sensitiveness, is sympathy direct awareness, is awareness sympathetic power" (BH 208). This direct relationship is one of organic sympathy, or love, in which the subject feels the feelings of others, the objects thereby exerting power directly on the subject without any intervening mechanism. "Surely God controls the world," writes Hartshorne, "not by hands, but by direct power of his will, feeling, and knowledge" (MVG 179).

The concrete nature of God, as supremely relative, directly feels the feelings of every individual in the universe. This is the world's influence on God, an influence that, as we have seen, God does not absolutely control. God, as the supreme form of creative freedom, determines how this data will be synthesized (NTT 82).

The best ruler is an intermediary in the universal interaction, able to moderate and harmonize actions because all that is done is done also to him, whose reaction to this action absorbs and transmutes all influences into a counter influence, integrative and harmonizing in tendency, discouraging excessive factors and encouraging insufficient ones. (DR 50)

What is clear is that while the difference between God and any finite cause is infinite, it is not absolute. This becomes clearer when we recall that the cause-effect relationship is the same as the object-subject relationship: "[T]o explain how something influences an experience, we have only to explain how this something comes to be an object or content of the experience" (LP 227). To change a subject one has only to change the objects that it experiences or "knows." Consequently, since God is the object-for-all-subjects, God can change the world merely by changing himself (CSPM 11–12; DR 139). God is the supreme instance of social influence, not a different type of influence.

One sense of the claim that God is a causal agent, then, is that the successive states of God's concrete nature impose restrictions upon the local agents. Self-causation, for God as for man, also entails the partial determination of others. As such God is an *efficient* cause. However, as noted above, God's action is not local in character. What then is determined through God's momentary creative syntheses? I believe that Hartshorne intends to say that God is establishing the laws of nature that function as a limitation on finite centers of creativity. The "outlines of the world-order, the laws of nature" are said to be "divine decrees" (CSPM 125). This is God's imposition of optimal conditions within which finite agents can operate, within which they can send each other particular goods and evils. Hence Hartshorne claims: "The only 'acts of God' we can identify . . . are the laws of nature. They make possible collectively coherent creative actions by the nondivine individuals and just this is the intent and need of the divine individual" (NTT 102). God's power is such as to be able to freely choose "the basic laws" of any logically possible world and to be able to fully know "whatever world results from the laws plus the choices of the creatures so far as left open by the divine choice" (CSPM 137).[32]

Thus far I have limited myself to a discussion of God's concrete nature which operates as an efficient cause. But God is also active in the world through his abstract nature as eternal final cause. Unlike the concrete nature, which is both cause and effect, the abstract nature is the purely abstract supreme cause. Hartshorne explicitly states that "God as efficient cause is past . . . while as effect he is present, and as eternal final cause he is abstract."[33] It is God's concrete pole that as past is efficient cause and as present is effect. The absolute pole is only final (and supreme) cause. "God as supreme (in the sense of universal) cause is what is universally required by other things and which itself requires only that the class of other things be not null" (PSG 501). That which is universally required is not any particular concrete state of God's being, but the wholly abstract essence of God. This essence is the divine character, the "primordial mind with an *un*acquired ideal, thus one which was never an effect" (PSG 502). It is the "unmoved mover" even of God himself (DR 82). The difference between God as concrete and abstract cause is brought out in the following quotation:

> The common factor presupposed by all possible world-states is the divine essence (not God, but His essence), the Cause of all things and effect of none, The Absolute. But the total concrete cause of *this* world is not merely the absolute divine essence; rather, it is God as having actually created and now possessing all previous worlds. (LP 273)

How is it that God's abstract nature functions as a final cause? Hartshorne recognizes that one needs ideal aims that relate one's life to something that transcends the finitude of one's own achievements. Self-worship, party-worship, and state-worship are the illegitimate substitutes for the truly adequate aim of serving the cosmic individual. It is God's nature as supremely relative that provides motivation for an individual. The "one primary good" is that "the creatures should enjoy rich harmonies of living, and pour this richness into the one ultimate receptacle of all achievement, the life of God" (DR 127–28). God is the beneficiary of created values and it is mankind's final end to contribute some value to the divine life that would otherwise be absent. "The future that ultimately matters is not particularly mine or yours, or even human, but cosmic and divine" (NTT 110). Thus it is the abstract nature of God, which establishes God as the everlasting One, the recipient of all values, that functions as the eternal final cause, persuading the world toward the all-inclusive, divine end.

## IV. CONCLUSION

Hartshorne's metaphysic establishes freedom as a fundamental explanatory feature of the world. It is essentially a social conception of freedom according to which our relations with others determine the scope of possibility for self-creation. Political freedom is, on this understanding, a special case of this ultimate metaphysical category. "The universal principle of freedom is that of 'self-determination,' as contrasted to 'determination by others.' Political freedom means that the behavior of citizens is in some important respects protected against determination by the rulers."[34] Hartshorne perceives the interrelationships between persons as illustrating the metaphysical principles of freedom and causation. Therefore, the questions concerning the place and extent of freedom and power in society and politics that bedevil the modern world can be answered only when one understands that our freedom and power are in fact restricted or local exemplifications of cosmic variables. Political power should therefore be patterned after the divine activity in the world. It is a question of establishing the proper limits to interference by others. Too little control would result in anarchy; too much control would stifle creativity. In either case, self-creativity would be impoverished, and this, in turn, would frustrate the divine aim at aesthetic beauty to which we all contribute.

*part three*

# PROCESS PHILOSOPHY
# AND POLITICAL THEORY

# 4

# The Individual and Society

In the previous section we outlined the fundamental principles of process philosophy. We are now in a position to turn our attention to an exposition and analysis of Whitehead's and Hartshorne's social and political writings. There are four main topics that we will address: (1) the relationship between the individual and society; (2) freedom, equality, and the ideal of democracy; (3) the use of force within and between states; and (4) progress and social development. In the course of our analysis we will supply their political ideas with historical context and depth by relating them to certain social and intellectual developments around the turn of the century. In addition, an effort will be made to demonstrate how the principles of process metaphysics support Whitehead's and Hartshorne's long-standing commitments to a modern liberal ideology.

## I. SCIENTIFIC MATERIALISM AND THE MECHANISTIC VIEW OF MAN AND SOCIETY

In the preface to *Science and the Modern World* Whitehead asserts that his study "has been guided by the conviction that the mentality of an epoch springs from the view of the world which is, in fact, dominant in the educated sections of the communities in question" (SMW ix). It is Whitehead's belief that the cosmology that has asserted itself for the last three centuries at the expense of other points of view has been that derived from science. The Lowell Lectures are an attempt to trace the emergence of the scientific world view since the seventeenth century. However, these lectures are more than a brief, though intriguing, history of ideas; they are at the same time a challenge to the scientific materialism underlying this development. With *Science and the Modern World* Whitehead steps into the world of metaphysics and undertakes what he considered to be one of the functions of philosophy, namely, that it be a "critic of cosmologies" (SMW ix).

Whitehead believed that all the variant systems within a philosophical epoch "unconsciously presuppose" some "fundamental assumptions" (SMW 71). During the modern period the unifying assumption is the concept of matter which has the property of simple location in space and time. "To say that a bit of matter has *simple location* means that, in expressing its spatio-temporal relations, it is adequate to state that it is where it is, in a definite finite region of space, and throughout a definite finite duration of time, apart from any essential reference of the relations of that bit of matter to other regions of space and to other durations of time" (SMW 84). What is most important in this statement, as Lewis Ford notes, is the claim of materialism that each particle of matter is externally related to every other particle.[1] Each particle can be said to be "here" in space and "here" in time "in a perfectly definite sense which does not require for its explanation any reference to other regions of space-time" (SMW 72). Both change and endurance are irrelevant to the essential reality of the material universe. Change and duration merely apply to "the fortunes of matter in its adventure through space" (CN 20).

The new philosophy of nature that emerged in the seventeenth century was heavily influenced by the theory of atomism. The atoms, which are permanent, are by nature simple, whereas the things that undergo change are complex. Complex entities are the product of the arrangement and rearrangement of the simple particles of matter. Matter is in itself "inert, i.e., without activity, and thus completely unable to initiate locomotion: matter *is moved*; it does not move itself."[2] Seventeenth-century proponents of atomism, such as Hobbes and Locke, believed

> (a) that all the changing material in the universe, even all apparent physical 'substances', consists of certain indivisible and imperceptible elementary particles; and (b) that the purely mechanical interactions between these atomic entities together with their own individual characteristics sufficiently explain all that happens and develops in nature.[3]

Whitehead describes this "fixed scientific cosmology" as one that "presupposes the ultimate fact of an irreducible brute matter, or material, spread throughout space in a flux of configurations. In itself such a material is senseless, valueless, purposeless. It just does what it does do, following a fixed routine imposed by external relations which do not spring from the nature of its being. It is this assumption that I call 'scientific materialism' " (SMW 25). Newtonian physics, with its "thorough-going doctrine of 'simple location' and 'external relations' " (AI 201), is an example of scientific materialism. "Newtonian physics," writes Whitehead, "is based upon the independent individuality of each bit of matter. Each stone is conceived as fully describable apart from any reference to any other portion of matter" (AI 200). Space and matter are the fundamental notions in this physical theory. Time is not an essential feature, but rather an accident, of the material. One is able, therefore, to abstract from change and to conceive of nature at a "durationless instant" (MT 199). At any given instant nature is characterized by the distribution of matter in space. The world is thus conceived as a succession of instantaneous configurations of matter, and the laws of motion, which Newton was concerned to express, govern the changes of this material configuration.

Alongside the new scientific cosmology there appeared new conceptions of human nature and society. Thomas Hobbes, perhaps the quintessential representative of seventeenth-century mechanistic materialism, constructed a theory in which human beings are self-maintaining machines, complicated examples of the universal principle of matter in motion. By means of the resolutive-compositive method of Galileo which he adopted, Hobbes resolved society into its simplest elements and then reconstructed those elements into a logical whole. "The resolving . . . was of existing society into existing individuals, and of them in turn into the primary elements of their motion."[4] In this way Hobbes attempts to assimilate the laws of human behavior to the laws of physics. In keeping with his materialism all aspects of human life, including human emotions and mental activity, are explained in terms of matter in motion.

Hobbes's political theory regards human nature as having been given with certain desires: to preserve its vital motion, to acquire power, to avoid death. The *natural* state of mankind is one of anarchy, a state of war "of every man, against every man."[5] Organized society, conversely, is an artificial construct, a man-made machine. It is prudential for an individual to enter into the social contract and thereby create a "mortal god."[6] "All society . . . is either for gain or for glory; that is, not so much for love of our fellows as for love of ourselves."[7] Society does not in any way contribute to a person's essential nature; rather it functions as the most effective means by which each individual can satisfy his or her natural interests. This is in keeping with Hobbes's materialistic "substance thinking" according to which relations are perceived as being external to a substance: "The substance is what it is independently of relations and then enters into relations. These relations do not affect its fundamental nature or existence."[8] Thus Hobbes found the metaphysical atomism of scientific materialism to be supportive of his interpretation of human beings as self-sufficient entities given with certain needs, purposes, desires, and interests that can only be satisfied in society ruled by an absolute monarch.

## II. ORGANIC MECHANISM AND THE ORGANIC VIEW OF MAN AND SOCIETY

### 1. Internal Relations and Holistic Social Theory

Whitehead's Lowell Lectures, as we already noted, are a *critical* account of the emergence of scientific materialism. As an alternative to this inadequate cosmology Whitehead offers his theory of "organic mechanism." Unlike materialistic mechanism which it seeks to replace, organic mechanism adopts a theory of internal relations. "Whitehead aims to develop a theory of mechanism, in which the activity of the whole can be affected by the interaction of the parts. But this is not a *materialistic* mechanism, whose parts are simply located bits of matter externally related to one another."[9]

The acceptance of internal relations is a central tenet of organic or holistic social theories. F. H. Bradley for instance argued (a) that entities are altered by the relationships into which they enter, and (b) that the parts qualify the whole and that the whole in turn qualifies the parts.[10] Bradley believed that all real relations are internal, external relations being merely the projection of our ignorance upon the world. Hence given *A R B*, *A* acquires some character *C* without which *A* would not be what it is. Every relationship in which *A* participates partly determines what *A* is. This is the heart of the theory of internal relations: entities are *necessarily* altered by the relations into which they enter. On the other hand, to mechanists . . . relations do not alter the entities that are related."[11]

The acceptance of internal relations is central to Whitehead's theory of organic mechanism. "[E]ach relationship enters into the essence of the event," he claims, "so that, apart from that relationship, the event would not be itself. This is what is meant by the very notion of internal relations. It has been usual, indeed, universal, to hold that spatio-temporal relationships are external. This doctrine is what is here denied" (SMW 180; see SMW 95).[12] D. C. Phillips argues against the reality of internal relations on the grounds that if one is to have knowledge of A one must know all of A's relationships because each relationship provides A with a defining feature. However, as Lucas points out, Whitehead only asserts, in refutation of pure logical atomism, that one's knowledge of an entity increases in proportion to the increase in one's knowledge of the relations between that entity and its environment.[13] As Whitehead says "A single fact in isolation is the primary myth required for finite thought, that is to say, for thought unable to embrace totality" (MT 12). Connectedness is of the essence of all things and "[a]bstraction from connectedness involves the omission of an essential factor in the fact considered" (MT 13). This idea that the parts cannot be understood in isolation from the whole is in keeping with holistic or organic social thought.

Hartshorne likewise acknowledges the reality of both internal and external relations. By a relation to A being external to another term B he means that B would have the exact same nature even if it was not related to A. "An external relation is only nominally a relation 'of' the term to which it is external. It is not that certain terms externally have relations, but that certain relations have terms, in such fashion that the terms, some of them, do not really 'have' the relations" (DR 65). Not every term is constituted by the relations which it is in; only the term to which the relation is internal possesses the other term as a constituent element. Hartshorne recounts Bradley's argument against external relations saying,

> If A is not, in its very being or identity, related to B, then we must relate A to the relation to B to get A really related. And this leads to a series of relations to relations to relations . . . a series which is vicious not only because it is infinite but because it can never arrive at a relation to B which really is A's. (DR 64)

Although Hartshorne disagrees with Bradley's claim that this argument proves that relations cannot be external to any of the terms, he does believe that it establishes that relations cannot be external to all of their terms. "For if no term is constituted by the relation, then the relatedness is additional to all the terms, and must be related to them by a further relation, and so on" (DR 64). Thus there must be internal relations as well as external relations.

Both Whitehead and Hartshorne affirm a theory of asymmetrical relations. Whereas scientific materialism holds that bits of matter exist independently prior to entering into purely external relations with other bits of matter, process philosophy claims that every occasion of experience is essentially related to the universe of actual entities that constitutes its environment. This has far-reaching implications for social theory. According to Hobbes each person possesses a fully formed nature independent of society. Instead of social groups conditioning what an individual essentially is, the features of the individuals, given independently of the social context, determine the ends of the society. Process philosophy rejects the Hobbesian supposition that an individual first exists and then subsequently enters into relations with others: "The human being is inseparable from its environment in each occasion of its existence" (AI 80). Each moment of creative synthesis arises in relation to the actual world. The notion of an individual in isolation from his or her wider environment is an abstraction. The fully concrete individual is the creative synthesis of the creativity of others; its nature is, in other words, a social product. Hence far from entering into social relations essentially immune to the community around us, "the richness of our individual experience depends upon the richness of the experience of others with whom we associate, the growth of our good is a function not primarily of competitive advantage but of communal well-being."[14]

Since human nature is a social product, society is no longer viewed as an artificial construct resulting from a hypothetical contract made between autonomous individuals, but as a wholly natural and necessary state of existence (AI 80-81). According to Lucas, Whitehead has demonstrated how a "doctrine of metaphysical holism stressing interdependence and reciprocal relatedness, could be developed without sacrificing freedom, pluralism, and a relative individuality for every actual entity in the system."[15] And although Hartshorne claims that all "clear thinkers" (LP 201) have turned away from holistic or organicist doctrines because of the consequences of symmetrical relatedness, this should not be taken to imply a rejection of organicism per se. While adhering to an "organic monism" in which the whole-parts relationship is asymmetrical, Hartshorne expressly rejects only those holistic theories that turned upon a theory of symmetrical relations. "Only by neglecting the time structure of the situation . . . have 'holistic' philosophies fallen into the confusion of a whole determining its individual parts. The symmetrical idea of 'interaction' between whole and parts is due to treating a complex of one-way relations en bloc" (LP 200).

## 2. Organicism in the Thought of Whitehead and Hartshorne

Before we turn our attention directly to Whitehead's and Hartshorne's views of society we must note some significant, but overlooked, differences between their understanding of organicism. In his mature metaphysics Whitehead distinguishes between a macroscopic and a microscopic meaning of organism.[16] The community of actual things is an organism in a continual state of expansion. Thus "the universe in any stage of its expansion is the first meaning of 'organism.' In this sense, an organism is a nexus" (PR 215[327]). This is the macroscopic meaning of organism. The microscopic meaning refers to the actual occasion "considered as a process of realizing an individual unity of experience" (PR 129[196]). The actual occasion repeats in microcosm what the universe is in macrocosm (PR 215[327]). We are thus explicitly supplied with two examples of organisms, the universe and each actual occasion.

It is interesting that these meanings of organism refer to extreme examples—the universe and the actual entity—omitting any reference to intermediary nexūs. Is a finite society, whether it be a tree, a human body, or a human community, an organism? *Science and the Modern World* leaves no doubt that it is:

> The concrete enduring entities are organisms, so that the plan of the *whole* influences the very characters of the various subordinate organisms which enter into it. In the case of an animal, the mental states enter into the plan of the total organism and thus modify the plans of the successive subordinate organisms until the ultimate smallest organisms, such as electrons, are reached. (SMW 115)

This idea is not confined to Whitehead's early metaphysical writings but is also found in his later "systematic" philosophy. In PR 287(440) he says that the organisms of the world are of two types: "one type consists of the individual actual entities; the other type consists of nexūs of actual entities." Not only the universe but finite nexūs as well are organisms. In a very enlightening passage from *Process and Reality* he writes:

> [I]n addition to the merely potential subdivisions of a satisfac-
> tion into coordinate feelings, there is the merely potential
> aggregation of actual entities into a super-actuality in respect to
> which the true actualities play the part of coordinate subdivi-
> sions. In other words, just as, for some purposes, one atomic
> actuality can be treated as though it were many coordinate
> actualities, in the same way, for other purposes, a nexus of
> many actualities can be treated as though it were one actuality.
> This is what we habitually do in the case of the span of life of a
> molecule, or of a piece of rock, or of a human body. (PR
> 286-87[439])[17]

It is important to be clear as to what Whitehead is and is not saying. What he is claiming is that a nexus of occasions is in some sense an individual organism which, for some purposes, can be treated as a whole, as one actuality. What he is not claiming is that this "super-actuality" has the ontological status of "true actualities." Such a claim would commit the fallacy of misplaced concreteness.

Perhaps we could say that organisms are of two types— occurrences and endurances. An actual entity, an occurrence, is an organic whole, a unity of prehensions which are its "parts." The becoming of an occasion is a creative synthesis of the data provided by its actual world and thus "in no sense is it the sum of its parts" (PR 140[213]). Yet an actual entity is itself part of one or more larger wholes which are endurances. These endurances are societies of occasions whose interrelatedness results in the emergence of distinc- tive characters or social patterns "which the separate factors in isolation or in haphazard juxtaposition do not presage."[18] As we saw in our initial summary of Whitehead's philosophy, a group of actual entities enjoys social order when they share in a common element of form as a result of their interrelatedness. "The self-identity of a society is founded upon the self-identity of its defining characteristic, and upon the mutual immanence of its occasions" (AI 262). Nancy

Frankenberry concludes that "nothing is explained apart from the whole, and no whole is explained as a mere sum of its parts. In the new paradigm, emergent behavior means that togetherness in nature signifies a creative synthesis in which dynamic components enter into internal relations such that a genuinely novel unity emerges with characteristic capacities and properties."[19]

If societies are properly conceived as "wholes" how are we to understand the interaction between the whole and its parts? In addition to internal relations, a further constituent idea of organicism is that the whole influences the nature of the parts. Given a theory of internal relations, the nature of the parts of a given whole are partially determined by the relational properties they possess among themselves. If the makeup of the whole is altered, for example through the addition of a further entity, then the parts will be changed through the acquisition of a new relational characteristic. "In other words, if the whole were different the parts would be different, and it is in this sense that the whole determines the nature of its parts."[20]

There is little doubt that Whitehead's theory of organic mechanism affirms the notion of a mutual interrelation between the whole and parts such that not only is "the part . . . constitutive of the whole" (SMW 181) but "the whole is evidently constitutive of the part" (SMW 181).

> [A]n individual entity, whose own life-history is a part within the life history of some larger, deeper, more complete pattern, is liable to have aspects of that larger pattern dominating its own being, and to experience modifications of that larger pattern reflected in itself as modifications of its own being. This is the theory of organic mechanism. (SMW 156)

The plan of the whole organism influences the subordinate organisms that enter into it. "[T]he molecules may blindly run in accordance with the general laws, but the molecules differ in their intrinsic characters according to the general organic plans of the situations in which they find themselves" (SMW 116). The whole, understood as the enduring organism up to that point, influences the aim of the successive parts which comprise the whole. How these subordinate organisms function, therefore, is in part determined by the larger enduring organism of which they are parts. Their *teloi*, or plans are partially determined by the *telos* of the whole.[21]

As Ford points out, "[o]rganic mechanism remains a permanent fixture in Whitehead's philosophy."[22] It finds expression in the general claim that an organism is dependent upon its wider environment for its continued existence. A specific reference can be found in PR 106(162) where we are told that "[t]he molecules within an animal body exhibit certain peculiarities of behaviour not to be detected outside an animal body."

It would appear safe to conclude that Whitehead advocates a new cosmological scheme in which the dominant scientific materialism is replaced with a modified organic or holistic theory of reality. Three fundamental tenets of organicism—the reality of internal relations, that the whole is greater than the sum of its parts, and that the whole influences its parts—are all present in the theory of organic mechanism and there is no suggestion that they were ever abandoned by Whitehead.

When we turn to Hartshorne's discussion of "wholes" and "organisms" we find some important differences from Whitehead. The position he defends is termed "organic monism" and it aims to replace the dualism of organic and inorganic wholes with a "relative dualism." "The assertion is not that all wholes are purposive or organic; but that, first, all well-unified wholes are organic, and second, that all wholes whatever both involve and are involved in organic wholes"(LP 192). Hartshorne's relative dualism differentiates between two types of wholes. An organism is defined as "a whole whose parts serve as 'organs' or instruments to a purpose or end-value inherent in the whole."[23] Such wholes are "well-unified." Being fully organic they are more than a collection. "[A] unitary organism in the narrower or more emphatic sense is one with a dominant member, which is the synthetic act, or rather act-sequence . . . " (LP 200-201). However, there is another type of whole that has "less unity than its most unified parts" and is therefore not an organism "in the pregnant sense" (LP 192) just described.[24] While not themselves "fully organic" such wholes can yet serve as "organs" for a more inclusive organism. Indeed, every finite whole is held to be composed of unitary organic events and is itself a part of the universal organism that is God.

The question, as Hartshorne points out, is one of *unity* (RSP 54). Only in so far as the whole is "well-unified" which is to say the product of a synthetic act, is it "fully organic." What qualifies as an organism in this sense? For Hartshorne the universe, with God as its synthetic act sequence, possesses such individual unity, as do all actual occasions. But what of finite societies of occasions? What type of "wholes" are they? Hartshorne says that a society of actual entities can be one of two types, namely, either a "democracy" or an "aristocracy." Only an aristocracy is a "unitary organism," because it possesses a dominant member that synthesizes the data of its parts. A human person is an example given by Hartshorne. Democracies, such as mountains, plants, and some lower forms of animals, lack a supreme, radically dominant member. Thus such societies are not super-organisms, but "quasi-organisms" (LP 193). Human societies are for Hartshorne also examples of a "democratic," and therefore quasi-organic, social structure (See RSP 38–39, 62–63). Elsewhere Hartshorne distinguishes between organisms considered from physiological and psychological standpoints (RSP 56–59). From the physical viewpoint a tree "really is a single organism," since the parts cooperate so as to preserve the whole, but Hartshorne adds that it is made such "by virtue of some purpose of the observer in carving out that much of his environment." From the psychical perspective it lacks the integration of an individual and is therefore only a "pseudo-organism." Hartshorne wants to avoid the term inorganic. Such societies are a mere collection of organisms, a democracy lacking the integration of its most unified members.

From this discussion I believe that we can detect important differences between Whitehead and Hartshorne concerning the nature of social unity and the relationship between the "part" and the "whole" in society. Hartshorne stipulates that a whole is "fully organic" only when it is "well-unified." This condition is met when the whole exhibits a unity equal to its most unified parts. At this point one thing becomes clear: no society *qua society* can be a fully organic whole. The reason for this is that every society is necessarily composed of actual occasions; therefore, for a society to be fully organic it would have to possess a unity equal to that of an actual occasion and this, clearly, is a condition that no society can meet. The only thing that can realize the organic unity of an actual entity is an actual entity.

The consequences of Hartshorne's line of reasoning are, in my opinion, unacceptable. For example, he writes that "an organism involves a plurality of entities contributing directly to the value of a single entity, the 'whole' " (LP 195). When considering a society, the "whole" is an individual entity. This strikes me as counter-intuitive, particularly when one considers the example of a human person used by Hartshorne. In practice, when it comes to the human person,

Hartshorne says that an individual is fully organic because of the synthetic act-sequence constituting his or her "stream of consciousness."

> My feeling at a given moment is one, that of my cells is many. The diverse cellular feelings become data for the unitary human feeling, and this feeling is the momentary "whole" summing up the antecedent states of "the parts" and subsequently reacting upon the later stages of these parts. Thus the many-one action is turned into a one-many action. Not the whole as collection of parts acts upon those very parts, but the one actuality which is my feeling now, and which reflects the actualities previously constituting my body, acts upon the many actualities which subsequently compose that body. (LP 200)

Notice that for Hartshorne the whole is the "unitary human feeling" or "my feeling now." But is it adequate to say that the whole person is that person's stream of consciousness? Hartshorne's analysis of the whole and its parts in the context of a society overlooks the limitations of a finite actual occasion. At any given moment the society of actual entities comprising a person's body are experiencing innumerable feelings. However the actual occasions constituting one's stream of consciousness cannot fully prehend any actual entity. They must be prehended under abstraction. On Hartshorne's analysis we must conclude that the multitude of bodily feelings that are not prehended by the dominant member of the complex society which is that person are not part of that "human reality" (LP 201).

I hold that Whitehead's position is to be preferred. He speaks of the "plan of the *whole*" influencing "the very characters of the various subordinate organisms which enter into it," that is, the parts (SMW 115). However, he does not identify the stream of consciousness with the plan of the whole. On the contrary,

> the *mental states enter into the plan of the total organism* and thus modify the plans of the successive subordinate organisms until the ultimate smallest organisms, such as electrons, are reached. Thus an electron within a living body is different from an electron outside it, by reason of the plan of the body. The electron blindly runs either within or without the body; but it runs within the body in accordance with its character within the

body; that is to say, in accordance with the general plan of the body, and this plan includes the mental state. (SMW 115–16; emphasis added.)

The general plan of the body *includes* the mental state but is not identified with it. The plan of the total organism is constituted by the plans of all its members; it is the harmony achieved through mutual cooperation. Thus the social whole is here understood as an endurance, not an occurrence.

It should be pointed out that like Hartshorne, Whitehead distinguishes between various types of aggregations of actualities. The lowest type is the nonliving, inorganic aggregation. The vegetable grade "exhibits a democracy of purposeful influences issuing from its parts" (MT 38). Such an organization lacks a center of experience "with a higher complexity either of expressions received or of inborn data" (MT 33). An animal has one center of experience expressing itself throughout the animal body. At the same time the body is a complex of centers of experience which are "imposing the expression of themselves on each other."[25] In the human grade of animal the central activity of enjoyment and expression has become radically dominant. Despite the similarity between Hartshorne and Whitehead concerning the identification of different levels of social organization, and notwithstanding Hartshorne's appeal to Whitehead for support of his classification (RSP 58), the use to which this analysis is put is distinctly different. For Hartshorne it is a matter of differentiating between levels of organic unity among societies— organic and "pseudo-organic." The differences among societies are not, for Whitehead, specifically differences in the level of organic unity which they achieve, but differences in the level of social co-ordination which does or does not permit the achievement of high levels of satisfaction, for example, consciousness, by "certain sets of its component members" (PR 100[153]). A democracy is no more nor less organic than an aristocracy. Both exhibit the organic unity of a society, an endurance.

Thus far we have seen that Whitehead and Hartshorne have replaced the materialist metaphysic of the seventeenth century with a social conception of reality. We have also seen, however, that their assessments of the organic nature of human society differ. Because a human society lacks the unity of a radically dominant member Hartshorne claims that it is not a fully organic whole but a collection of parts. A human society cannot therefore be considered to be a whole that influences its parts. Whitehead, on the other hand, holds that the plan of the total organism, understood as an endurance and not as an occurrence, is a harmony that emerges from the plans of its parts and, because it is a society and therefore has temporal duration, affects its own parts. In the following section we will begin to observe the correspondence that exists between these different organic conceptions of reality and their social and political theories.

## III. PROCESS PHILOSOPHY AND MODERN LIBERALISM

### 1. Organicism and the New Liberals

The move toward an organic conception of human nature and society was not peculiar to Whitehead and Hartshorne. Recent historians of liberal thought have emphasized the monumental developments within that tradition from the time of J. S. Mill until the First World War. Far from being a static dogma, liberal ideology was a dynamic theory which developed over time. Thus while classical liberals such as Bentham generally viewed man as "essentially independent, private and competitive beings who see civil association mainly as a framework for the pursuit of their own interests," modern liberals such as Mill and Hobhouse are "more apt to stress mutual dependence over independence, co-operation over competition, and mutual appreciation over private enjoyment."[26]

The metamorphosis of liberalism around the turn of the century was the result of a confluence of many forces that were at work in British society. Among these forces was a growing preoccupation in some circles with questions of social reform in an effort to alleviate the harshest effects of industrialization. Unlike many groups in nineteenth-century Britain, the new liberals were not ivory-tower ideologues and did not pretend to theorize in a vacuum.

> They dealt with acute problems such as dire poverty, unemployment, and disease, which constituted the immediate challenge to the policy-makers of the period. Their achievement lies in the quiet yet impressive way in which they combined the major intellectual tendencies of the time, to form a powerful framework within which to tackle those concrete issues.[27]

Foremost among these intellectual tendencies were the biological concepts of evolution and the social organism.[28] It was these theories which the Social Darwinists were using to argue that "[p]rogress in the natural and social world alike resulted from the free adaptation of individual to environment; [therefore] the laws of evolution pre- scribed a policy of Individualism."[29] Given the influence of Darwin's theories upon the intellectual climate during the late Victorian period, no social ideology that hoped to gain general acceptance could fail to come to terms with them.[30] It was thus incumbent on the new liberals to demonstrate that biological theory supported their social and political programs.

The organic model of society developed by the new liberals is based on the claims that individual development within society is interdependent and that the differing personalities of the members of society complete each other. [31] These claims are closely related and are both central to Hobhouse's social theory. By organic interdepen- dence Hobhouse means that the condition for the growth and continued activity of each part is not fulfilled by its own internal constitution but by its relationships with the other parts.[32] The same point is made in *Liberalism* when he says: "A thing is called organic when it is made up of parts which are quite distinct from one another, but which are destroyed or vitally altered when they are removed from the whole."[33] Note that for Hobhouse, even as for Whitehead, the affirmation of organicism does not entail a denial of the individ- uality of the parts. An individual's environment affects his or her essential nature without, as Hartshorne says, "dissolving all definite structures into ineffable unity . . . " (LP 201). This relative determi- nation of the parts within an organic structure is brought out clearly in the following passage:

> The organic whole is the system formed by several . . . [inter- dependent] parts in permanent relation, and it is one in which each part is determined—in a degree at least sufficient for the maintenance of the system—by the requirements of the whole, while the whole is determined in respect of some of its features by the requirements of each part.[34]

Hobhouse attempts to demonstrate that a proper understanding of society avoids the extremes of one-sided collectivism and one-sided individualism. "By a one-sided collectivism is intended the theory which conceives the life of the community as something qualitatively different from and superior to the lives of the component individuals."[35] Hobhouse repeatedly stresses that society has no "mystical psychic unity," no distinct personality transcending that of the individual members of society.[36] This is not to deny society a collective life and character; however, the unity is constituted by the various interrelationships that bind the members together. The life and well-being of a nation is nothing other than the life and well-being of its citizens. "In all cases the good, if it is real at all, is ultimately to be enjoyed by individuals."[37] Green made the same point when he wrote: "Our ultimate standard of worth is an ideal of *personal* worth. . . . To speak of any progress or improvement or development of a nation or society or mankind, except as relative to some greater worth of persons, is to use words without meaning."[38] The value of collective aims and achievements is to be tested by their consequences for the lives of individual persons. "What is sound in the collective life," writes Hobhouse, "is that which completes the personal and carries it on to a higher harmony of wider sweep."[39]

While it is true that "the life of the nation has no real existence except as the life of the individuals composing the nation, a life determined by their intercourse with each other, and deriving its peculiar features from the conditions of that intercourse,"[40] it is a mistake to regard the nation merely as an aggregate of individuals. Hobhouse refers to this error as "one-sided individualism," a belief "which attributes to the individual as against society anything which really belongs to him only as a member of society."[41] This form of individualism, which I have referred to as "atomistic" individualism, finds expression in the doctrine of natural rights. Natural rights theorists argue that rights are "something absolute and fixed, a remainder that is left out of the original stock of human nature after the deductions necessary for concluding the social contract."[42] Hobhouse on the other hand regards the idea of rights outside of society as self-contradictory. Following Green he argues that rights are defined by the common good and obtain their authority from their contribution to social welfare, that is, harmony.[43] Consequently, far from hindering or conflicting with the common good, they are the conditions necessary for the promotion of social harmony. "The fulfillment of each personality is a constituent element of the common good, and the individual may justly claim the conditions necessary to it, the forbearance of others, and their aid in so far as the general conditions of the community allow."[44]

The new liberals generally held that an organic theory of society would avoid the social conflict that follows from either the suppression of individuality under abstract collectivism or the disregard of the common good under abstract individualism.

> If in one sense society is clearly greater than the individual, there is another sense in which the individual may stand above society, and any reconciliation of personal and social claims must reckon with this relation. The problem then is to conceive the heightened claims of personality as to make them not disruptive of the social order but working constituents of social harmony.[45]

The advantage of the organic analogy is that it envisages a social unity based upon interlocking differences among the parts. "The organic relation is one of mutual service," claims Hobhouse. "In its most complete expression it is a harmony wherein the intrinsic tendencies of each part assist one another in their fulfillment, or . . . co-operate spontaneously in a system by which in turn their own energies are maintained."[46] Organic unity does not reduce its members to a common type, but allows their "intrinsic tendencies" to complement one another thereby constituting the wider social harmony. That organic synthesis or harmony, also called the "common good," is the whole in which the good of the individual parts is preserved and yet transcended.[47] It is that "higher order . . . within which individuality has full play. . . ."[48] Strictly speaking, states Hobhouse in a footnote, "the Common Good is neither the sum of individual 'goods' as independently determined, nor another kind of good opposed to them. It is the harmony of which each individual good is a constituent."[49]

The social ideal is thus the organic harmony in which the full personal development of every member of society is realized. For Hobhouse, as for Green, this ideal is the *telos* of human action; it is the ideal by which he linked his ethics to his political theory. He advances a "theory of ethical evolution which makes the collective progress of humanity the supreme end of conduct. . . ."[50] Hobhouse defines the good as "a harmony of anything that in the widest sense may be called experience with feeling."[51] Evil is the experience of disharmony or conflict of feeling. Such disharmony can occur between one's own feelings or between two feelings in different individuals. In a passage that exhibits close affinities to process thought, and which clearly reveals the social nature of the individual, Hobhouse adds:

> If there is anything in the nature of Mill's social feeling within me there is a traitor in my camp, and the division between my neighbour and me is reflected in a division of my own feelings. These feelings, if given full scope and drawn out into all their consequences, compel me to include my neighbour, and with him in the end all men whom my action may affect, in the harmony that I can be satisfied with as really good, and to recognize any disharmony within this world of felt experience as evil. . . . [52]

It is this social feeling, this feeling of essential relatedness to one another, that carries the "burden of obligation."[53] Disharmony is not adequately dealt with by repression of one of the feelings. "[O]nly that can be reasonable and finally held good in which such collisions are overcome."[54] This ideal harmony, while unattainable by humanity, remains the criterion by which the good and right are determined. This brings us back to his theory of rights. Human rights are "partial expressions of ethical truth"[55] which experience has shown to be necessary for personal development. In other words, human rights (and their correlative duties), are the necessary conditions for achieving a harmonious "experience with feeling" and as such form the moral order recognized by society. Social progress lies in the harmonization and completion of the rights acquired by human beings.

> Treating the full development of humanity, the unfolding of the powers of mind, the coming to itself of the human spirit, as the final cause of life, the ultimate aim of action, and the canon by which right and wrong are to be judged, the evolutionist estimates institutions by their bearing on this supreme end.[56]

This subordination of politics to ethics is one of the primary features of the new liberalism.[57] "Through the ethical conception of the community as an organization of rationally co-operating individuals, the liberal belief in unimpeded development of individual faculty was complemented by a collectivism expressing mutual responsibility and social solidarity."[58]

### 2. Process Philosophy and Organic Social Thought

When we turn to Whitehead and Hartshorne we discover that the social and political implications of their organic philosophy parallel features of modern liberalism as presented by Hobhouse. It is Hartshorne's belief, for instance, that philosophy in America has arrived at a metaphysics, namely process or "neoclassical" metaphysics, "in which human freedom and human consciousness are given a congenial setting, unfavorable both to collectivism and to anarchic individualism . . . " (CAP 12). Hartshorne contends that "suitable working ideas are in principle derivable from neoclassical metaphysics" (CAP 13), which will enable us to avoid both the Scylla of collectivism to which the communists have fallen victim as well as the Charybdis of individual self-interest into which the "Free World" has been swept. In a passage strongly reminiscent of Hobhouse's writings Whitehead also denounced abstract collectivism as

> a perversion of doctrine concerning the social character of humanity. The worth of any social system depends on the value experience it promotes among individual human beings. There is no one American value experience other than the many experiences of individual Americans or of other individuals affected by American life. A community life is a mode of eliciting value for the people concerned. (ESP 52; see PR 108[165].)

As with Hobhouse, this is not to deny that a society has a collective life and character. For Whitehead the social whole is the pattern of interrelationships that unites the members and that elicits value for the true individuals. "[T]he cohesion of social systems depends on the maintenance of patterns of behaviour; and advances in civilization depend on the fortunate modification of such behaviour patterns. Thus the infusion of pattern into natural occurrences, and the stability of such patterns, and the modification of such patterns, is the necessary condition for the realization of the Good" (ESP 83–84).

The organic character of reality also entails for Whitehead a rejection of abstract individualism. "The whole concept of absolute individuals with absolute rights, and with a contractual power of forming fully defined external relations," he asserts, "has broken down" (AI 80). What is particularly interesting is the way in which Whitehead, like Hobhouse, connects the theory of natural rights with a belief in absolute individualism. According to natural rights theory, a right is something that an individual possesses irrespective of the social reality that then obtains; rights are attributed to the individual, says Hobhouse, "as though they were part of his skin, or one of his limbs."[59] The new liberal position, however, is that individual rights are, like the individuals themselves, social products.

The principle of rights in Whitehead's philosophy, as Douglas Sturm has perceptively noted, closely resembles the organic philosophy of Hobhouse and Green.[60] Rights are not independent of society and, consequently, are not to be regarded as ends in themselves. The new liberals subordinate rights to ethics arguing that rights "owe their validity to the functions they perform in the harmonious development of society."[61] A genuine right is one that is compatible with the common good which is the ethical ideal of society. I maintain that Whitehead also subordinates rights to ethics and that the theory of absolute rights is open to the same criticisms that he levels against the notion of absolute laws of nature and moral codes. Scientific and moral theories are the product of abstraction; they are "myths" that reflect a finite perspective on reality. The formulation of such myths involves the selection of some details of the environment as important while other details are suppressed as irrelevant. As such they are not wrong but unguarded. The problem with all such formulations, including theories of human rights, is that they generally suffer from exaggeration. "The notion of the unqualified stability of particular laws of nature and of particular moral codes is a primary illusion which has vitiated much philosophy" (MT 18). The same illusion impairs political philosophy when rights are understood in abstraction from their social environment.

Whitehead flatly asserts that "moral codes are relevant to presuppositions respecting the systematic character of the relevant universe" (MT 18). Again, in AI 374 we read: "The details of these codes are relative to the social circumstances of the immediate environment. . . . " Whitehead is quick to add that this does not mean that morality is completely relative. On the contrary, "[m]orality is *always* the aim at that union of harmony, intensity, and vividness which involves the perfection of importance for that occasion" (MT 19; emphasis added). As was the case with Hobhouse, moral codes are the myths which wide experience has shown will further the aims of a society at its ideal, and as such they are essential for civilization. What is to be avoided is the exaggerated claim that there is

> one behaviour-system belonging to the essential character of the universe, as the universal moral ideal. What is universal is the spirit which should permeate any behaviour-system in the

circumstances of its adoption. Thus morality does not indicate what you are to do in mythological abstractions. It does concern the general ideal which should be the justification for any particular objective. (MT 20)[62]

Both Whitehead and Hartshorne, having rejected abstract collectivism by locating value firmly within individual experience, and having rejected abstract individualism by affirming the social basis of such experience, claim that morality consists in the maximization of experience. Each philosopher provides his own version of the principle of utility.[63] According to Hartshorne, *"To be ethical is to seek aesthetic optimization of experience for the community."* [64] For Whitehead, "Morality consists in the control of process so as to maximize importance. It is the aim at greatness of experience in the various dimensions belonging to it" (MT 19). Both philosophers are thus advocating a teleological ethic: that action is good and right that seeks to maximize valuable experience.

What is valuable experience? "If we know what experience is, at its best or most beautiful," writes Hartshorne, "then and only then can we know how it is right to act; for the value of action is in what it contributes to experiences" (CSPM 303). A beautiful experience is one in which there is a mutual adaptation, or harmony, of feelings. However, harmony alone is not sufficient for the realization of "great value." What is also necessary is intensity which "depends upon contrast, the amount of diversity integrated into an experience. Thus aesthetic value is found in diversified, harmonious experiences" (CSPM 303; see RSP 100). Beauty is "a *balance* of unity and variety" (CSPM 304).[65]

Whitehead also provides an aesthetic analysis of value. "The teleology of the Universe is directed to the production of Beauty" (AI 341). This is the general ideal that justifies any particular objective or goal. By beauty he means the unification of prehensions so as to produce a harmonious satisfaction. The aim of this adaptation is twofold: (1) the absence of mutual inhibition among the prehensions (the minor form of beauty); and (2) the additional introduction of new contrast of objective content through the synthesis of its various prehensions (the major form of beauty). "In other words," writes Whitehead, "the perfection of Beauty is defined as being the perfection of Harmony; and the perfection of Harmony is defined in terms of the perfection of Subjective Form in detail and in final synthesis" (AI 325). This "perfection" of subjective form is defined in terms of "strength" which has two aspects: (1) "Massiveness" which is the breadth or variety of detail brought into effective contrast; and (2) "Intensity Proper" which is "comparative magnitude without reference to qualitative variety" (AI 325). In the major form of beauty the parts contribute to the massive feeling of the whole while the synthesis leads to a heightened intensity of feeling of the parts. It appears that where Hartshorne spoke of beauty as the balance of unity and variety, Whitehead in similar fashion speaks of beauty as the harmony of detail and final synthesis.[66]

Since valuable experience is identified as beautiful, right action is determined by its ability to promote beautiful experiences.[67] Hartshorne distinguishes clearly between intrinsic and instrumental value: "Ethical value, goodness, is not the value of experiences themselves, but rather the instrumental value of acting so as to increase the intrinsic value of future experiences, particularly those of others than oneself" (CSPM 308). Aesthetic value is a metaphysical principle; therefore, each instance of creative synthesis, in so far as it realizes a unity in diversity, will possess some intrinsic value. The extent to which an occasion is also moral depends on the degree to which its activity aims to promote the value of future experiences. Hartshorne is quick to add that although distinguishable, intrinsic and instrumental goodness are intimately related.

> An ethically good act is good in two senses: it contributes to harmony and intensity of experience both in agent and in spectators. A good will enjoys a sense of harmony between self and others (insofar, virtue is indeed its own reward); and its consequences, if it is wise and fortunate as well as good, will be to enhance the possibilities in the community for intense and harmonious experiences.[68]

Moral goodness therefore involves the pursuit of beauty in future occasions including those that transcend one's own personal future.

Similarly Whitehead claims that parts of an occasion's objective content can be called "beautiful" because of their contribution to the perfection of the occasion's subjective form. Beautiful means "the inherent capability for the promotion of beauty when functioning as a datum in a percipient occasion" (AI 329). This is significant because it establishes the same distinction between intrinsic and instrumental value encountered in Hartshorne's thought. Intrinsic value is the beauty attained by an occasion through the unification of its prehensions into a determinate satisfaction. Instrumental value, or beautifulness, is an entity's contribution to aesthetic experience in future occasions. Whitehead also recognized that this division is somewhat artificial. For instance, immediately after distinguishing between the entity's subjective aim at intensity of feeling in the immediate subject and in the relevant future, he adds:

> This double aim . . . is less divided than appears on the surface. For the determination of the *relevant* future, and the *anticipatory* feeling respecting provision for its grade of intensity, are elements affecting the immediate complex of feeling. The greater part of morality hinges on the determination of relevance in the future. The relevant future consists of those elements in the anticipated future which are felt with effective intensity by the present subject by reason of the real potentiality for them to be derived from itself. (PR 27[41]; see PR 350[531])

Again, we read that an entity's importance is its emotional worth "embodying in itself derivations from the whole, and from the other facts, *and embodying in itself reference to future creativity*" (MT 160; emphasis added). Thus no absolute division is possible between beauty and beautifulness.

What is the significance of Whitehead and Hartshorne's ethical principles for their organic theories of society? Recall that for Hobhouse the social ideal is an organic harmony in which every member achieves the full development of his or her capacities. Social institutions are judged according to their tendency to promote or hinder progress toward this ideal. Hobhouse believes that this social ideal requires that society, in some sense, be conceived as an organic whole. The good of society is the common good which is the harmony of the good of the parts. I believe that Whitehead's conception of organicism enables him to adopt a social theory almost indistinguishable from Hobhouse's. Hartshorne, on the other hand, while certainly supporting many of the aims and ideals of modern liberalism, develops a more individualistic social theory in so far as it emphasizes the "quasi-organic" nature of human society.

Hobhouse and the new liberals generally wanted to say simultaneously that the good is something enjoyed by individuals alone and that in society there is a harmony of individual goods called the common good. This harmony is a unity in diversity; it is, to use the

aesthetic terminology of process thought, beautiful. As for Hartshorne, we noted that he readily acknowledges the intrinsic worth of
fully organic wholes. Such a unitary organism is a synthesis of its
parts and as such achieves a "balance of unity and diversity." Actual
entities, cells, the human person, and ultimately the universe itself
are all fully organic wholes and hence are intrinsically valuable. But
what is the value of "quasi-organic" wholes such as human societies?
"If there are wholes which are directly valuable in and for themselves, there can be groups of these wholes which are valuable not
directly, but for the sake of their members, or of some larger whole"
(LP 194). Human social structures are of purely instrumental value. In
themselves such structures are neither good nor bad; they are good or
bad only to the extent that they assist or retard the realization of
beautiful experience by the members of society. What Hartshorne's
social theory lacks is the notion of a common good on the level of
human societies, and to that extent it harks back to classical liberal
conceptions of society.[69]

However, although his organic monism leaves no room for the
development of a notion of the common good on the level of human
society, Hartshorne is yet able to reject an ethic of self-interest because of
his dipolar conception of God. Abstract individualism and abstract
collectivism are two ways in which human relations can be falsified.
Even an ethics of enlightened self-interest cannot, in Hartshorne's
opinion, arbitrate between the conflicting claims of individuals. "There
seem to be two possibilities only," says Hartshorne, "the good of the
greatest number, self-included, or some superindividual unity" (BH 32).
But is the good of the greatest number one good? "Can there be value
in a sum of values unless there is a valuation which summates them,
which embraces them together in a single good" (BH 32–33)? Having
denied that society or mankind as a whole can be such a summation
Hartshorne concludes that the real solution is to see God as the
integrating subject of the universal community.

> The conception of the ultimate or cosmic organism is the remedy
> for two great errors of political thought, abstract individualism
> and abstract or mythical collectivism. Neither the human indi-
> vidual nor any human class or race is an absolute end, but only
> that whole in which men and nations and all existences have
> their place and value. We are members one of another because
> we are members of one ultimate body-mind, one inclusive,
> unborn, and imperishable organism. (LP 214; see BH 76–77)

Hartshorne believes that the classical conception of God as immutable is in part responsible for these political errors and that a solution for them will only be found when mankind comes to acknowledge the divine relativity as well as the divine absoluteness. "Man cannot live without ideal aims which relate his endeavor and his suffering and his joy to something more lasting and more unitary than the sum of individual human achievements taken merely at face value" (DR 148).[70] If God is not recognized as the final end of all our efforts, then we will inevitably treat something finite as though it were absolute. "What ensues is Lenin worship, party worship, state worship, self-worship, despair, sensuality, or some other vagary" (DR 148).

Hartshorne's doctrine of God provides a further metaphysical justification of his utilitarian ethics. Why should we be interested in promoting the welfare of other individuals? It is not in itself sufficient to say that the social structure of reality is such that to limit our aim at our own future good is an irrational limitation of our efforts. For if humanity is itself finite then in the end one's contributions to mankind are going to pass away.

> Be the aim Nirvana, the Classless Society, the Welfare State, Self-realization, the query is never silenced, what good is it, from the cosmic and everlasting perspective, that one or other or all of these aims be attained for a time on this ball of rock? . . . Only through a relationship to the Everlasting Itself . . . can the query concerning the aim of life have an answer which avoids giving rise to a still more ultimate query. (LP 132)

The argument that we should seek to maximize beauty in the world generally is a rational aim only if "all lives whatever are embraced in or contribute to a mysterious but real and abiding unity."[71] Thus Hartshorne cannot accept that the collective progress of humanity is "the supreme end of conduct" as Green and Hobhouse would argue.[72] It is the life of God that alone provides humankind with a rational aim. Yet having said this, Hartshorne's metaphysical utilitarianism still results in the subordination of politics to ethics. Social structures are to be evaluated on the basis of whether or not they further the cosmic aim at beautiful experience: "[F]or only by thinking of God as the maximal value of all variables can we see clearly the direction in which man must move to reach higher values of these variables" (BH 37).

As for Whitehead there is no doubt that he too saw human societies as instrumentally valuable. In his article, "An Appeal to Sanity" he states: "A community life is a mode of eliciting value for the people concerned. . . . The beauty of a family is derivative from its members. The family life provides the opportunity; the realization lies in the individuals. Thus social life is the provision of opportunity" (ESP 52). Social life is valuable in so far as it provides opportunity for individuals to realize their potentialities. Again, in AI 376–77 he says that while particular codes of morality reflect the special circumstances of the concrete social structure, underlying such codes are more general principles. "These are the principles of the generality of harmony, and of the importance of the individual." Although at first sight conflicting, these principles support one another in an organic harmony:

> The antithesis is solved by rating types of order in relative importance according to their success in magnifying the individual actualities, that is to say, in promoting strength of experience. Also in rating the individual on the double basis, partly of the intrinsic strength of its own experience, and partly on its influence in the promotion of a high-grade type of order. (AI 376–77)[73]

Finally, evidence that Whitehead perceived social order to be of instrumental value can be found in his essay "Mathematics and the Good." There we read: "In itself a pattern is neither good nor bad. . . . The point I am emphasizing is the function of pattern in the production of Good or Evil in the finite unit of feeling which embraces the enjoyment of that pattern" (ESP 85).

Thus far Whitehead is in full agreement with Hartshorne and Hobhouse who also held that the beauty of a society is derivative from its members. Things are a bit less certain when we ask in what sense Whitehead entertained a notion of the common good. Without doubt there are several arguments that parallel those employed by Hartshorne. For example, concerning the phrase "the greatest happiness of the greatest number" Whitehead asks, "But what is meant by the addition of the Happinesses of different occurrences? There is no occurrence with the Happiness of this addition sum. At least, if there be such an occurrence, it ought to be indicated in the principle, and this indication will lead us in the direction of the discarded Platonism" (AI 51). Again, in ESP 52 he writes: " It is true that there is a mystic sense of the co-ordination and eternity of realized value. But we here approach the basic doctrine of religion. To attach that co-ordination of value to a finite social group is a lapse into barbaric polytheism." As with Hartshorne, so too Whitehead rejects the deification of society through its conceptual misrepresentation as the final *telos* of individual action. Of this there can be no doubt. The immortality of the World of Action is only derived from its transformation and preservation in the divine nature. "What does haunt our imagination is that the immediate facts of present action pass into permanent significance for the Universe. The insistent notion of Right and Wrong, Achievement and Failure, depends upon this background. Otherwise every activity is merely a passing whiff of insignificance" (ESP 72).

However, unlike Hartshorne he also makes statements that suggest that a human society is itself a harmony of detail and final synthesis. Consider, for example, Whitehead's rather Hegelian comment that "[e]ach society has its own type of perfection, and puts up with certain blots, at that stage inevitable." He then adds, while speaking in the context of social perfection: "All realization of the Good is finite, and necessarily excludes certain other types" (AI 375). As we saw earlier, societies as well as individual entities are said by Whitehead to have a *telos* which is here described as its own type of perfection and is said to be a realization of "the Good." A few pages later we are told that the moral code is "the behaviour-patterns which in the environment for which it is designed will promote the evolution of that *environment* towards *its proper perfection*" (AI 377; emphasis added). Not only individual entities, but the environment as well, that is, a society, can be properly said to have its own perfection. Moral codes are the behavior-patterns that will bring the society to perfection through its members. In this way the whole enables the parts to realize their full individuality, and this in turn leads to the perfection of the whole. As with Hobhouse and Green, the ideal is an organic unity or harmony in which the full development of each individual is simultaneously the means to the full development of every other person. "Morality of outlook," asserts Whitehead in PR 15(23),

is inseparably conjoined with generality of outlook. The antithesis between the general good and the individual interest can be abolished only when the individual is such that its interest is the general good, thus exemplifying the loss of the minor intensities in order to find them again with finer composition in a wider sweep of interest.

What is absolutely clear in this passage is that the general good or common good is not the sum of individual goods but a higher harmony in which the good of every part is synthesized. Ultimately that harmony is the "Harmony of Harmonies" which is God himself, but Whitehead's organic conception of reality appears to allow for the experience of social harmony on the finite level.[74] Hobhouse saw the ideal of collective life as that which *completes* the personal rather than dwarfs it, and which carries one to a "higher harmony of wider sweep."[75] So too Whitehead believes that ideally the general good involves the perfection of the parts through their enjoyment of a "wider sweep of interest." In his discussion of civilization Whitehead likens human society to a work of art in which the details of the ccmposition

> make their own claim to individuality, and yet contribute to the whole. Each such detail receives an access of grandeur from the whole, and yet manifests an individuality claiming attention in its own right. . . . Each detail claims a permanent existence for its own sake, and then surrenders it for the sake of the whole composition. (AI 364)

There is evidence then that Whitehead perceived an organic conception of human society to involve a transcendence of the means/end distinction characteristic of utilitarian thought. Given the social nature of reality he concludes that morality involves the abolition of the antithesis between individual interest and the common good. It is in the pursuit of maximal future beauty, which is Whitehead's definition of morality, that one realizes one's own true good.[76] Green's argument for morality and the common good reflects a similar line of reasoning. Morality, for Green, consists in the realization of an ideal that one presents to oneself. Understood thus, moral action "is an expression at once of conscious contrast between an actual and possible self, and of an impulse to make that possible self real; or, as it is sometimes put, it is a process of self-realisation, *i.e.* of making a possible self real."[77] This "possible" or "real" self is further identified with God.

Green believes that in virtue of the principle of divine realization in man, "man has definite capabilities, the realisation of which . . . forms his true good."[78] "[T]he perfection of human character—a perfection of individuals which is also that of society, and of society which is also that of individuals—is for man the only object of absolute or intrinsic value. . . ."[79] Although a complete account of these capabilities cannot be provided, Green does attempt to specify the form that human self-realization necessarily takes.[80] Of paramount importance is Green's refusal to acknowledge a "fundamental dichotomy between personal and public good. . . ."[81] As we saw earlier, Green admits that the divine idea can only be realized in persons and that our ultimate standard of worth is an ideal of personal worth; but such a realization "can only take place in and through society."[82] "[I]t is only in the intercourse of men, each recognised by each as an end, not merely a means . . . that the capacity is actualised and that we really live as persons."[83] The development of personality requires a social environment in which individuals treat one another as ends in themselves. "They are interested in each other *as persons* in so far as each . . . finds satisfaction for himself in procuring or witnessing the self-satisfaction of the other."[84] The self which the moral agent seeks to realize is a social self; therefore, concludes Green, an individual's true well-being is necessarily a social well-being, a well-being in which the opposition of good for self and good for others does not enter into consideration.[85] This is what Green terms the common good. It is that social order in which the fulfillment of each person's capabilities entails the fulfillment of every other person's as well.

Green's argument for the identity of the individual and the common good is thus grounded upon his theory of human nature. Given that the individual's good is defined as that which satisfies his or her interest, Green's desire to reconcile personal interest and morality ineluctably leads to an identification of the individual's interest with the social interest. Since society provides the context in which the individual pursues his or her interests, and since mankind's social nature unites each person with others, Green, like other modern liberals, concludes that the perfection of one person is inconceivable apart from the perfection of all persons. Individual salvation coincides with corporate salvation. Genuine self-development cannot, therefore, be purchased at the expense of development in others.[86]

By identifying social and individual interests Green avoids a preferential theory of interest such as that generally found among utilitarians. His position, claims Roberts, is similar to Rousseau's:

"[W]here Rousseau held that the individual's real will is the general will, as opposed to his actual will, even if he does not recognize it, Green believes that the individual's essential interest, even if he is unaware of it, is the social interest."[87] I suggest that his position and argumentation are also similar to Whitehead's. According to Whitehead's process metaphysics, each actual entity seeks its satisfaction in the realization of a particular ideal which the subject presents to itself.[88] The process of concrescence is thus a process of self-realization in which an "ideal" self is made real, that is, its "interest" is satisfied. In so far as each occasion of experience achieves a degree of beauty in its satisfaction, it can also be said to realize its "good."

The question we need to ask of Whitehead is whether the good of the individual can conflict with the general or common good. The distinction drawn by Whitehead between beauty and beautifulness implies that on occasion such a conflict can occur. "Of course the present can be sacrificed to the future," Whitehead unambiguously asserts, "so that Truth or Beauty in the future can be the reason for the immediate attenuation of either" (AI 309). Given that morality is concerned with the maximization of beauty, we are seemingly forced to conclude that morality may require the sacrifice of one's personal good. Yet Gamwell argues: "If the best decision does not maximize beauty in the present, maximal beauty cannot be the good. But maximal beauty must be the telos of the universe, otherwise there is no point in pursuing it. In short, the result is absurd."[89]

With Gamwell I believe that the logic of Whitehead's organic theory of society naturally leads to an identification of the individual's interest with the social interest. The notion of an individual-in-isolation is an abstraction; therefore, to speak about the individual's good without reference to society is equally an abstraction. The "real" self is an individual-in-relation, a social self, whose "true" good is a social good. Other individuals are not merely means to our own satisfaction but are ends in themselves. By our very constitution as individuals-in-relation there can be no separation between our good and the common good; our good is constituted by the pursuit of the good in others. It is not just that society functions as the datum for our own satisfaction, and therefore our pursuit of maximal beauty in others will rebound favourably upon us.[90] That is not always the case. Rather, owing to the aesthetic character of value the pursuit of maximal future good itself enhances the subject's satisfaction. The process of self-creativity, by virtue of the subject's conceptual anticipation of the future, is the teleological aim at some ideal in the future.

And yet this aim, claims Whitehead "is not really beyond the present process. For the aim at the future is an enjoyment in the present. It thus effectively conditions the immediate self-creation of the new creature"(MT 228).[91] The subject's anticipation of the future contributes to its experience. The broader that interest in the future the more these anticipatory feelings will contribute to the massiveness, and therefore beauty, of the present experience. In this way morality, "which is inseparably conjoined with generality of outlook," qualifies the beauty achieved by the moral agent. By pursuing the common good, which is a harmony of the good of all the parts, the moral agent loses "minor intensities" which she might have experienced by focusing on her own future, only to find her true good in the "wider sweep of interest."[92] In *Adventures of Ideas* we read: "The general health of social life is taken care of by formularized moral precepts, and formularized religious beliefs and religious institutions. All of these explicitly express the doctrine that the perfection of life resides in aims beyond the individual person in question" (AI 373). Morality involves the pursuit of the "general health of social life," and it is in one's aims at a common good that transcends one's individual life that the perfection of life resides. By locating one's own good within the harmony of the common good one avoids as much as possible any disharmony between oneself and others that would lead to a diminution in the beauty of one's satisfaction. For this reason one must look for one's own true development within the context of a social order that provides for the full development of all the members. Hence, as with Green, the individual's essential interest, even if he or she is unaware of it, is the social interest, and failure to identify one's own good with the common good leads to a sacrifice of one's real self.[93]

It would appear then that Whitehead vacillates in his description of the relationship between the individual and society. This vacillation results from the shift in emphasis that he makes in his analysis of social relationships. To emphasize the primacy of the individual he refers to the instrumental character of social order as the locus of opportunity for self-realization. Yet he also wants to allow for a real unity within finite societies including human social arrangements. That such societies can be said to express a common good in which the good of the individual members can find full realization follows from his organic theory of society discussed previously. The social organism has a *telos*, a perfection, a good which is not reducible to the mere sum of the aims and values of the individual members of that society. To this extent Whitehead fully shares the perspective of the modern liberal organicism of Green and Hobhouse. Hartshorne, on the other hand is less well equipped to construct a theory of the common good because of his steadfast refusal to attribute purpose and intrinsic value to that which is not fully individual. For Hartshorne, moral obligation requires the idea that we contribute to some whole of value of which our own satisfactions are only a part (RSP 63). However, the only whole that he will allow beyond the level of the human mind is the cosmos itself, that is, God. Whitehead, on the other hand, accepts the reality of intermediary wholes. These social units have their own *telos*, their own common good, to which the finite agent contributes. Yet, like Hartshorne, he also accepts that the ultimate *telos* of the creative process is God.

One practical consequence of this difference between Hartshorne and Whitehead can be seen in their different perceptions of human rights. Because a common good cannot be found at the level of human society there seems to be a permanent hostility between the state and the individual in Hartshorne's political theory. Between the two there is needed

> a mighty *mediator*, which can equally *sanction* the delegation of vast powers to the state and the withholding of vast powers, to be divided among private individuals or groups, including groups of cooperating consumers. In this way a healthy balance will be possible between the highly imperfect private citizen and the highly imperfect public official. Each will have enough power to "stand up" to the other. (BH 36; emphasis added.)

In this revealing passage we see how Hartshorne has employed his dipolar conception of God to endorse a classical liberal political conception of the division of power between state and citizen. God is supremely relative as well as absolute, the cosmic individual, and therefore God is the fully organic whole that harmonizes the values of the lesser individuals. Far from seeing society even ideally as a synthesis of the aspirations of finite individuals, Hartshorne implies that God must act as a mediator between the citizens and the state. The synthesis lies outside society and within God who alone is the common good. The common good is identical with the cosmic good; as a consequence, it is inappropriate to expect a reconciliation of individual goods on the level of human society. The good of any finite society, no matter how broadly conceived, cannot be regarded as a criterion of the good of the individual members of that society. On the level of human society the good of the individual is a social good only in the sense that it is conditioned by society, not in the sense that the individual's good is indistinguishable from the good of the social organism. Hartshorne's understanding of the individual and society accepts that the good of individual persons may be mutually exclusive. Because of the fundamental opposition between individual and society there must be a division of power and this means that the individual possesses rights *against* society (BH 32).

Whitehead's organic conception of society enables him to overcome the opposition between state and citizen which remains in Hartshorne's more individualistic account of human society. In a speech on women's suffrage delivered in 1906 he says: "[T]he chief and noblest of the external activities of human beings is concerned with the life of the State, that great organism on whose well-being depends the nature of the opportunities which life can offer to each individual" (LEW 37). The state is an "organism" in whose well-being the opportunities for the self-development of all its members is found. This social ideal is a harmony of individual ends. No "mighty mediator" is therefore necessary to sanction a balance of power between two opposing forces. On this understanding of society human rights, like moral codes, are relative to the environment in which they are formulated and have as their goal the perfection of that environment. In place of a *balance* of power which enables individuals to stand up to one another Whitehead advocates a *harmony* of interests, a common good in which the individual finds his or her perfection. There is no need of any individual rights against society in Whitehead's view, for every true moral right is a necessary condition for the full self-development of each individual relative to his or her wider environment. Whitehead's organicism thus reflects the modern liberal ideal of a harmony between the individual and society. "Rights are relative to the well-being of society," argues Hobhouse, "but the converse proposition is equally true that the well-being of society may be measured by the degree in which their moral rights are secured to its component members."[94] Modern liberal social theory aims at reconciling "the rule of right with the principle of the public welfare. . . . "[95]

I would like to note, by way of conclusion, a rather interesting result of our investigation thus far. An examination of our philosophers' comments on the relationship between the individual and society reveals, in addition to numerous points of correspondence that we might expect to find, a rather subtle divergence of opinion. Whitehead's social philosophy appears to be more holistic and communitarian than Hartshorne's; Whitehead seems more eager than his American counterpart to emphasize the harmonious and cooperative aspects of society. Hartshorne's social theory, on the contrary, is more individualistic, laying greater emphasis on the tragic and competitive qualities of life. This observation becomes even more intriguing when one realizes that this difference of opinion in social philosophy parallels a divergence in their metaphysical systems. Whereas Whitehead treats all societies, including human societies, as "wholes" that exhibit the organic unity appropriate to endurances, Hartshorne makes an important metaphysical distinction between "fully organic" and "pseudo-organic" societies. Human social structures are unavoidably "pseudo-organic," as are all finite societies inclusive of human persons; consequently, there is no common good below the cosmic level to which we all contribute and in which we can find a harmony of personal interests. On the level of finite human societies the true interests of individuals are mutually exclusive. Because of this unavoidable conflict God sanctions a decentralization of power which, according to Hartshorne, finds its appropriate expression in a system of individual rights.

Metaphysical speculation, I have argued, is not performed in a vacuum. Whitehead explicitly acknowledges that all forms of human thought, including speculative philosophy, are conditioned. Moreover, it is clear that in his own constructive philosophical endeavors Whitehead unabashedly argued by way of analogy and imaginative generalization from his understanding of human nature and society. All of this raises an interesting query: is it possible to discover in the life-situations of our philosophers anything that might have contributed to their different estimations of organicism? I believe that David Nicholls, in a couple of recent articles, has identified some very basic environmental factors that might shed some light on this question.[96] Nicholls argues that "a particular concept used about God becomes predominant at a given period of history in a given social situation and that this concept is often closely related to the political discourse of the time, which in turn is dialectically related to the social context in which it operates."[97] In the United States, respect for the federal constitution coupled with a pluralist ideology has fueled an assault upon the traditional or "classical" image of deity as an impassible, omnipotent monarch.[98] For example, William James, who along with John Dewey, Whitehead, and Hartshorne is treated as a representative of this predominantly American theological tradition, concludes in *The Pluralistic Universe* (1909) that "[t]he vaster vistas which scientific evolutionism has opened, and the rising tide of social democratic ideals, have changed the type of our imagination, and the older monarchical theism is obsolete or obsolescent. The place of the divine in the world must be more organic and intimate."[99] Despite their many differences, these members of the American theological tradition are united in their call for a new conception of deity, and in their constructive efforts they offer images of God that are closely linked to their social and political beliefs.

Generalizations about entire theological or philosophical movements frequently fail to see the trees for the wood; yet they can also provide valuable insights concerning the lay of the land. In highlighting federal democracy and the accompanying pluralist ideology as two environmental factors that have conditioned theological reflection in the United States, I believe that Nicholls has helped to provide an explanation for some philosophical differences between Whitehead and Hartshorne. Hartshorne's greater emphasis on the individual and his refusal to regard human society even ideally as a "whole" with a common good that is inclusive of the true goods of its members, reflects his social location in the United States. The dominant social and political reality which has constituted Hartshorne's immediate environment has been one that idealizes among other things pluralism, democracy, a federal system of government with its system of checks and balances so that each branch of government can "stand up" to the others, and individual freedom. I suggest that these dominant social and political ideals have been consciously or unconsciously appropriated by Hartshorne and incorporated within his own worldview, and that his flight of metaphysical speculation, as seen for example in his understanding of organicism, has been conditioned by the historical reality from which it has taken off.[100]

As for Whitehead, while he lived in America and wrote his metaphysical theories at Harvard, he was and always remained by his own admission, "a typical example of the Victorian Englishman" (ESP 88). The late Victorian era was a time in which "some of the harshest features of capitalism were present, together with a growing challenge to the economic and social system on the part of the labor movement. The only way the capitalist state could avoid revolution was by mitigating some of the most brutal consequences of the system."[101] The end result, says Nicholls, was the emergence of a paternalistic state and a welfare conception of God. What is particularly significant for our purposes is to note that a driving force behind many of the movements for social reform and the rationale for interventionist legislation enacted by the British government was an organic conception of society such as that found among the new liberals. Thus Whitehead's understanding of human nature and society were formulated in an environment that was sympathetic to organic interpretations of the state and this, I believe, is reflected in his later metaphysical generalizations.

In arguing that Whitehead and Hartshorne were influenced in their constructive philosophical efforts by the images of the state that were dominant in their respective environments I am not intending to imply that their ideas are "mere" reflections or an epiphenomenon of society. What I am claiming is that an inquiry into the connection between process philosophy and the social and political locations of process philosophers—in this case those of Whitehead and Hartshorne—might shed light on the values and ideals that are implicit in their metaphysics. I hope to provide additional support for this contention with an analysis of their views on democracy, equality, freedom, and coercion in the following chapters.

# 5

# Freedom, Equality, and the Ideal of Democracy

## I. FREEDOM AND EQUALITY

In our initial examination of Whitehead's and Hartshorne's thought we observed that the notion of freedom is a key principle in their philosophical theories. Freedom is an example of what Hartshorne terms a cosmic variable (BH 112); it is a property that to some degree is possessed necessarily by all entities. "Nature is a hierarchy of freedoms, if freedom is real at all."[1]

Given the universality of freedom, political and social freedom within human society are treated by Hartshorne simply as special cases of this general category. His arguments on behalf of social and political freedom parallel perfectly the metaphysical principles outlined earlier. Thus the principles relevant for determining the nature and scope of freedom within human society are, in Hartshorne's opinion, simply restricted applications of metaphysical axioms. Take, for example, the following argument presented in his article, "Politics and the Metaphysics of Freedom": "It is obvious that in all societies men have some political freedom, if relatively unimportant aspects of behavior are considered. Thus indeterminism (positing limits to determinism by others) rather than determinism is true, politically speaking."[2] This clearly echoes Hartshorne's detailed arguments for relative indeterminism. Just as freedom is an ultimate principle exhibited to varying degrees throughout the natural world, so political freedom is exemplified throughout the spectrum of possible political systems. Totalitarianism, in the literal sense of a government's *total* determination of its citizens' activities, is impossible.[3] A similar position is taken with regard to social freedom. Here we are concerned, not with the determination of the individual by the government alone, but with one's multifarious social relationships: "How much can I determine as to my own life, and how much do others decide for me, not simply as rulers, but as relatives, neighbors, employers, and so on?"[4] Social freedom is more general than strictly political freedom; yet, like its political counterpart, social freedom is an expression of the ultimate metaphysical category of freedom. "[T]he social case of freedom is special only in the sense that human society is special among societies in general."[5]

When considering human freedom, the practical question, according to Hartshorne, is one of *degree*:

> [H]ow much self-determination (rather than determination by rulers) is there, in what important respects of behavior, and— perhaps above all—how much definite assurance is there in advance as to the boundaries of freedom, that is, are there recognized limits to governmental interference, guaranteed "rights" to make one's own decisions?[6]

Hartshorne provides us with two examples: that of the slave and that of the individual who is overly dependent upon his or her parents. In both instances, the individual has some degree of self-determination; however, each of them lacks the degree of freedom "proportionate to his human capacities of thought and imagination."[7] Social and political freedom must be proportionate to the mental capacities characteristic of the human species.

This raises the question of how the ideals of freedom and equality are related to one another. Given that the practical question is one of degree, do the various differences between human beings imply that varying degrees of freedom should be granted to different people? Liberal political theorists tend to respond to this challenge by searching for a feature common to all human beings.

> Although modern liberals certainly believe that individual natures differ, they also hold the traditional liberal view that all men share a similar nature and, consequently, their differences—unlike, for instance, those separating Plato's classes or citizens—do not mark off radically different types or grades of existences. Whether the claim has been that we are all God's children, all rational beings or all creatures capable of pleasure and pain (thus, incidentally,

extending similitude to non-human animals), liberals have in-
sisted that whatever differences individuals manifest, they are
essentially the same sort of beings.[8]

The claim to equal liberty is thus upheld by establishing a fundamental equality among individuals. The problem with this argument is
that people, in fact, tend to be only roughly equal in the way
suggested. Whatever trait is put forward as common to all people
turns out to be unequally distributed among them. As Gaus notes, "a
pressure is thus usually exerted to convert what would seem to be a
continuum into a dichotomy."[9]

Hartshorne's understanding of the relationship between liberty
and equality closely resembles the typical liberal position as described
by Gaus. According to Hartshorne, there are two kinds of differences
among individuals: physical contrasts, such as race and sex, and
psychical and behavioral characteristics. He argues that the gross
material differences of race or sex are inappropriate criteria for
evaluating persons and for imputing inequality. Racial and sexual
characteristics tell us little about the human capacities an infant is
born with. Within every large group of people identified by such
physical traits alone one can find examples of genius and stupidity,
criminal and saintly behavior. The extreme differences of achievement are between individuals rather than groups, and thus he
concludes that there is no justification for regarding any particular
race or either sex en bloc as being inferior in capacities.[10] What
differences there are in the achievements of such groups can better be
explained in terms of the opportunities provided to them for the
development of their potentialities.

It is important to observe that Hartshorne does not believe that
there is any "literal, unqualified sense in which all creatures in
human shape are of equal worth."[11]

> When it is said that human beings are "born equal," it can
> hardly be meant that there is no difference in value between a
> congenital idiot, which will never exhibit human behavior at
> all—never employ words or other symbols in the human
> fashion—and a normal child. If an idiot is a precious individual,
> why not a donkey? Is the mere human shape a proof of value?[12]

He rejects arguments to the contrary premised on humanity's supposed immortality or status as children of God: "[B]eing human, in

any but the crudely physical sense, is a matter of degree."[13] However, apart from the most extreme cases, such as the congenital idiot or hopelessly confirmed criminal, it is impractical to take into consideration, either socially or politically, the differences in worth between adult human beings. This is because no one is competent to judge the relative importance of the innumerable ways in which people differ. "Large groups of persons classified together on the basis of physical traits having no known relation to inborn mental or moral capacities are to be presumed virtually equal in such capacities, and therefore in essential human worth."[14] Thus, while absolute equality is not a valid notion, "[r]acial oppression, the 'subjection of women,' the denial of opportunity to children of the poor cannot be justified by appealing to any known inequalities of capacity or merit."[15] For some purposes equality retains a "practical absoluteness."[16]

Although human beings are not literally equal, our inability to judge their relative worth leads Hartshorne to claim that the ideal of equality should be considered absolute for all practical purposes. But why, we might wonder, can we not ascertain a person's worth? The metaphysical justification appears to be twofold: First, the value of an individual is not fixed. At each moment in a person's life there is a new synthetic experience that results in the emergence of new values. Consequently, even if we could determine a person's worth at a given moment we would have to revise our findings almost immediately. Second, for Hartshorne the question of value is in part relative to the perspective of the subject. The creative synthesis of the subject is within a universal process and the value of the subject (its "importance" in Whitehead's terminology) is partly relative to its place in, and contribution to, that process. Each subject will therefore evaluate a given individual differently, the only absolute perspective being that of God.[17]

Hartshorne declares his agreement with Thomas Jefferson's claim that human equality amounts to a common inferiority to God and a common superiority to other creatures. The equality of human beings resides in their common inequality to God and the rest of creation. That which distinguishes the human species from other creatures is our rationality which is revealed in our symbolic power and, more specifically, in human speech. "Our equality," writes Hartshorne, "as a common inferiority to God, whose nondiscursive knowledge must put him above language, and a common superiority to the speechless brutes, extends no farther than the symbolic power."[18] This symbolic power, which can be expressed in a multi-

tude of ways including language, pictures, and mathematical nota-
tion, is universal to every large group of human beings and gives
humanity its radical superiority over the rest of the known creation.

In his article "Politics and the Metaphysics of Freedom" Hartshorne provides a parallel explanation of basic human equality. There
he points out that "freedom comes from participation."[19] By this he
means that freedom depends upon social relatedness. The richness in
content of an individual experience is derived through its participation in other experiences. "The scope of . . . self-determination
. . . depends upon the level of complexity, the range of diversity, in
the participations open to the individual."[20] Among humans there is
a basic mutuality of participation, the essential sign of which is
language.

> It is true that some men have a more limited language than
> others, and have less power of participation than others. When
> we are dealing with actually feeble minded or insane persons, or
> with infants, we are for some practical purposes not dealing
> with human beings at all. Essential mutuality is lacking. But
> apart from these extreme cases, any inequalities in participatory
> power which exist are too uncertain, fluctuating, and equivocal
> to justify the supposition that some men are in relation to other
> men as men are to animals.[21]

Thus the inequalities between people, as real as Hartshorne believes
them to be, are, apart from some extreme cases, too uncertain to be of
practical consequence.

What consequences does this innate equality among persons
have for political freedom? First, and most obviously, Hartshorne
regards many of the differences that have historically been used to
discriminate between groups of people, such as color and sex, as
irrelevant to freedom. Since human beings are roughly equivalent in
participatory power, political structures should be adjusted so as to
give all citizens equal political freedom. Second, Hartshorne says that
because no one is radically superior to anyone else in participatory
power, or sympathy, and because we are all limited in attention span,
when it comes to our needs "each man must in good part look to
himself, simply because no one else could have time and energy,
even had he the ability, to do it for him."[22] Here we find the
ingredients for the liberal doctrines of tolerance and individual
self-reliance. Each individual is the best judge of his or her own needs

and purposes; therefore, we should display tolerance toward others as they seek to realize their personal preferences. "No one else feels and knows the needs and desires of an individual as intimately and constantly as that individual does. Hence each person should be permitted to design his or her life-style so far as this is compatible with others doing the same" (IOGT 226). This is the ideal of freedom, the economic version of which is laissez faire (IOGT 226). In addition, this requires a political system that permits citizens to identify their own needs and interests, and grants them the (negative) freedom to pursue those purposes (so far as it is compatible with others doing the same). As was mentioned earlier, the practical question of freedom is one of degree:

> [H]ow much self-determination (rather than determination by rulers) is there, in what important respects of behavior, and—perhaps above all—how much definite assurance is there in advance as to the *boundaries of freedom,* that is, *are there recognized limits to governmental interference, guaranteed 'rights' to make one's own decisions?*[22]

Obviously, a highly centralized government such as that found in the Soviet Union is anathema to Hartshorne. The members of the Politburo do not possess the superior participatory power required to decide for the ordinary Russians what their needs are, and which would justify the banishment of dissenters to prison labor camps: "The former are not more than men, the latter not less. And if the rulers of Russia were really super-human, they would understand the need for greater autonomy and for the honest expression of differences of thought and feeling which are the natural modes of human mutuality."[24] Finally, just as the individual rather than the state is the best judge of a person's needs, when it comes to personal welfare the individual should depend not on the state, but on his or her own efforts to satisfy those needs.

The basic point that Hartshorne is arguing is that there is no innate subservience of one group of human beings to any other group. He attempts to clarify this by providing two examples of such natural subservience. First, the cells of the human body are innately subservient to the human individual to whom they belong. These cells are inferior sorts of individuals which are by nature under the command of the human self. Second, the individuals that constitute the entire universe are innately subservient to God. What is being denied, therefore, is that one man can be to another as a cell is to [a] man, or as any man is to God. A born imbecile is presumably born to an inferior position, but not even this case is nearly as radical as the two proposed paradigms of inequality. And all men sufficiently normal to have anything like average symbolic capacity are appropriately dealt with as participants in a cooperative process of conscious valuation and purposive activity. They should have, if not literally "equal respect" for each other, sufficient respect so that [it] is not very appropriate even to raise the question of a distinction. Primarily one confronts a fellow, only secondarily if at all a superior or inferior.[25]

It should be clear by now how Hartshorne's perception of the relationship between liberty and equality compares with that of liberalism. Like traditional liberals, Hartshorne locates human equality in a feature common to all human beings, namely, their symbolic power. Yet he readily admits that not all people possess this capacity to the same extent; being human in this all-important sense is a matter of degree. But apart from extreme cases such inequality is practically irrelevant for social or political issues. We must clearly understand that Hartshorne is not repudiating a distributive theory of justice; his argument is the practical one that we are incompetent to determine individual worth except in the most extreme cases. In these cases it is right and proper to restrict the liberty of the individuals in question. Hartshorne is also arguing that the typical criteria used for denying people certain freedoms, namely race and sex, are in fact unjust precisely because there are no distinguishable differences in innate capacities between large groups of persons. The only distinguishable differences are between individuals, and then, as we have seen, only extreme cases exhibit any degree of precision. Thus Hartshorne sidesteps the problem of our unequal possession of some defining trait by offering the practical argument that we are limited in our competence to judge individual worth and therefore limited in our right to restrict individual freedom.

It would appear that in Hartshorne's estimation the principles of process metaphysics support the typical liberal notion of equality before the law. Evidence that such a strand of classical liberal thinking exists in Hartshorne's social theory can be found in his brief discussion of the ideals of equality and liberty presented in the concluding chapter of *Creative Synthesis and Philosophic Method*. There Hartshorne claims that, given the aesthetic matrix of value, the most complete and purely human relations are between equals. The ideal of friendship is the harmonious relation of two equal, but no doubt deeply contrasting, human beings. This fact provides the ideals of social equality with a sound basis; however, this ideal "has to take its chances with several others" (CSPM 314). Hartshorne has in mind the competing ideals of self-development and liberty. The ideal of self-development is that

> each individual shall have opportunity to make the best possible use of innate powers. That these powers are in numerous important ways highly unequal seems reasonably certain, in the present state of our genetic knowledge. If well-endowed and poorly-endowed individuals . . . have equal opportunities to do their best, the result will not be a society of equals in the sense required for friendship. (CSPM 314)

There are two features of this argument that should be noted. First, Hartshorne is now offering an argument against social equality, understood as an equality of results, that has for its major premise a belief that the "innate powers" of people are in fact "highly unequal." This is in sharp contrast to his extensive arguments in favor of political equality which are based on the contrary belief in the fundamental equality of people apart from extreme cases. Where significant inequality was previously the exception, it has now become the rule. Second, this argument invokes a distributive principle according to which individuals should have equal access to the external means to self-development. The equality among people that Hartshorne is now concerned with is neither an equality of innate capacities nor an equality in the results of self-development, but in the opportunities people have to develop those capacities. Equality of opportunity as an ideal could lead to a policy of state intervention in order to ensure that each person's access to the means to self-development is proportionate to his or her innate capacities. However, the same practical consideration that provides Hartshorne with his basic argument in favor of political equality prohibits him from taking such a position. Because of the difficulty in determining with regard to innate capacities whether an individual is or is not well-endowed, not to mention the limited sympathy that we all have for the needs of other people, the state lacks the ability even if it had the will to allocate resources on an individual basis; the best the state can do is to allow equal, that is, impartial access by individuals to that which is necessary for personal development, for example, material resources. Equality of opportunity, an ideal by which the new liberals defended state intervention on behalf of the socially disadvantaged, ends up being for Hartshorne a justification for the classical liberal conception of equality before the law. People have an ''equal opportunity'' for self-development in the purely negative sense that there are ''recognized limits to governmental interference.''[26] Individuals, for example, have an equal right to private property which they are free to use in order to satisfy their needs and realize their purposes as they perceive them, that is, self-realization. Moreover, given the practical problem of ascertaining what an individual's innate capacities are, it is difficult to see how Hartshorne could allow the state the right to limit an individual's accumulation of the means for self-development, for any such limitations might restrict the self-development of an especially well-endowed individual.[27]

In his discussion of self-development Hartshorne mentions two additional factors that make it virtually impossible that the ideal of social equality will be realized in the future. First, in keeping with the basic belief of process philosophy that the character of an individual depends upon its environment, Hartshorne argues that even if infants were equally endowed in their innate capacities, without comparable environmental conditions they would not remain equals. Second, and more significantly, he claims that a society of equals will not be forthcoming if competitiveness is neccessary to induce individuals to exert themselves. If Hartshorne is correct and competitiveness does provide individuals with a valuable impetus to realize their potential for personal development, then social policies that unduly dampen the fires of healthy competition must be avoided. The important questions that then need to be addressed are what constitutes *healthy* competition and what policies or programs will *unduly* dampen that competition. Liberals, who have traditionally been concerned to foster individuality or ''character,'' frequently defend competition in the economic sphere because survival is a strong inducement to personal development! As a result, conservative liberals often denounce both the welfare state and the redistributive state on the grounds that they demotivate individuals. The welfare state, by guaranteeing its citizens an economic minimum, is accused of encouraging dependency and sapping the energies of self-reliance necessary to personal development.[28] The redistributive state, which

guarantees (that is, enforces) a strict equality of results among its
citizens or at least sharply limits the potential differential between
the best and least well off members of society, demotivates the
well-endowed individuals because they do not appear to benefit
from their efforts.[29] Hartshorne's support of competition as an
inducement to personal development, together with his preferential view of what constitutes personal development—our "needs
and purposes"—and his belief that self-reliance is the primary
means by which those needs will be met, reveals the conservative
strain in his political thought.

The ideal of social equality "has to take its chances" not only
with the ideal of self-development, but also with that of liberty.
"Anything like strict equality of opportunity," he claims, "would
have to result partly from coercion, since those who have advantages are likely to strive to retain them for themselves, or for
relatives or favorites" (CSPM 314). A *strict* equality of opportunity,
that is, a positive guarantee that all citizens will have access to
those things that are necessary to the development of their
individual powers or capacities rather than an equality of opportunity understood negatively as an equality before the law, would
require the coercion of those whom society has advantaged. Thus
coercion can be added to the list of practical problems that in
Hartshorne's estimation surround the ideal of social equality. The
need for coercion, the state's unavoidable insensitivity to individual needs and purposes, the basic inability of people to determine
the extent of a given individual's innate capacities, and the need of
competition to induce self-development, all lend support to the
traditional liberal doctrine of equality before the law and an
"umpire" conception of the state. Moreover, it is interesting to
observe that although a redistribution of opportunity, of power,
can only be achieved at the expense of the liberty of those who
currently have advantages, Hartshorne does not appear to regard
the exercise of those advantages on behalf of family and friends as
coercive. This is understandable if Hartshorne treats equal opportunity as a negative concept, as the absence of legal restrictions on
the exercise of one's will, and if one's capacities are no longer
simply taken as a person's innate abilities, but also include the
advantages that a person acquires in society. People are to be given
equal opportunity to realize all of their capacities— including their
acquired social advantages—and to restrict their "self-realization"
in this expanded sense is to diminish their freedom. To turn

opportunity into a positive concept, as the equal *ability* for all people to realize their *natural* capacities, will place restrictions on the exercise of one's socially acquired advantages. Indeed, equal opportunity in this positive sense means that by definition no one will possess "advantages" that others do not share.

Social equality, therefore, is not an overriding ideal that can be given "an absolute right of way without sacrificing other ideals . . . that seem as well-founded" (CSPM 314). While a leveling of *political* inequalities follows from Hartshorne's belief in the practical equality of human beings, *social* and *economic* inequalities naturally follow from the "highly unequal" innate powers among individuals. Such innate inequalities will ensure that inequalities in worth will persist, and any attempt to completely do away with them will necessitate the sacrifice of another ideal, that of freedom. Claims for equality must therefore be defended in the face of other competing ideals.

Evidence that I am not misrepresenting Hartshorne is to be found in his recent affirmation of the Friedmans' classical liberal position on equality and liberty. Milton and Rose Friedman distinguish between three concepts of equality that have governed human thought in different periods of American history. The first sense is termed "equality before God."[30] Here, like Hartshorne, they refer to Jefferson and the Declaration of Independence. They explicitly deny that innate personal equality is meaningful in any literal sense, and refer to Jefferson's belief in an elite class among human beings. Equality before God means that each person is precious and as such possesses inalienable rights, these being life, liberty, and the pursuit of happiness. In other words, equality before God finds practical expression in political equality. Hartshorne, of course, also denied that there was any literal equality among human beings either in their capacities or in their value to God. While discussing the idea of equality before God he writes, as if he had the Friedmans in mind: "I am not forgetting Jefferson, for whom I have deep admiration and who was a theist. But Jefferson spoke of 'natural aristocrats.' . . . He disbelieved in aristocracy by inheritance. But he saw that some people are nobler than others and some are vastly more skillful" (IOGT 229). Although not literally equal, Hartshorne defends through the principles of process philosophy the intrinsic value of every person and, with the exception of a minority of extreme cases, the basic equality of human beings in terms of their participatory power. Through principles such as these Hartshorne attempts to justify the leveling of political inequalities. The primary issue here, for Hartshorne as well as for the Friedmans and for Jefferson, is one of *individual rights*. Equal rights flow naturally from our fundamental equality before God; all persons have been "created equal" and have thereby been "endowed by their Creator with certain unalienable rights." Hartshorne likewise appeals to God in order to legitimate equal rights; God is "a mighty mediator, which can equally sanction the delegation of vast powers to the state and the withholding of vast powers, to be divided among private individuals or groups . . . " (BH 36). Whereas the concept of the divine right of kings functions to legitimate political inequalities among human persons, Hartshorne's God and his process metaphysics legitimate the ideal of political equality and the possession of guaranteed individual rights.

The second sense of equality identified by the Friedmans is "equality of opportunity." By this they mean that "[n]o arbitrary obstacles should prevent people from achieving those positions for which their talents fit them and which their values lead them to seek."[31] This understanding of equality "is manifested particularly in economic policy. The catchwords . . . [are] free enterprise, competition, laissez-faire. Everyone . . . [is] to be free to go into any business, follow any occupation, buy any property, subject only to the agreement of the other parties to the transaction."[32] Equality of opportunity thus means for the Friedmans, even as for classical liberalism of the nineteenth century, free-market capitalism.

The third, and final, concept of equality is "equality of outcome," which has as its goal "fairness."[33] They insist that whereas government measures to promote the first two forms of equality promote liberty, government measures to achieve "fair shares for all" reduce liberty. "The use of force to achieve equality will destroy freedom, and the force, introduced for good purposes, will end up in the hands of people who use it to promote their own interests."[34] It is a "myth" that free-market capitalism increases inequalities and is a system whereby the rich exploit the poor. On the contrary, they argue that it is within centrally planned societies that the gap is widest.[35] It has been the masses who have supposedly benefited most from the high productivity of the capitalist system. Thus any attempt by the state to secure equality of outcome will lead to a diminution of freedom and economic welfare for all citizens.

The extensive similarities between Hartshorne's understanding of freedom and equality in *Creative Synthesis and Philosophic Method* and the Friedmans' discussion of these same topics in *Free to Choose* are obvious. In a recent book Hartshorne himself praises the Friedmans, claiming that their "distinction between equality of opportunity and equality of results and benefits is important" (IOGT 229). He continues by underscoring his agreement with their case "against the view that equality of benefits can be maximized without seriously curtailing freedom and diminishing the goods available for all. We must to some extent take our chances in life, and equal attainments and perquisites cannot be guaranteed. Communist societies show nothing of the kind" (IOGT 229). Whereas in *Creative Synthesis and Philosophic Method* social equality, equal opportunity for self-development, and freedom are given the appearance of being equally well-founded ideals, none of which can be given an absolute right of way, it is now clear that equality of benefits is an inferior ideal—if an ideal at all—that can only be realized by *seriously* curtailing freedom and diminishing economic productivity. Freedom is curtailed because social equality would require a redistribution of power; people would not be able to enjoy the perquisites that they have acquired. The goods available for all will likewise diminish because in the absence of competition, without the inducement of rewards in the form of personal advantages or perquisites, without the incentives provided by a capitalist market economy, individuals will not be motivated to exert themselves. Yet while equality of results is not a valid ideal, Hartshorne accepts the ideals of political equality (based on our common inequality to God) and equality of opportunity which, like the Friedmans, he takes to be a negative concept, that is, the absence of "arbitrary obstacles" to self-realization. "Not birth, nationality, color, religion, sex, nor any other irrelevant characteristic should determine the opportunities that are open to a person—only his abilities," say the Friedmans. In other words, equality of opportunity "simply spells out in more detail the meaning of personal equality, of equality before the law."[36] Hartshorne's acceptance of political equality and equality of opportunity as legitimate ideals is clearly expressed in his article "Individual Differences and the Ideal of Equality." There he concludes that since

> we know little about an infant's inborn capacity, since also there
> are no manifest physical marks of the essential human traits,
> since, further, people cooperate willingly only if they feel
> themselves treated as ends and as the reflective decision-making
> creatures they are, and, finally, since human abilities and moral
> worth are hard to judge, the only principles upon which we can

expect a community to agree permanently are those of universal opportunity and universal participation (near idiots and criminals apart) in the collective decisions.[37]

In his arguments on behalf of liberty and equality Hartshorne ends up defending a position virtually indistinguishable from that of the Friedmans and of classical liberalism generally. This is particularly interesting given that historically classical liberalism has adhered to an atomistic theory of human nature and a mechanistic view of society, both of which have been challenged by process philosophy. Whereas we might have expected Hartshorne to develop arguments for freedom and equality from the idea of the social relatedness of individuals—as for example are found among the new liberals[38]—instead we discover him defending these values because of our *lack* of sympathy, because of the inadequacy of our social feelings for one another, because we are, in fact, "almost stone blind to the lives of others, even those close to us. . . . "[39] Consequently, those political and economic systems that secure for its citizens equal rights and erect no artificial barriers to self-development are in harmony with the nature of reality itself. For a philosopher who stresses the social nature of reality as much as Hartshorne does, it is astonishing to find him so vigorously emphasizing our isolation from and insensitivity to other human beings. Yet as we shall see, this emphasis also lies behind several of his arguments on behalf of democracy.

## II. THE PRINCIPLE OF DEMOCRATIC RULE

The lack of sympathy among human persons for the feelings of others is an unavoidable attribute of human nature by which Hartshorne legitimates the liberal democratic vision of equality and liberty. Yet, while unavoidable, process philosophy does not consider insensitivity to be a property that deserves admiration. Sympathetic dependence on others rather than independence from others is a sign of excellence. It is this belief—that relativity is also a positive quality that should be attributed to deity—that lies behind Hartshorne's dipolar theism. "The eminent form of sympathetic dependence can only apply to deity," asserts Hartshorne, "for this form cannot be less than an omniscient sympathy . . . " (DR 48). As one descends the scale of being each subject will display a degree of dependence that is appropriate for that level. It is inappropriate, therefore, for human persons to try to sympathize with all life. Each of us will as a matter of necessity sympathize most with that small group of family, friends, and associates nearest to us.

The belief that dependence upon others is a negative attribute unworthy of deity and, therefore, that God's absoluteness entails that God is in no sense dependent upon creation, is a tenet of "classical" theology strongly opposed by process philosophers and theologians. What is particularly interesting is the way in which this concept of God has been linked with images of the state and society. Whitehead, for instance, is well aware that in our efforts to express our understanding of ultimate reality human beings have applied to God imagery that coheres with the accepted political realities of the time. Religious thinkers in the ancient Near East "could find no way better to express themselves than by borrowing the characteristics of the touchy, vain, imperious tyrants who ruled the empires of the World. In the origin of civilized religion, Gods are like Dictators" (MT 68). In other words, the connection between imagery of God and of the state is not purely accidental; social and political structures provide a primary analogate by which people are able to understand the cosmos. As for the concept of God as self-sufficient, an idea that classical theology has derived from Greek philosophy, in classical Greek thought both God and the *polis* were thought of as autarkic. "It is noteworthy," says Nicholls, "that this strong emphasis upon self-sufficiency should emerge at a time when there was particular concern with the relationship between the small city state and the larger Greek community."[40] Nor is it purely coincidental, he adds, "that the notion of God's self-sufficiency has been challenged most vigorously by philosophers and theologians from the United States, where interdependence among the several units of the federation is a long-standing phenomenon."[41]

Hartshorne also believes that there is a connection between the image of God as self-sufficient in classical theology and political realities; however, his approach is basically Idealist since he argues from the idea of God to political systems while ignoring the way dominant political structures can encourage certain interpretations of reality. One of the difficulties in relating democracy to religion, he claims, is "that God is usually conceived rather as a supertyrant, the sponsor of all lesser tyrannies than as the superdemocrat, the inspiration of democracy; or again, that God as the absolute, imparts to His believers an absolutistic attitude which conflicts with the relativity essential to democratic tolerance and mutuality."[42] Similarly, when he comes to discuss the "practical applications" of his social conception of God at the end of *The Divine Relativity* he lists some of the "deficiencies of inherited religions," among them being "[p]ower worship—the divorce of the notion of supreme influence from that of supreme sensitivity, in the concepts both of deity and of church and state authority" (DR 148). Through the assertion of God's sheer absoluteness, God's self-sufficiency, and the denial of process in the divine consciousness, classical theology idealizes a tyrant conception of God which infects ecclesiastical and political authority. Hartshorne does not consider it a coincidence that "stateolatry" chiefly arose "in countries where Roman Catholicism is well represented; in the first instance, a country almost entirely Roman Catholic. Nor should we forget Hitler's Catholic origin" (BH 34). Roman Catholicism provided Fascism with a context in which "power and necessity have been exalted above love and freedom as final explanatory concepts" (BH 30).

Behind the image of God as a tyrant or despot resides the belief that the creation, as God's subject, should be dependent upon God's will while the divine ruler should not in any sense be dependent upon the wills and fortunes of others (DR 42). Hartshorne labels this "the transcendentalized absolute negation of the principle of the democratic rule, which is that the ruler should in a sense also be subject and the subject in a sense also ruler."[43] A key principle of process philosophy is that every individual is both active cause as well as passive effect, and that God is the supreme or eminent instance of this metaphysical truth. This social conception of reality is held by Hartshorne to be a sounder principle both *politically* and *theologically*:

> [H]e who is most adequately influenced by all may most appropriately exert influence upon all. The best ruler is an intermediary in the universal interaction, able to moderate and harmonize actions because all that is done is done also to him, whose reaction to this action absorbs and transmutes all influences into a counterinfluence, integrative and harmonizing in tendency, discouraging excessive factors and encouraging insufficient ones. (DR 50)

Thus process philosophy's "metaphysics of freedom," based as it is on a social conception of reality, is also a "metaphysics of democracy." Hartshorne goes on to say that the "democratic idea of rule . . . is an ideal of equality only by virtue of the fact that men are essentially of one species in their capacity to absorb influences [and] therefore in their right to exert power" (DR 50-51). Because all fully human beings are approximately equal in their participatory power, that is, in their ability to absorb influences, there is no innate right for any to rule over his fellows. The argument appears to be that the right to exert power (cause) is exactly proportionate to one's ability to receive influences from others (effect): "[T]he totalitarian state is an abomination because it places unlimited power where there cannot be anything like unlimited understanding and love . . . " (BH 37). Among human beings, therefore, only that system that allots to each citizen equal freedom to determine the destiny of his or her society is just. Hartshorne believes that democracy is that system.

It is interesting that for Hartshorne the democratic idea of rule is an ideal of equality *only* by virtue of the fact that human beings are essentially equal in sensitivity. In other societies the same ideal may be reflected in an *unequal* distribution of power owing to an innate inequality between individual members within that society. To understand this we must recall Hartshorne's metaphysical distinction between monarchical and democratic types of societies. In a monarchical society there is a radically dominant member which is the synthetic act-sequence uniting the organism. A democratic society, such as a plant, lacks any such dominant member. Two examples of monarchical societies, which we will recognize from our discussion of equality, are the human person and the universe. In both cases there is a ruling member that is the natural overlord of the subservient individuals comprising its "body." However, Hartshorne's defense of human equality, as we have seen, involves the denial of any innate subservience between "reasonably normal adults. . . . "[44] All human beings, as Jefferson said, are born free and equal; therefore, the institutions of slavery and kingship cannot be justified by any appeal to nature or to divine right.

> All human rule over persons is by convention, custom, conscious decision; it is not established by blind instinct, like that of brain and muscle cells to express human thought and feeling. Human social and political arrangements belong to a very different order than such instinctive subordinations, being always in part deliberate or voluntary.[45]

Human societies, lacking as they do a dominant unifying member, are "democratic." Therefore the democratic idea of rule, according to which one's right to exert power is proportionate to one's ability to be influenced by others, is properly expressed in a political system that distributes power equally among society's members.[46]

In a "monarchical" society, on the other hand, the same principle is properly expressed in an unequal distribution of power. The universe is a monarchical society in which God is the unifying member. But the divine rule over the universe does not violate the democratic idea of rule:

> [I]f there be a being supreme in sensitivity, in nonapathy, in cognitive relativity, then no man who understands what he is doing will wish to deny this being supreme power, least of all on the basis of the democratic principle. For to say God is supremely sensitive is to say that in his rule he allots to us a privilege of participation in governing which goes infinitely beyond a mere ballot. It means that with every decision, however secret, that takes place in our minds we are casting a vote which will surely be taken account of and will surely produce effects in the divine decisions. (DR 51)

We find ourselves in the peculiar situation where the supreme *monarchy* is simultaneously the eminent example of the *democratic* principle! This should hardly surprise us. Given the principle of social relatedness, it would appear that all metaphysical monarchies *necessarily* exhibit the democratic ideal. By definition the dominant member of a monarchical society is innately superior to its subordinate members in its power of participation. Thus the most powerful member is the most sensitive as well. That feature which makes a society monarchical is the very feature that causes it to exemplify the democratic idea of rule. The language that Hartshorne uses to describe the interaction of ruler and ruled in a monarchical society might strike us as odd given that it is characterized by the democratic principle: "The cells of the human body are, we may say, not only innately inferior, but innately subservient, to the human individual to whom they belong. Theirs not to reason why, to vote for or against their predesignated ruler, or to propose changes in the institution of his rule."[47] As with God and the world, so also here the innately inferior subject is not to question the policy decisions of its master.[48] According to the democratic principle, the eminent influence is also to be eminently influenced; power is to be proportionate to sympathy. In a monarchical society the dominant member is by definition the most sensitive entity; therefore, there is no need to erect safeguards against its dominion. It is with democratic societies (in the metaphysical sense), in which no individual is innately more sensitive than another, that the danger of misproportioned power is greatest. In such societies the democratic ideal is observed by providing the members with an equal voice in decisions that affect the body politic; in a monarchical society the same ideal is expressed by an inequality of power.

We can conclude, then, that Hartshorne saw process philosophy as providing metaphysical support for a democratic political theory. Such support is founded first and foremost upon its social conception of reality of which God is the preeminent example. Power should be proportionate to sensitivity. Yet this is not the sole argument that process metaphysics can muster in defence of democracy. I suggest that there are at least three additional (although related) arguments and that their use by Whitehead and Hartshorne lends further support to the claim that process thought legitimates the ideals of modern liberalism. It is to these arguments that we must now turn.

### 1. Democracy and the Distribution of Freedom

In his criticism of dipolar theism, Merold Westphal takes issue with the political models used by Hartshorne to strengthen his case for a neoclassical conception of God. Hartshorne, like Whitehead, claims that the absolute deity of classical theism is the "transcendentalized admiration of politico-ecclesiastical tyranny . . . " (DR 50). "But is it not the case," asks Westphal,

> that our admiration of democracy and our dislike of tyranny and despotism presuppose the limitations of human knowledge and goodness? Because power tends to corrupt and because no one person is sufficiently wise to govern alone we share the responsibility and privilege of governing. Is it so clear that in a society with one member whose goodness, power, and wisdom were perfect . . . we would wisely prefer democracy to (benevolent) despotism?[49]

Westphal's argument for democracy is a purely protective one: democracy is a better form of government than a benevolent despotism because of the "limitations of human knowledge and goodness," because power tends to corrupt, and because no one alone possesses sufficient wisdom to govern well. Our preference for democracy is justified in Westphal's opinion only because it *protects* us from the misuse of power by imperfect creatures.

In his reply Hartshorne emphatically asserts that democracy is preferable to a benevolent despotism "if the tyrant is to determine everything."

> For then the "citizens" would not really determine anything, and it would be a mystery how they could even know what "determine" or "decide" means. The value of democracy—surely this is commonplace—is not merely that the right decisions are more likely to be made, but that the process of deciding, which in principle is life itself, is distributed instead of monopolized.[50]

The problem with Westphal's criticism is that it assumes the value of democracy to reside solely in its protective function. As we shall see below, Hartshorne, too, extols the protective virtues of democracy; however, he rightly points out that as an explanation of the value of democracy this feature alone is inadequate. Democracy also has value because it preserves the freedom of the individual.[51]

Within a democratic society political freedom is distributed rather than monopolized. Here two points need to be made, one economic and the other metaphysical. First, Hartshorne exhibits a marked hostility toward all forms of monopoly, and in particular toward those in the economic sphere. The "only ideal" is a balance of power between the citizen and the state. "It involves the transfer of the present fanatical hatred of socialism (balanced by an equally fanatical hatred of competition) to the one object deserving of hatred—private monopoly . . . " (BH 36). Having said this, Hartshorne refers the reader to Henry Simons's "brilliant" (BH 38, n.10) pamphlet, "A Positive Program for Laissez Faire." Turning to Simons's pamphlet we find statements such as the following:

> [P]olitical liberty can survive only within an effectively competitive economic system. Thus, *the great enemy of democracy is monopoly, in all its forms:* gigantic corporations, trade associations and other agencies for price control, trade unions—or, in general, organization and concentration of power within functional classes.[52]

Simons's belief that monopoly is the great enemy of liberty is echoed throughout Hartshorne's own writings. In his review of Simons's pamphlet Hartshorne argues that if the individual is to be protected from exploitation then there must be free competition within society.[53] This will require that those businesses that cannot operate competitively, for example, the utilities, railroads, and so forth, must be socialized. Complete socialization, however, is "illiberal" and will inevitably lead to totalitarianism. State socialism simply transfers the power of privately owned monopolies into the hands government bureaucrats, and there is consequently no net increase in freedom for the private citizen. Comments such as these make it clear that by the time Hartshorne wrote *Beyond Humanism*, which is one of his earliest publications, he was already firmly committed to a modified laissez faire economic theory.

Given Hartshorne's obvious dislike of political and economic monopolies it is interesting that the repudiation of monopolistic power as an ideal is also a characteristic feature of his metaphysical theory. "Unqualified monopoly is always bad, even in the eminent case. Or rather, there can be no eminent monopoly of power."[54] Hartshorne claims that a monopoly of power is "the most undesirable thing imaginable; or rather it is the unimaginable and indeed inconceivable absolutizing of an undesirable direction of thought."[55] As we saw earlier, according to process thought God's power is unsurpassable, but it is not absolute and therefore should not be identified with the sheer monopoly of power. The value of every entity resides in its power of self-creativity. Since no individual is totally lacking in power those social arrangements that would monopolize power, be they political or economic, run counter to the structure of the universe itself. It is because freedom and power are cosmic variables (of which God is the eminent but not sole example) that democracy is to be preferred above even the most benevolent despotism.

## 2. Democracy and the Protection of Personal Interests

In our earlier discussion of Hartshorne's views concerning liberty and equality we noted that he defends political equality on the grounds that people are limited in their power of participation or sympathy. We are, for all practical purposes, equal in our inequality before God and apart from a few extreme cases, there is no innate subservience among human persons. Consequently, everyone who is capable of doing so should be free to participate equally in the collective decision-making process.

What Hartshorne is in effect providing is a protective argument for democracy. Each of us is vastly more sensitive to our own needs and purposes than of those around us; therefore, we are not only best suited to determine what those needs are, but we cannot presume for a moment that other people, including government officials, will be sensitive to and will take into consideration our own interests. This is especially true given Hartshorne's belief that

> [t]he will to power is inherent in man. For on the one hand man is conscious of an infinite ideal, and on the other hand it is always easier for him to conceive of the good in terms of his own than of others' realization. And . . . the inability of men to understand one another except very partially and abstractly makes the necessity of entrusting our affairs largely to a few executives (a condition of efficiency) a bitter necessity. (BH 73–74)

Hartshorne clearly does not cherish any utopian dreams about the withering away of the human struggle for power. On the contrary, he appears to view politics as an unending competitive struggle between numerous partial and limited understandings of the good, each of which usually, although not inevitably, emphasizes its own interests. Because of our relative lack of sympathy for one another each of us tends to universalize his or her own limited perspective of the good, a perspective that naturally favors one's own interests. Given, as we saw in the previous chapter, that Hartshorne's organicism does not really provide for an understanding of the common good on the level of human society in terms other than the sum of individual goods, it is not surprising that he should see politics as a competitive struggle between different basically self-interested views of the good. For this reason political participation is vital if we are to ensure that our interests are not overlooked. Ideally this would take the form of direct democracy since it would ensure that one's voice was heard. Unfortunately, efficiency makes it a "bitter necessity" that a few executives be granted political power out of proportion to their participatory power. Our limited ability to conceive of the good in terms of our neighbor's realization entails that even a representative government may fail to serve the general interest. Thus mankind's lack of sympathetic power means not only that no one has an innate right to rule over others, but also that every person must be allowed to participate in political proceedings if their interests are not to be overlooked.

The claim that democracy is the form of government best suited to protect the interests of its citizens was perceived by liberal democrats in the first half of the nineteenth century as the strongest if not sole argument in favor of the democratic system. According to C. B. Macpherson liberal democratic theory builds upon assumptions derived from the capitalist market society and the laws of classical political economy, namely, a model of man as a maximizer of utilities and model of society as a collection of individuals with conflicting interests.[56] Such assumptions led Bentham, for instance, to conclude that society is a collection of individuals incessantly seeking power over each other. The sole security that citizens have against the natural and unavoidable selfishness of their governors is the power to remove them through frequent elections. ''[W]ith the single exception of an aptly organized democracy,'' he writes, ''the ruling and influential few are enemies of the subject many: . . . and by the very nature of man . . . perpetual and unchangeable enemies.''[57]

The protective argument does not require Bentham's extreme pessimism about human nature. J. S. Mill, who provides a similar argument for democracy as ''the ideally best form of government,''[58] has a more positive view of human nature. ''We need not suppose,'' he asserts, ''that when power resides in an exclusive class, that class will knowingly and deliberately sacrifice the other classes to themselves: it suffices that, in the absence of its natural defenders, the interest of the excluded is always in danger of being overlooked. . . . ''[59] An extreme egoistic individualism, therefore, is not necessary for the protective argument to work; the more cautious claim that people are limited in their sensitivity to others and consequently that there is a danger that the needs of some might be overlooked is sufficient. Hence Mill concludes that ''the rights and interests of every or any person are only secure from being disregarded when the person interested is himself able, and habitually disposed, to stand up for them.''[60] Each is the best guardian of his or her own interests.

Mill's belief that individuals generally prefer themselves to others does not mean that everyone is equally insensitive to the needs of others. On the contrary, he considers communism practicable among the elite of mankind, implying that such people have overcome the natural preference of themselves to others, or of those nearest them to those farther away. Mill could adopt a theory of plural voting precisely because some individuals are superior to others in ways that are directly relevant to the political process. Since everyone is the best guardian of their own interests, reasons Mill, everyone should have a voice in the government's exercise of power. However, voting is more than defensive; it also determines policy which affects the lives of others. Since everyone is not equally capable of ascertaining the general interest, as opposed to their own interests, the opinions of those who are better qualified by virtue of their superior intelligence should be given greater weight: "[T]he opinion, the judgment, of the higher moral or intellectual being, is worth more than that of the inferior. . . . "[61] Consequently, Mill advocates a system of plural voting, the better qualified being given more votes than the less qualified. "[T]hough every one ought to have a voice—that every one should have an equal voice is a totally different proposition."[62]

Hartshorne's protective argument for democracy is more akin to Mill's than to Bentham's. Hartshorne has a more optimistic view of human nature, acknowledging the reality of social feelings and rejecting Bentham's egoistic theory of behavior. "Absolute selfishness is nonsense, and it is worth realizing that this is so." Even so, he continues, "[e]ach person must still incline to take himself and his intimates more seriously than he takes human beings in general."[63] Rulers do not act purely out of self-interest; but because of the limited nature of their sensitivity there remains the danger that the needs of some individuals will be inadvertently neglected. Although Hartshorne rejects the extreme egoism of Bentham's theory of individualism in favor of a relative individualism, the classical liberal view of society as a collection of individuals with conflicting interests has been largely retained: each of us tends to conceive of the good in terms of our own realization. To ensure that our interests are not disregarded by insensitive and selfish bureaucrats, governmental officials must be made accountable to the electorate. "Bureaucrats will be more or less selfish (claiming to be beneficent), ignorant, stupid, or insensitive; and we must economize in the extent of our reliance on their discretion, backed as it is by the coercive police power. To forget this coercive aspect is to lose any claim to the title of liberal" (IOGT 228).

Although Hartshorne develops a protective argument for democracy similar to Mill's, he does not follow Mill down the path of plural voting. The reason for this is that with regard to sympathetic power "there is no vast difference between superior people and most people."[64] Since Hartshorne appears to operate according to the principle that the right to exert political power should be proportionate to one's power of participation, there is no justification for the inegalitarian distribution of votes defended by Mill. Everyone is basically equal in their sensitivity to others and therefore in their ability to ascertain the general interest. Hartshorne's position reflects the egalitarian ideal of American democracy according to which everyone is considered to be equally capable of participating in politics up to the highest level.[65] And yet he does not believe that everyone should be allowed to exercise political power. Some people, for example, confirmed criminals, should not get any vote at all. In extreme cases where individuals lack the capacity to "weigh ends and means and compare values" they should be excluded from the process by which the collective decisions that affect them are made.[66] It is also worth pointing out that whereas for Hartshorne extreme cases must be evaluated on an individual basis, Mill claims that ascertaining who is the wiser or better person is "a thing impossible as between individuals, but, taking men in bodies and in numbers, it can be done with a certain approach to accuracy."[67] Thus votes were allotted primarily on the basis of one's occupation, a basis that Hartshorne would have found unacceptable.

### 3. Democracy and Self-Development

The primary argument offered by modern liberals on behalf of democracy is that, like liberty, political participation encourages the citizens' self-development or education. In his justification of democracy Bentham claims to take human beings as he finds them and then seeks to arrange political structures so as to constrain human nature to work for the common good. In fact, however, he takes human beings as he finds them in a capitalist market society which assumes that mankind is by nature an "infinitely desirous consumer of utilities. . . ."[68] But with Mill a new concept of human nature was introduced into liberal thinking, namely, that of mankind as "an infinite developer of his human attributes."[69] The Locke-to-Bentham perception of human nature was rejected by the new liberals in favor of an ethical conception which assumed "not only that each individual was equally entitled to the opportunity to realize his human essence, but also (as against the Greeks) that men's capacities were substantially equal, and (as against the medieval tradition) that they were entitled to equal opportunity in this world."[70] Mill entertains a vision of humanity's moral improvement and claims that a democratic system is the means to that improvement in as much as it maximizes each individual's ability to use and develop his or her essentially human capacities. "Human nature is not a machine," writes Mill, "to be built after a model, and set to do exactly the work prescribed for it, but a tree, which requires to grow and develop itself on all sides, according to the tendency of the inward forces which make it a living thing."[71] Utopia cannot be imposed upon the people; rather they must discover it for themselves. Participation in politics is a means to individual improvement, and thereby the improvement of society as a whole.

According to the new liberals political participation is educative because citizens are confronted with interests that differ from their own and this exposure to a variety of perspectives on various issues expands their understanding and appreciation of the problems confronting the larger group, be it local or national. By this process each person becomes aware of his or her status as a member of a larger community and of the common good in which they participate with others. Our fraternal feelings, or sympathies, which stem from our "deeply-rooted conception" of ourselves as social beings and natural desire for "harmony between . . . [our] feelings and aims and those of . . . [our] fellow creatures," are strengthened.[72]

An example of this line of argument can be found in Whitehead's speech at the annual meeting of the Cambridge Women's Suffrage Association. There he took issue with Asquith's claim that the political influence of women would be destroyed if they were given the vote: "Their influence as a class, at present, is necessarily irresponsible and often uninformed. When they have the vote they will take themselves seriously, and form their opinions with a sense of responsibility." Whitehead continues:

> During the last General Election nothing has struck me more than the educative effect of the vote upon the agricultural labourers in the village in which I live. They listened to both sides with care and attention, and their random political ideas were transformed into an instructed body of opinion. (LEW 38)

Thus participation in the decision-making processes of society is educative because it stimulates interest in wider issues and provides an opportunity for the expansion of one's perspective on the larger social group.

Even if we grant that participation in public affairs is educative because it develops an appreciation for other viewpoints on issues of general concern, one might still question whether *political* participation is specifically necessary. Could not such an awareness be achieved without giving people a voice in the decision-making process? John Dewey tackles this problem by arguing that the responsibility one takes for the collective decisions of society, and the common deliberation this requires, makes political participation a particularly good means, though not the sole means, of educating a personality.[73] The aspect of responsibility requires that the citizen have the right to participate actively in politics; simply to be informed about the issues is insufficient. With a process metaphysics we can support the link between personal development and full adult suffrage by appealing to the second aspect of an entity's subjective aim, namely, its aim at intensity in the relevant future. A subject is partly responsible for the effects of its decisions on future occasions of experience; furthermore, the anticipation of this effect qualifies the present subject's intensity of experience. Thus by increasing the responsibility of the individual, that is, the scope of future relevance, one is increasing the potential contribution that anticipatory feelings can make to an individual's development. Political participation, which brings with it responsibility for the welfare of the nation, also brings with it a unique potential for personal development.

A further point needs to be made concerning the benefits that democracy brings for the development of its citizens. According to process thought intrinsic value lies in the free self-creativity of each experient occasion: the process of deciding is in principle "life itself."[74] From this principle of process metaphysics Hartshorne draws the following political conclusion:

> Statesmen know that beyond a certain point interference with the lives of citizens does more harm than good, and this not solely because of the weakness or stupidity of statesmen but also because of the meaning of good as self-activity. This is part of the reason for the ideal of democracy, that people need first of all to be themselves, and this self-hood no tyrant, human or superhuman, however benevolent, can impose upon them. (LP 204)

A benevolent despotism is inferior to a democratic system of government precisely because the good can only be the result of the free decision of an individual. In a similar vein Whitehead writes:

> The basis of democracy is the common fact of value-experience, as constituting the essential nature of each pulsation of actual-

ity. Everything has some value for itself, for others, and for the whole. This characterizes the meaning of actuality. By reason of this character, constituting reality, the conception of morals arises. We have no right to deface the value-experience which is the very essence of the universe. (MT 151)

The experience of every individual is the realization of some value. Whitehead believes that democracy is preeminent among political systems for the promotion of value-experience among its citizens. There is a close connection between politics and morals. A totalitarian regime subordinates the individual to the community with the result that "human nature is dwarfed" (ESP 52). Totalitarianism is consequently immoral because the value experiences of those subject to it are defaced. The full development of human nature requires that society provide the opportunities necessary for self-realization.

This is the justification of that liberalism, that zeal for freedom, which underlies the American Constitution and other various forms of democratic government. It is the reason why the "totalitarian" doctrine is hateful. Governments are clumsy things, inadequate to their duties. A wise government makes provision for the interweaving of alternative forms of community life. (ESP 52–53)

However, while society can provide an environment conducive to individual development, such development cannot be coerced. The value experience of each "pulsation of actuality" is ultimately the result of the self-creativity of the individual concerned.

The notion that there is an important relationship between self-activity and intrinsic value is an idea common among modern liberals also. The idealists Green and Bosanquet in particular emphasized that personal character could only be developed through *self*-control. "No one can convey a good character to another," writes Green. "Every one must make his character for himself. All that one man can do to make another better is to remove obstacles, and supply conditions favourable to the formation of a good character."[75] Hobhouse similarly argued that self-development required that the person's character be the product of his or her own will. It is only through persuasive action "on a man's reason and feelings" that his good is to be sought.[76] "To try to form character by coercion is to destroy it in the making. Personality is not built up from without but grows from within, and the function of the outer order is not to create it, but to provide for it the most suitable conditions of growth."[77] The good, for Hobhouse even as for process philosophy, is inseparably linked to self-activity, and the democratic theory of government holds that a "vitalizing element" is obtained through the active participation in the community's affairs. Good government obtained from the hand of a benevolent despot lacks this vitalizing element.[78]

## III. CONCLUSION

On the basis of the preceding analysis I believe that we can justifiably conclude that Hartshorne and Whitehead considered process theology to provide a metaphysical foundation for liberal democracy. Four different although related arguments in favor of democracy can be distinguished: (1) First, Hartshorne asserts what he terms the "democratic idea of rule" according to which he who is most adequately influenced by all may most appropriately exert influence upon all. Given that human beings are essentially equal in sensitivity, that political system which permits all people to participate equally is to be preferred. (2) Whereas the first argument was based on the metaphysical claim that power should be proportionate to one's ability to sympathize, the second argument is grounded on the related metaphysical claim that no entity is entirely lacking in power. In place of the divine despot Hartshorne and Whitehead established a social conception of deity which has as its corollary the belief that finite entities have a genuine power of creativity. Democratic systems reflect this fact by distributing rather than monopolizing political power. (3) In many ways the third argument is the obverse of the first one. Instead of focusing on the equality of sympathetic power among human persons, the protective argument focuses on their general lack of sensitivity. Because God is eminently relative we are in no danger of being unjustly treated by God. The same cannot be said of people whose sensitivity is incomplete. A democratic form of government, it is argued, is best able to protect us from the insensitivity of others. (4) Finally, not only do all finite creatures have power, but this power is the power of self-creativity. Valuable experience involves self-creativity and this cannot be achieved through coercion. Democracy provides citizens with the freedom necessary for self-realization.

It is this latter argument which is, within the liberal political tradition, characteristic of modern liberalism. Modern liberals such as

Hobhouse, Green, and Mill did not reject the arguments used by classical liberals to justify democratic structures (although they did tone down the misanthropic tenor of the protective argument), but they gave preeminence to the developmental argument. Human nature is a social product and democracy, they argued, provides the most suitable environment for the full development of that nature. When we compare Hartshorne with such modern liberal theorists, we see that he not only reproduces both the protective and developmental arguments for democracy but adds some of his own which correspond to his process ontology. Whitehead, on the other hand, concentrates upon that argument that is distinctive to modern liberalism, namely, the developmental argument. Perhaps Hartshorne's use of the protective argument is evidence of his leaning toward a more classical liberal theory in contrast to Whitehead's fully modern liberal perspective. Too much weight cannot be given to this evidence in support of such a claim because of the small amount of Whiteheadian material on both equality and democracy. Even so, while on its own wholly inadequate, it may appropriately form part of a cumulative argument. Therefore having drawn attention to this point we must proceed to an examination of their positions concerning the use of coercive force by the state and between societies.

# 6

## State Intervention and
## International Relations:
## The Use of Coercive Force

The introduction of a social conception of human nature was a turning-point in nineteenth-century liberal political theory. Human beings were no longer viewed as essentially consumers and appropriators of utilities, but as exerters and developers of their capacities. The negative conception of liberty as the freedom to act according to one's desires was replaced by a positive conception of liberty as the ability to develop one's innate capacities. And whereas the early liberals defended the democratic ideal on the grounds that it afforded the best protection against the sinister interests of those in power, the new liberals were prone to see in the democratic franchise an implement for the education of society's less developed individuals. Yet it was the issue of state intervention that brought into focus most sharply the significance that the new understanding of human nature had for liberal thought.

It is my intention in this chapter to provide a careful exposition of Whitehead's and Hartshorne's attitudes toward the use of coercive force by the state. This analysis will provide further evidence of their substantial link with the liberal tradition. However, it will also highlight significant differences between Whitehead and Hartshorne further supporting my contention that Hartshorne is committed to a more classical form of liberalism than Whitehead.

## I. INTERVENTION AND THE OPTIMIZATION OF FREEDOM

In *Adventures of Ideas* Whitehead says that human communities are struggling with two types of compulsion: natural necessities and necessities for social coordination (AI 87). He goes on to list three ways this social coordination is produced: instinctive habit, compulsion by other members of the society, and reasonable persuasion. Compulsion by other members of society is not limited to the strictly political compulsion of the state, but includes the coercive aspect of our general social relations. This is the question of social freedom as described at the beginning of the previous chapter.

As we have seen, for process metaphysics there is always a mixture of self-determination and determination by others in human relationships. Not only is absolute freedom an impossibility, but from a process perspective, were such a condition conceivable, it would hardly be ideal. Not only do our relationships with other individuals determine the area of real possibility open to us for self-determination, and thus restrict our freedom in a negative sense, but they simultaneously provide us with the necessary data for a rich experience, and thus enhance our freedom in a positive sense. In Hartshorne's words, "[t]he social limitation upon freedom is what gives it positive content and value."[1] The problem of social freedom is an aesthetic one and reflects the metaphysical fact that the creative process is a creative synthesis. It is creative in that the past does not fully determine what values will be realized in the present occasion; but it is also a synthesis since the occasion depends upon the data it prehends in order to achieve intense experiences.

Although coercion is an unavoidable element of social interaction, we should remember that what limits our freedom is other freedom: "[F]reedom is causality in the making, causality is crystalized freedom, the influence of past acts of self-determination by countless creatures upon this act now taking place" (LP 307–308). Hartshorne explains the tragic aspects of existence by reference to his theory of freedom. An individual is self-active, and since "what is really many must act as many," the harmonious activity of the many cannot be guaranteed.[2] There are multiple centers of individuality and freedom, and therefore a multiplicity of decisions and relationships irreducible to a single decision. Some of these relationships will be characterized by social harmony, and others by discord; but the character of any particular relationship is partly a matter of chance.

No absolute coordination of creaturely decisions is possible. To guarantee harmony "the cosmos must completely coerce the lesser individuals, that is, must deprive them of all individuality. Existence is essentially social, plural, free, and exposed to risk. . . . "[3] Thus for the details of our existence we depend upon the choices that others make. Every individual is fate for other individuals, divine providence being a "superfate" (LP 314) for us all. Hence, because of the social nature of existence, tragedy is in principle, although not in particular, an unavoidable fact of human social life.

In general, tragedy is the unavoidable consequence of a world in which there are multiple centers of creative freedom. In this instance, tragedy is unfortunate but accidental, a product of chance. However, not all tragedy is accidental. The cross of Jesus symbolizes for Hartshorne the supreme tragedy in the world. The world is tragic "not only because conflict is inevitable between free and ignorant beings, but because there is an inner conflict in men between their will to serve a common good and their desire to promote a private or tribal goal" (RSP 149). This is the meaning of sin. Tragedy is not only a matter of chance; it can also be a matter of choice. As such it is not the unforeseen consequence of the decisions made by many free beings, but the result of a conflict of interests within a single individual.

While tragedy is in principle unavoidable, it does not follow that the scope for tragedy is beyond control. This overlooks divine providence which, according to Hartshorne, means not that God determines what will happen in its full definiteness, but that God places limitations on the operation of chance. Without God's ordering, without the divine providential activity, "individuals could not form even a disorderly world, but only a meaningless, unthinkable chaos in which there would be neither any definite good nor any definite evil. This is the same as no world. With God there is an order, a world in which good and evil can occur."[4] Creatures have freedom because of, and not in spite of, the limitations that God imposes upon the creative order. The successive states of God's concrete nature limit the possibilities available for realization by finite agents. God "controls, checks, encourages, redirects" (LP 203) the impulses that are produced by finite individuals. God's concrete states are the divine reactions to finite actions by which God "absorbs and transmutes all influences into a counterinfluence, integrative and harmonizing in tendency, discouraging excessive factors, and encouraging insufficient ones"[5] By this activity God establishes a situation that provides for a maximal surplus of opportunities over risks. If God were to allow more freedom then the increase in risks would exceed that of opportunities gained. Similarly, additional restrictions would result in a larger decrease in opportunities than in risks. Thus God's universal activity establishes at each moment conditions that express the optimal risk-opportunity ratio.

Hartshorne draws a very close analogy between divine and political authority, between the image of God and the image of the state. In the previous chapter we saw how the "despot" conception of God advanced by classical theology can undergird nondemocratic political systems. Process metaphysics, on the other hand, with its social conception of God, legitimates the "sounder" political principle of democracy. But the analogy between God and the state does not stop here. Hartshorne now adds that what God does for the universe, the state should do for human society; God's activity in the world is a model for the exercise of power by the state. "What God can do, and because he is good does do, is to set the best or optimal limits to freedom (as any good government will do, in its drastically more limited providence)" (RSP 41). A similar parallel between the activity of God and the state is drawn in the article "A Philosopher's Assessment of Christianity" where he writes: "The question confronting God's love is this: Within what limits can the creatures be allowed to be their own and each other's destinies? It is these limits of freedom which provide for the cosmos the predictability which legal forms aim to achieve for human society."[6] The perfection of the divine activity consists in God's exerting an "optimum of control" and thereby "maximizing the promise of freedom."[7] God establishes a "golden mean" between risk and opportunity. Similarly, the proper function of government is to establish an environment that optimizes the opportunities of its citizens. Like the divine ruler, human government should control, check, encourage, and redirect the impulses originating from its citizens. Good government, then, is *not* characterized by insensitivity to the needs of its citizens. Society must arrange and continue to rearrange itself so as to optimize the opportunities for development for all its members.[8] The best government is the one that is sensitive and responsive to its citizens' needs. The proper adjustment of chance and love "requires that destructive conflict arising from incompatibility of values should be mitigated without paying too high a price in loss of individuality, from which spontaneity, chance, and danger cannot be eliminated" (RSP 108).

One criterion of good government, then, is that in response to the needs of its constituents the government should supply sufficient coercive force to ensure the maintenance of an ordered environment without unduly restricting the options of the citizens for self-development.

It is unclear how far Hartshorne intended to push the analogy between the divine governance of the universe and good state government. For example, we recall that God does not intervene in particular situations to send us particular evils; rather, divine action "establishes an order in which creatures can send each other particular goods and evils" (NTT 120). The question is whether, for Hartshorne, good government is similarly characterized by such "universal" action. In other words, should a government intervene in affairs of particular citizens, or should its legislation be applicable to the whole body politic? If the latter is the case, as the analogy suggests, then this would further secure equality before the law as a political ideal. That Hartshorne did have such an analogy in mind is supported by a passage in *The Logic of Perfection:* "To rule is to sway all by a *common* influence; but something must, in each individual case, be freely added to constitute the response to the influence. Ruling or governing is always the imparting of certain *common* characters or limits to the self-determining of the ruled or governed" (LP 231; emphasis added). The principles of good government are thus special instances of the metaphysical principles outlined in our third chapter on freedom and causality. Causality, we will recall, is the restriction of logical possibility. Within the range of real possibility determined by the cause there will be factors *common to the entire set.* These features are "conditional necessities," that is, features that invariably will be realized by the event. However, the event is not fully determined by its antecedent causes. There remains an element of "chance," an element of uncertainty that follows from the self-creativity of the event. Similarly, government should ensure that certain "common characters or limits," that is, rights, are shared by the citizens thus retaining a level of social order within which citizens are free to act. At the same time, however, government must avoid an excessive restriction upon the freedom of its citizens: "[P]eople need first of all to be themselves, and this self-hood no tyrant, human or superhuman, however benevolent, can impose upon them" (LP 204).

Whereas Hartshorne explicitly refers to the coercive use of force by government to maintain an optimal risk-opportunity ratio, Whitehead speaks of the "double significance" of the "compulsory domin-

ion of men over men": "It has a benign effect so far as it secures the
co-ordination of behaviour necessary for social welfare. But it is fatal
to extend this dominion beyond the barest limits necessary for this
co-ordination" (AI 108–109). For Whitehead, even as for Hartshorne,
political philosophy cannot escape the doctrine of the golden mean:

> Unrestricted liberty means complete absence of any compulsory
> co-ordination. Human society in the absence of any compulsion
> is trusting to the happy co-ordination of individual emotions,
> purposes, affections, and actions. Civilization can only exist
> amid a population which in the mass does exhibit this fortunate
> mutual adaptation. Unfortunately a minority of adverse individ-
> ual instances, when unchecked, is sufficient to upset the social
> structure. A few men in the whole cast of their character, and
> most men in some of their actions, are anti-social in respect to
> the peculiar type of any society possible in their time. There can
> be no evasion of the plain fact that compulsion is necessary and
> that compulsion is the restriction of liberty.[9]

A civilized society cannot rely predominantly upon coercion to
maintain itself. While circumstances might compel a government to
override the rights of its citizens that society, as Hobhouse noted, "is
for the time moving backwards in the scale of civilisation.[10] Coercion
has a stultifying effect on society because it represses the spontaneity
of its members. Instead of tolerating novelty, a minority attempts to
impose a standard pattern upon the majority. The result is a failure by
the citizens to develop their natural capacities and a consequent lack
of adventure and social development. Reasonable persuasion, presumably, does not produce the same pathological consequences.[11]
Instead it provides an environment "within which the higher mental
activities and the subtler feelings can find their use and their
enjoyment" (AI 87). Unfortunately, not everyone will act in the
interests of the common good, and therefore some restraints will be
necessary to ensure a minimal level of social coordination. This idea
is expressed most clearly by Hartshorne when he asserts that "the
state and society must hold out rewards, including negative ones or
punishments, just to the extent that the minimal requirements of
social behavior out run the amount of love that can be presupposed
in men generally."[12] Both philosophers, therefore, agree in principle
with Hobhouse's claim that law is essential to liberty. "Law, of
course," writes Hobhouse, "restrains the individual; it is therefore

opposed to his liberty at a given moment and in a given direction. But, equally, law restrains others from doing with him as they will. It liberates him from the fear of arbitrary aggression or coercion, and this is the only way, indeed, the only sense, in which liberty *for an entire community* is attainable.''[13]

What Whitehead and Hartshorne are advocating is a balance between corporate and individual responsibility. This was a common emphasis among Idealists and new liberals alike although the different theorists did not always strike the same balance. Idealists such as Green, Arnold Toynbee, and Bernard Bosanquet had a fundamental concern for the character of the individual.[14] Hence while the government had a responsibility for providing citizens with the minimal requirements necessary for self-development, it must not ''interfere with the growth of self-reliance . . . with the moral autonomy which is the condition of the highest goodness. . . . ''[15] In an extended passage reminiscent of Hartshorne Green writes:

> It is one thing to say that the state in promoting these conditions must take care not to defeat its true end by narrowing the region within which the spontaneity and disinterestedness of true morality can have play; another thing to say that it has no moral end to serve at all, and that it goes beyond its province when it seeks to do more than secure the individual from violent interference by other individuals. The true ground of objection to 'paternal government' is not that it violates the 'laissez faire' principle . . . but that it rests on a misconception of morality. The real function of government being to *maintain conditions of life* in which morality shall be possible, and morality consisting in the disinterested performance of self-imposed duties, 'paternal government' does its best to make it impossible *by narrowing the room for the self-imposition of duties* and for the play of disinterested motives.[16]

Among the new liberals Hobhouse presents us with a similar position. Where there is a harmony in social relationships individuals cooperate freely together and this results in a ''heightening and fulfilling [of] their natural capacities.''[17] However, to some degree, constraint as well as cooperation is involved in every society. ''High organisation may be achieved on these lines,'' writes Hobhouse, ''but at a cost to social vitality proportioned to the degree of constraint exerted, and in the extreme case ruinous.''[18] Since repression leads to a diminution of the vitality within society that is located within individuals, the state should limit its action to securing those *common ends* in which uniformity or concerted action is necessary and which cannot be secured without compulsion.[19] Overlegislation and too much corporate responsibility is thus equally dangerous as underlegislation and too little responsibility.

## II. INTERVENTION AND THE CRITIQUE OF LAISSEZ FAIRE CAPITALISM

Both Whitehead and Hartshorne acknowledge the necessity of governmental coercion to maintain an acceptable social order in which individuals may prosper. The metaphysical justification of this position is found in their social conception of reality and in the ideal of individual self-creativity. Human beings are not atomic individuals externally related to each other, but elements in an organic system which are in part constituted by their relations to their environment. As Hartshorne describes it, we are "fate" to one another, we determine in part one another's destiny.

The social conception of reality, and the possibility of tragedy inherent in it, helps us see why Whitehead and Hartshorne, like the modern liberals, criticize the early liberal faith in laissez faire capitalism. Whitehead describes the "political, liberal faith of the nineteenth century" as "a compromise between the individualistic, competitive doctrine of strife and the optimistic doctrine of harmony. It was believed that the laws of the Universe were such that the strife of individuals issued in the progressive realization of a harmonious society" (AI 41). Similarly, Hartshorne says that classical economics misunderstands the true nature of tragedy and thus displays two "almost metaphysical deficiencies":

> On the one hand, it toys with the idea of an invisible hand which always and infallibly brings beneficent results out of individual motivations; and on the other, it toys with the idea that human beings should resign themselves to being, outside of family relations, simply selfish and calculating, rather than beings whose very core is love or social solidarity. (RSP 108)

Classical economists argue that the pursuit of individual interests will ultimately produce the best overall society. "Self-interest, if enlightened and unfettered, will, in short, lead . . . to conduct coincident with public interest."[20] With the idea of an "invisible hand" classical economists separate chance from tragedy. What happens is not seen to be the chance product of numerous free decisions but is invariably the best consequence for all concerned. Hartshorne readily accepts the classical liberal belief that the market is "a marvelous mechanism for usefully coordinating actions in ways not intended by the actors . . . " (RSP 108). What he denies is that it removes the element of chance from human relations, and therefore that the tragedy that is produced by the market is somehow necessary. The market is not itself "an absolute or all-sufficient mechanism" (RSP 108); it must be supplemented by other controls such as state intervention.

While state intervention is unavoidable, Hartshorne repeatedly warns readers against excessive government control such as is found, for example, within socialist countries. "Marxian planning and dictatorship," he writes, "seem excessive limitations upon the chance-spontaneity of the many, and Marxian solidarity seems to ask both too much and too little of human love" (RSP 108). In other words, socialist societies excessively restrict human freedom, they overlook the natural limitations of human sympathy, and they ultimately subordinate the individual to the group.[21] What is required is a balance between unbridled competition and state socialism. Hence, rejecting both blanket socialistic and antisocialistic dogmas— neither of which can be "justified by the genuine absolutes" (RSP 108)—Hartshorne defends a mixed economy consisting partly of socialized industries and partly of free competition among private enterprises (RSP 47).

What is particularly interesting in Hartshorne's criticism of laissez faire capitalism and state socialism is the criterion by which he determines their inadequacy, namely, *competition*. Why is it that pure laissez faire capitalism is not by itself a sufficient mechanism for producing the best society? Because left to itself capitalism produces monopolies that stifle true competition and economic freedom (BH 35–36). Similarly, state socialism assumes its own form of monopolistic power: "[A] state machine having nearly all the economic power would *be* the totalitarian state—the antithesis of liberty, whether secular or religious, and however democratic in form the state might pretend to be."[22] Hartshorne concludes that "to expect planning to supersede competition entirely is to forget the real truth in the religious sense of the sinfulness and limitations of man. . . . "[23]

In defending a mixed economy in the name of effective competition against the dangers of monopolistic power posed by laissez faire capitalism and state socialism Hartshorne is acting as a spokesman for the economic program of Henry Simons. In 1934 Simons wrote a pamphlet that he describes as "a defense of the thesis that *traditional liberalism* offers . . . the best escape from the moral confusion of current political and economic thought and the best basis or rationale for a program of economic reconstruction."[24] The tract is a reiteration of the "Old-fashioned" liberal position against not only "Communists and Fascists," but also against the " 'liberal' reformers" of his day.[25] Simons believes that the "real enemies of liberty in this country are the naive advocates of managed economy or national planning"[26] and that "none of the precious 'freedoms' which our generation has inherited can be extended, or even maintained, apart from an essential freedom of enterprise—apart from a genuine 'division of labor' between competitive and political controls."[27] Consequently, the greatest danger to democracy, as we noted in the previous chapter, is *monopoly:* "[P]olitical liberty can survive only within an effectively competitive economic system."[28]

A political policy of laissez faire, "and the correlative political philosophy, nineteenth-century liberalism,"[29] are judged to be the only secure defense against totalitarianism. By laissez faire Simons does not mean that the state should adopt a completely hands-off policy with regard to the economy; on the contrary, through positive economic legislation the state must liberate the free-enterprise system from those powers that hinder the operation of market forces. The state's responsibility for promoting laissez faire is properly exercised as it acts to establish and maintain the legal and institutional framework necessary for a genuinely competitive economy. If this is done properly then the state will not need to regulate the heart of capitalism, namely, the freedom of contract.[30] In a few instances— where "it is impossible to maintain effectively competitive conditions"[31]—it will be necessary for the state to assume ownership and management control of an industry or utility. However, in the vast majority of cases, the proper regulative agency is not the state but effective competition within a free capitalist market.

Hartshorne's support of Simons's political policy of "positive" laissez faire, not to mention his brand of "Old-fashioned" liberalism, was not a brief infatuation but a deep, lifelong commitment. He described "A Positive Program for Laissez Faire" as "brilliant" (BH 38) in 1937 and continued to extol its "wisdom" (IOGT 227) as late as

1983. Like Simons, Hartshorne believes that liberalism is the only guarantee of personal freedom: "Let religious persons take warning," he writes in his review of Simons's pamphlet, "that only liberalism renounces the totalitarian state *in principle!*"[32] The reason for this is that in a liberal society political and economic power are distributed rather than monopolized. According to Gaus, it is characteristic of classical liberals to claim "that a 'competitive economy based on private property is the institutional *guarantee* of freedom.' Here the idea is that the dispersion of power that results from a private property market economy protects civil and political liberty against encroachment by government."[33] This is precisely the line of argument advanced by Simons and Hartshorne. Simons advocates a " 'division of labor' between competitive and political controls,"[34] a point that is reiterated by Hartshorne and given added support by an allusion to the principles of process metaphysics:

> [T]here never can be bureaucrats so superior to ordinary people that they can be trusted to monopolize the decision-making process so far as the distribution of goods is concerned. Economic power and political power must not be too much concentrated in the same hands. No bureaucrat can be to citizens as a human mind is to the cells of its body, or as God is to the cosmos. (IOGT 228)

Hartshorne maintains that the ideal of freedom finds economic expression in laissez faire capitalism, while the economic version of the ideals of equality and fraternity is socialism (IOGT 226). In evaluating the merits of these alternative economic systems he concludes:

> Socialist societies have done rather poorly on the side of production, and have been far from libertarian, or consistently equalitarian or fraternal. Non-socialist societies have in some cases been brilliantly productive, with more internal freedom than socialist ones, though with very considerable inequalities and class conflicts. (IOGT 227)

To this he adds that Marxism has exceeded capitalism in its support of tyranny and colonialism. "If by its fruits a policy is to be judged," he concludes, "the case for Marxism is not impressive, whatever Sartre and Merleau-Ponty, for example, may say by way of special pleading" (IOGT 227). There can be no mistaking where Hartshorne's sympathies lie, despite his rather lame attempts to appear evenhanded in his criticisms of capitalism and Marxism. And although Hartshorne says that he wants to move beyond the dichotomy of capitalism and socialism (CAP 236); the fact that he sees Simons (and to some degree the Friedmans) as offering a balanced alternative demonstrates his solid support for a (slightly) modified capitalism. Simons's proposal of "a dual or mixed economy consisting partly of vigorous socialization of large industries, and partly of equally vigorous competition between private enterprises" is not a "timid compromise" but is, in keeping with his aesthetic matrix of value, a bold use of contrasts that will produce more vital harmonies (RSP 47).

Hartshórne readily admits that capitalism is in need of reform. "[C]apitalism *in its present-day form* is ugly—and doomed" (RSP 47), he claims. But the use of italics to qualify his criticism of capitalism demonstrates his underlying commitment to the capitalist economic system. It is not private property, or the creation and expropriation of surplus wealth, or competition, or even the inevitable inequalities that result from free-market competition that makes capitalism "ugly"; the problem with capitalism is that if left completely alone it produces private monopolies that destroy competition, and it is the absence of competition that leads to "very considerable" inequalities among people.

> In a time of loose talk about the "fallacy of profits," it is worthwhile to have it pointed out in trenchant fashion that the only demonstrated fallacy lies in monopoly-profits, which are profits as the reward not of efficiency but of extortion. Also that, although competition is harsh, it is not necessarily harsher than political struggles for power can be under socialism, both within the state and between states; while the really insufferable thing is profiteering through monopoly, which not only forces wages down but forces prices up, whereas competition, where it really exists, tends to keep wages and prices in fairly reasonable relation to each other.[35]

When there is true competition market forces will keep a proper balance between wages and prices; and since profits will not be inflated by wage reductions and artificial increases in prices, excessive inequalities between the owners of capital and wage laborers will not occur. When they are not extortionate, profits are in Hartshorne's opinion beneficial since, as we have seen, they provide an incentive to develop one's abilities and thereby indirectly increase productivity. Thus the form of capitalism that Hartshorne inveighs against is an "oligarchic" capitalism (CAP 236), which is not truly competitive.

Hartshorne not only supports Simons's positive program for laissez faire, he also gives it religious legitimation: "Although Professor Simons does not say so, I believe it could be shown that *religious economics must be liberal economics.*"[36] This is especially evident when one compares Hartshorne's understanding of the proper role of the state in the market with his interpretation of God's activity in the world. "Laissez faire saw Providence in competition, as a mechanism for producing social good out of relatively shortsighted and selfish actions," writes Hartshorne. "Pure socialism sees in man himself, especially in those men set in positions of power, the equivalent of Providence."[37] What these have in common is the mistaken belief that providence—either the "hidden hand" of the market or socialist "planning"—will eliminate chance. However, providence, properly understood, "is not the prevention of chance, but is its *optimization*" (DR 137; emphasis added). The proper role of the state is not to try to eliminate chance, but to establish a golden mean between chance of evil and chance of good, between risk and opportunity for its citizens. For Hartshorne, as for Simons, this entails establishing the legal and institutional framework necessary for genuine competition in the economy. A system in which there is true competition optimizes the freedom and opportunities for all. The state should not attempt to send particular citizens good and evil, but to establish an order in which citizens are free to send each other particular goods and evils. Inevitably, there will be tragedy: "Not everyone will be successful in competition" (IOGT 228). However the state is not concerned directly with individuals; it is the market that is to determine the distribution of goods. The state's role is to "optimize" the risk-opportunity of the market by ensuring that it remains truly competitive.

I suggest that Hartshorne's image of God and the role of divine providence is a projection of the capitalist marketplace onto the universe at large. According to Hartshorne, God's providential activity does not guarantee that some ideal course of events will occur; it does not eliminate chance. "Only the conditions under which the local agents determine local happenings are optimized by deity; the result is not ideal, for the local agents are not optimally wise or good, and cannot be." In other words, God "turns creatures loose to be each other's destiny, within wise limits of natural law" (NTT 121) even as the state, within its much more limited providence, turns *citizens* loose to be each other's destiny within wise limits of *civil* law. The only acts of God we can identify are the laws of nature (NTT 102), and it is these laws that establish an order in which creatures are free to send one another particular goods and evils.

In establishing the laws of nature God's concern is to maximize the total welfare, or beauty, in the universe. God is not concerned, that is, with the distribution of goods among finite creatures. "The future that ultimately matters is not particularly mine or yours, or even human, but cosmic and divine" (NTT 110). God's concern for the successes and failures of finite beings is finally in what they contribute to the divine life; God will make the most of them for us "only as items in the inclusive reality, members of the inclusive society" (NTT 110). Thus the justice of God is the justice of the liberal democratic state that oversees the competitive struggle in the capitalist market. God displays the impartiality of the state which acts "universally" to ensure equality under the law. I agree with Thomas Nairn that for Hartshorne God does not, as Moskop puts it, "will that some individuals be forced to suffer in order to promote the greatest happiness for the greatest number."[38] Yet this is not to say that God is not willing that some individuals suffer in order to promote the greatest good for the greatest number. A government that willed that certain individuals be forced to suffer would be unjust, even if thereby the greatest good of the majority was promoted; however, a government would not be considered unjust if, in treating all people impartially, that is, equally under the law, some individuals suffered as a consequence. Divine providence is just such a picture of liberal government writ large. God is *willing* that some individuals suffer, although God does not himself *will* that any particular individual suffer. It is not divine providence that "wisely decides how much and when each creature ought to suffer" (LP 314). The function of divine providence is "to set limits to the free interplay of lesser individuals . . . " (LP 314). As creatures compete with one another in the cosmic marketplace to realize their needs and purposes as they see them, some individuals will inevitably suffer. God's aim is to establish by law the maximal risk-opportunity ratio for that marketplace and then let the "whip of competition"[39] decide everyone's particular fate.

Hartshorne's philosophy, I conclude, is not simply a "metaphysics of democracy" (DR 50), but more specifically a metaphysics of *liberal* democracy. In the previous chapter we discovered that God is the supreme example of the "democratic idea of rule"; now we observe that divine providence is conceived in terms of the state's role in maintaining a truly competitive economic market. God is presented in the image of a properly functioning liberal democratic state which employs its legal powers to ensure that there is neither too much freedom (laissez faire) nor too little freedom (socialism) for its citizens. Furthermore, I suggest that the connection that Hartshorne makes between the image of God and capitalism extends even beyond the parallels between God and the liberal state. Since God is supremely relative, God is also the ultimate beneficiary of the universal marketplace. In other words, God is presented in the image of the cosmic entrepreneur who seeks through an optimization of the risk-opportunity ratio to maximize the return on his investment, namely, the beauty of the universe itself. The distribution of "wealth" (so to speak) in the universe is not God's ultimate concern. However, since every creature is part of the divine portfolio and ultimately pours the richness of its achievements into the divine life itself, God is not indifferent to the weal or woe of any creature.

## III. INTERVENTION AND POSITIVE LIBERTY

Toward the end of the nineteenth century it had become clear that unbridled competition was not producing the harmonious society envisaged by the seers of classical liberalism. On the contrary, as Hobhouse concluded, experience made clear that "liberty without equality is a name of noble sound and squalid result."[40] Whitehead shared these sentiments exclaiming that "[t]he mere doctrines of freedom, individualism, and competition had produced a resurgence of something very like industrial slavery at the base of society" (AI 42). Some of the tragic results of capitalism, far from being necessary, were from a process perspective the consequence of society's failure to provide adequate limitations to the possibilities of social interaction between its citizens. Thus Whitehead asserted that "no one now holds that, apart from some further directive agency, mere individualistic competition, of itself and by its own self-righting character, will produce a satisfactory society" (AI 44). How society is to achieve a harmonious coordination is not determined. Several proposals, including educating the directing classes, governmental regulation of the conditions of employment, and state ownership of the means of production, have been tried. What remains true, however, is that despite their preference for power as persuasion, Whitehead and Hartshorne believed in the necessity of limited state intervention in order to secure an optimal environment in which citizens can fully develop their capacities.

In their rejection of pure laissez faire capitalism and support of the state's role in partially regulating the social relationships among its citizens, our philosophers are reaffirming ideals espoused by modern liberalism. "The whole conception of the state . . . as an instrument for the active adaptation of the economic and moral environment to the new needs of individual and social life, by securing full opportunities of self-development and social service for all citizens," Hobson asserts, "was foreign to the Liberalism of the last generation."[41] The old liberalism had a negative attitude toward the state. An excessive emphasis was placed upon the negative aspect of liberty which consisted in the absence of restraint while neglecting the positive aspect of liberty as the presence of opportunity.[42] This was encapsulated in the golden calf of liberal ideology, namely, the so-called "freedom of contract." State legislation that sought to regulate the conditions on which two or more parties could agree a contract was thought to constitute undue interference with the "supposed inherent right of every man to do what he will with his own."[43] Thus, for example, the reform acts that limited the conditions under which certain types of labor could be bought or sold, that limited the number of hours women and children could work in the factories, and regulated the health and safety conditions of the workshops were resisted on the grounds that they interfered with each person's freedom to use his or her capital or labor power as each saw fit. Moreover, by endeavoring to protect people who should be able to protect themselves, the old liberals claimed that interventionist legislation "tends to weaken their self-reliance, and thus, in unwisely seeking to do them good, it lowers them in the scale of moral beings."[44]

The new liberals, on the contrary, beginning with Mill (in some moods) and Green, emphasized the positive aspect of freedom. Negative theories of freedom operate on an opportunity-concept: "[F]reedom is being able to do what you want, where what you want is unproblematically understood as what the agent can identify as his desires."[45] Positive theories of freedom operate on an exercise-concept. Freedom consists in being able to exercise certain capacities and thereby effectively determine the shape of one's life. When we speak of freedom, writes Green,

> [w]e do not mean merely freedom from restraint or compulsion. We do not mean merely freedom to do as we like irrespectively of what it is that we like. We do not mean a freedom that can be enjoyed by one man or one set of men at the cost of a loss of freedom to others. When we speak of freedom as something to be so highly prized, we mean a positive power or capacity of doing or enjoying something worth doing or enjoying, and that, too, something that we do or enjoy in common with others. We mean by it a power which each man exercises through the help or security given him by his fellow-men, and which he in turn helps to secure for them.[46]

Freedom properly understood is not merely the absence of external restraints but also involves the positive realization of one's capacities as part of the common good. Negative freedom alone is what Hobhouse calls an "unsocial" freedom, that is, "the right of a man to use his powers without regard to the wishes or interests of any one but himself."[47] Social freedom "is a freedom that can be enjoyed by *all* the members of a community, and it is the freedom to choose among those lines of activity that do not involve injury to others."[48] It is Green's contention that negative liberty is properly conceived as only a means to an end, namely, the "liberation of the powers of all men equally for contributions to a common good. No one has a right to do what he will with his own in such a way as to contravene this end."[49] True freedom, therefore, is not necessarily preserved by minimizing the activity of the state as proponents of a negative theory of liberty suggest.[50] Within a free-market economy the freedom of contract ends up being the freedom of one party to use its superior power to coerce the weaker party into accepting an agreement that aims, not at the best interests of all concerned, that is, the common good, but at the partial interests of the dominant individual or group. Consequently, just as "the uncharted freedom of one would be the unconditional servitude of all but that one,"[51] so the "restraint of the aggressor is the freedom of the sufferer. . . ."[52] Because of their positive conception of liberty the new liberals maintained a positive attitude toward the state. The state was one among many forms of collective action for the improvement of life.

> [T]hough Liberals must ever insist that each enlargement of the authority and functions of the State must justify itself as an enlargement of personal liberty, interfering with individuals only in order to set free new and larger opportunities, there need remain in Liberalism no relics of that positive hostility to public methods of co-operation which crippled the old Radicalism.[53]

Similarly Ritchie said that

> [a]ll salutary State action must be such as will give individuals so far as possible the opportunity of realizing their physical, intellectual, and moral capacities. In a genuine and honestly worked democratic State, State action and individual liberty will no longer be opposing principles; . . . individual liberty will exist, not in spite of, but by means of State action."[54]

State intervention is now seen as necessary to the effective realization of personal liberty.

There is much which would suggest that process philosophy adopts a purely negative conception of liberty. For example, as we noted in the previous chapter, Hartshorne says that political freedom is a question of degree, and he is concerned to ask if there are "recognized limits to governmental interference, guaranteed 'rights' to make one's own decisions."[55] Similarly, Whitehead's talk of the "double significance" of coercion, with its claim that dominion must not be extended "beyond the barest limits necessary" to secure social coordination, recalls Mill's desire for a "maximum degree of non-interference compatible with the minimum demands of social life."[56] I suggest, however, that such a reading neglects the fundamental insistence of process philosophy on the self-creativity of the individual. No doubt, as Berlin himself recognizes, every interpretation of the word liberty must include a minimum of negative liberty.[57] Yet the absence of restraints is not itself a sufficient condition of liberty. This point is brought out well by Green. The wandering savage, he writes, is the most free of all men if by freedom we mean the absence of restraints imposed by other human beings. Yet the condition that makes the savage free is the very condition that impoverishes his life. Submitting to the restraint of society "is the first step in true freedom, because the first step towards the full exercise of the faculties with which man is endowed."[58] Likewise, process thought holds that depth of experience depends upon the provision of an ordered and rich environment. The freedom of Green's savage results in the experience of "triviality." True, our freedom is in one sense limited by our social environment for, as we saw in our discussion of societies in Whitehead's philosophy, the social environment must be permissive of an individual's self-realization. And yet we also saw that the past not only limits our potential for self-realization, but also *supplies* us with the data necessary for the attainment of satisfaction. "The social limitation upon freedom is what gives it positive content and value."[59] Human freedom, in the sense of one's ability to exercise one's capacities, requires that one be a part of an ordered society. Only such an environment will provide a person with the opportunities for self-creativity by which his or her innate powers can be developed.

Further support for the claim that process philosophy supports a positive theory of liberty can be adduced from a comparison of comments made by Whitehead and the new liberal Herbert Samuel. In his *Memoirs* Samuel writes:

> [A]s more thought was given to the meaning of liberty—which Liberalism existed to serve—it was seen that liberty was not a matter only of national independence, or of constitutional democracy, or of freedom of thought and religion . . . but that there could be no true liberty if a man was confined and oppressed by poverty, by excessive hours of labour, by insecurity of livelihood . . . To be truly free he must be liberated from these things also.[60]

Whitehead makes a very similar comment when discussing freedom in *Adventures of Ideas*:

> When we think of freedom, we are apt to confine ourselves to freedom of thought, freedom of the press, freedom for religious opinions. Then the limitations to freedom are conceived as wholly arising from the antagonisms of our fellow men. This is a thorough mistake. The massive habits of physical nature, its iron laws, determine the scene for the sufferings of men. Birth and death, heat, cold, hunger, separation, disease, the general impracticability of purpose, all bring their quota to imprison the souls of women and of men. . . . The essence of freedom is the practicability of purpose. Mankind has chiefly suffered from the

> frustration of its prevalent purposes, even such as belong to the
> very definition of its species. (AI 84)

Liberty is more than the absence of restraints imposed by our fellow
citizens; it also involves the "practicability of purpose." This is an
exercise-concept of liberty. When it comes to the realization of the
purposes that belong to the very definition of the human species,
poverty, disease, and physical constraints imprison the soul as surely
as those limitations that arise from the dominion of men over men.

Of course Whitehead is well aware that poverty, hunger, and
disease are conditions exacerbated by human social and economic
relations. In his article "The Study of the Past—Its Uses and Its
Dangers," he criticizes modern industry because of its consequences
for individual freedom. "Under our present industrial system
. . . freedom is being lost. This loss means the fading from human
life of values infinitely precious to it. The divergent urges of different
individual temperaments can no longer find their various satisfactions in serious activities" (ESP 116-17). Practicability of purpose is
lost because of the scale of modern industry with its "iron-bound
conditions of employment" (ESP 117). Whitehead suggests that our
"industrial and sociological statesmen" should study "the preservation of freedom for those who are engaged in mass production and
mass distribution. . . . It is a study requiring penetrating insight so as
to distinguish between the realities of freedom and its mere show,
and between hurtful and fruitful ways of freedom" (ESP 117). Under
present industrial conditions negative freedom is both "hurtful" and
a "mere show." It is a "grim joke to speak of freedom" in the
industrial world: "All that remains is the phantasm of freedom,
devoid of opportunity" (ESP 117). What is necessary is for
corporations to adapt their mode of functioning so as to provide
real freedom for the worker, that is, opportunities for the individual development of capacities. "My point," Whitehead says, "is
that in our economic system as now developed there is a starvation
of *human impulses,* a denial of *opportunity,* a limitation of *beneficial
activity*—in short, a lack of *freedom*" (ESP 120; emphasis added).
Freedom is clearly here understood in a positive sense. And as a
result of this failure by our economic system to promote every
individual's true freedom there is "an excess of irritability in the
social organism" (ESP 120).

It should be noted that Whitehead, like Hartshorne, does not
advocate the abolition of capitalism, but only its modification:

My line of argument up to this point is not the preliminary to an attack on great commercial corporations. These organizations are the first stage of a new and beneficent social structure. My complaint is that in the two or three generations of their existence on their present scale, they have functioned much too simply. They should enlarge the scope of their activities. (ESP 119)

Whitehead's position is essentially the same as the rest of the new liberals. Both he and Hartshorne, along with the new liberals, "continued to maintain the traditional radical view that the interests of capital and labor were ultimately one. Such a view, of course, is essential to any scheme of reformed capitalism, or at least to any theory that hopes to effect change through piecemeal reforms."[61] In the end, as Macpherson has perceptively noted, the new liberals rejected the market conception of human nature while retaining a modified market itself. It is precisely this that vitiates the new liberals' developmental model of democracy: "A system which requires men to see themselves, and to act, as consumers and appropriators, gives little scope for most of them to see themselves and act as exerters and developers of their capacities." He adds that liberal-democratic theorists after Mill "showed even less recognition . . . of any fundamental incompatibility between capitalist market relations and the equal possibility of individual self-development."[62]

## IV. INTERVENTION AND PERSONAL DEVELOPMENT

Without adequate protection, the liberty of the strong results in the oppression of the weaker members of society. Perhaps it might be argued that the strong must also be free to develop their capacities and that governmental intervention places an undue restriction upon the well-endowed which runs counter to the general aims of society. Hartshorne's belief that tragedy is inevitable, that individual goods are mutually exclusive, and that competition may be necessary to induce individuals to exert themselves, provides grounds for suspecting that he would sympathize with such an argument. It is a metaphysical principle that "every good excludes some possible good" and consequently "[s]omething must always be renounced that would not be valueless if realized." This principle has according to Hartshorne "political applications" (IOGT 224, 225). The nature of these applications, although not specified by Hartshorne, are clear. While the state is responsible for establishing the optimum risk-opportunity ratio within its area of jurisdiction, the members are left free to compete among themselves in their efforts to realize their opportunities for self-creativity. The social nature of existence, together with the incompatibility of finite values, means that in such a competitive world A's success means B's failure.[63]

As we have seen, Hartshorne's thought at times leans perceptively toward the classical liberal position. The idea of personal development as competitive, an idea based on his belief that tragedy is inevitable, seems to be one of those points. However, he also makes statements that show a divergence from classical liberalism. While some tragedy is unavoidable, there is also a form of tragedy that stems from "an inner conflict in men between their will to serve a common good and their desire to promote a private or tribal goal. Some conflicts are chosen where a less destructive, more fruitful form of interaction is known."[64] Hartshorne is suggesting that the supreme tragedy (sin) is a failure to realize those forms of interaction that produce a wider harmony, pursuing instead a path that is known to involve the sacrifice of the common good to a private goal.[65]

What are we to make of these two different attitudes? It appears that Hartshorne falls between classical and modern liberalism. The individualism of the classical liberals is evident in his emphasis on the inevitability of conflict between partially free beings. Conflict is unavoidable owing to the social nature of reality and the incompatibility of individual goods. What practical consequences follow from this? "To try so to act that no conflict results is to adjust oneself to fairyland, not any real world. . . . What we have to do is to prefer the less deadly. The more constructive or fruitful forms of conflict" (RSP 148–49). A stress on the tragic element in the world leads Hartshorne to propound a policy of semiacquiescence to human conflict. Our aim and the function of the state should be to limit the scope for conflict among individuals as they compete for the realization of their own goods. The idea of a harmonious realization of individual aims is consigned to "fairyland." Conflicts, and hence trade-offs, are the stuff of reality. Thus he concludes that "[e]very legislative act excludes things which for some are genuine values. *Always* someone loses or suffers. This is an element of tragedy inherent in process itself" (RSP 99; emphasis added).

Although Hartshorne lays considerable stress upon the tragic nature of process, his acceptance of competitive individualism is tempered by his concept of God. Hartshorne sees that we are not just dealing with society and competition, but also with God, and when God is brought into consideration this alters one's perspective. Pure self-interest is ruled out because we are all part of the one divine life; competition must therefore be balanced by an ideal of harmony. We are enjoined to pursue the general welfare of humanity because that welfare, as a whole, is "effectively enjoyed by a single subject in a single satisfying experience" (DR 133). Our ultimate purpose is to serve God, which we do by promoting the creative process, by contributing to the general welfare or common good. Within the common good each person's own future happiness is included so far as compatible with that of others.

While tempering competitive individualism, the introduction of God into the equation does not make the common good noncompetitive. The pursuit of our own self-development can in theory conflict with a similar pursuit by other members of society. "No one individual can decide unilaterally that there shall be harmony; for an individual cannot give up all personal preference and conform purely passively to the preferences of others. To be an individual is to have and act upon some distinctive preference or other."[66] Hartshorne leans toward a theory of the good according to which "the nature of one's self-interest is solely a matter of preference, so that one's happiness is defined in whatever way one pleases."[67] This is a characteristic feature of classical liberalism. "[T]he goals of liberalism can be succinctly stated. In general, they are that as many individuals as possible realize as many of their private preferences as possible."[68] Part of what it means to contribute to the common good is to respect the freedom of others to actualize their private preferences. God's aim "seems to be zestful creaturely activity, the creation of intense and predominantly harmonious experiences, in order that these may be appreciatively appropriated by the divine love, of which our own love is a faint image."[69] To love another person is to respect their freedom and to accept their decisions as objects of appreciative awareness.[70] Therefore we love God when we respect the freedom of our neighbor to act upon his or her preferences; in other words, we demonstrate our love for God by our adherance to the liberal value of tolerance. Of course, there are limits to such tolerance: "each person should be permitted to design his or her lifestyle *so far as this is compatible with others doing the same"* (IOGT 226; emphasis added). In the event someone's actions violate this basic liberal principle then Hartshorne identifies our love for God with the use of coercive force in its defense! It is this that underlies his attack on pacifism in "A Philosophy of Democratic Defense" where he argues:

> [I]f one loves A, B and C, and if A can be prevented from killing or torturing B and C only by being threatened with loss of his own life, then there is an enforced choice between *A's interest and those of B and C,* and this is not less true because all the interests, including A's, have, through love, become as one's own. What love does mean is that, in killing A, one destroys or defeats a part of oneself, as it were, but with the sole alternative of seeing an even larger part of oneself doomed to frustration.[71]

Notice that Hartshorne has apparently no difficulty in suggesting that the killing or torturing of B and C is a legitimate interest of A. This is only possible because Hartshorne adopts a preferential theory of self-interest, so that A's true interests are whatever A thinks they are. A is to be restrained, not because he has misconceived his true interests, but because B's and C's personal preferences just happen to outweigh A's legitimate interests. Owing to the incompatibility of individual preferences, conflict is unavoidable; consequently, the most free beings can do is to "harmonize themselves together as best they can"[72] within the parameters of the liberal ideal of mutual tolerance.

What we see in Hartshorne's writings is an attempt to moralize a competitive marketplace by introducing a concept of God as supremely relative. This enables him to criticize individualist laissez faire as one-sided while maintaining a firm commitment to a slightly modified capitalism. In becoming consciously aware that the values realized through our own and others' free self-creativity contributes to a common good (that is, God) we should—out of our love for God—be tolerant of other people in their pursuit of "zestful" activity. The ideological functioning of Hartshorne's dipolar theism is patently obvious. Take, for example, the following discussion of the importance of contrast in life:

> The importance of contrast is not confined to art. . . .
> Schemes of life which attempt to reduce everything to a

uniformity of any kind must be examined to see if they do not threaten the essential vitality of life's harmonies. For instance, it may be a good thing to have strict economic equality between some groups in society, pure communism—e.g., among monks. But any proposal to universalize strict equality is perhaps a proposal to render life insipid in this respect. (RSP 46-47)

Economic equality is opposed on the grounds that it makes life insipid; similarly, individualist laissez faire is "ugly." If we love God we will want to maximize self-creativity and will support a mixed economic system that will "produce more vital harmonies" (RSP 47). Thus by positing the existence of God as the common good to which we all contribute as we are able, Hartshorne's dipolar theism functions ideologically to legitimate the existence of inequalities and a class society produced by capitalism.

A modern liberal would object that Hartshorne's emphasis upon conflict stems from his inadequate grasp of the organic nature of society and of the common good. What Hartshorne has done is to emphasize the metaphysical principle that freedom *limits* freedom at the expense of the equally important principle that our environment *provides* us with our real potentialities. The past both limits and supplies.[73] An emphasis on this latter aspect opens the way for entertaining the ideal of a common good that is noncompetitive.

In contrast to Hartshorne's claim that the exclusion of possibility from actualization is necessarily tragic Hobhouse argues that not every development of the individual is socially desirable, but only those that are in accordance with the conditions of social harmony. "For after all," he writes, "it is not every development of every faculty that can reasonably be desired for the sake of progress. There are mischievous as well as benevolent talents capable of cultivation, and if we are asked for a test to distinguish the two, we can give none more simple than that of the capacity of harmonious working in an ordered society."[74] The development of the aristocracy, for example, or of the bourgeoisie, is not an adequate form of development because it involves the suppression of others. Such developments are, according to Hobhouse, only partial:

[W]hat there is of social progress in them does involve a development of individuals, while, on the other hand, in so far as the life of any member of society is cramped and mutilated by

them, there is social stagnation and decay. Any such development is not fully harmonious. Gain on one side is set off by loss
on another. The problem of true social progress is to find the
lines on which development on one side does not retard
development on another, but assists it.[75]

Similarly Green argues that while it is possible for an individual to
realize himself in ways that make the world wonder, yet the social
effect of such individual realizations may be the hindrance rather than
the development of the human spirit. This is not to deny that such a
person

> is living for ends of which the divine principle that forms his self
> alone renders him capable, but these ends, because in their
> attainment one is exalted by the depression of others, are not in
> the direction in which that principle can really fulfill the promise
> and potency which it contains.[76]

The notion of a common good that is noncompetitive dominates
the minds of modern liberals such as Hobhouse and Green. The good
of the individual cannot be considered in abstraction from the good of
everyone else. The salvation of each is dependent upon the salvation
of all. Hence Green writes that "the idea of a perfection, of a state in
which he shall be satisfied, for himself will involve the idea of a
perfection of all other beings, so far as he finds the thought of their
being perfect necessary to his own satisfaction."[77] In a similar vein
Hobhouse declares that "for the rational man there is no harmony
within the self unless as a basis of harmony with other centres of
experience and feeling, and the realisation of any one self is regarded
only as an item in the development of society, that is in a Common
Good."[78] Far from accepting the inevitability of trade-offs whereby
A's success means B's failure, modern liberals hold that true development is cooperative rather than competitive. Individual development made possible through the suppression of other members of
society is an inadequate form of development. Social progress involves the development of a form of order that promotes this
common good.

Only those individual developments that promote the development of other members of the society are good. The lopsided
development of a portion of society must be avoided, either by
self-restraint or governmental coercion. Mill expresses this well in a
lengthy passage from *On Liberty:*

In proportion to the development of his individuality, each person becomes more valuable to himself, and is therefore capable of being more valuable to others. There is a greater fullness of life about his own existence, and when there is more life in the units there is more in the mass which is composed of them. As much compression as is necessary to prevent the stronger specimens of human nature from encroaching on the rights of others, cannot be dispensed with; but for this there is ample compensation even in the point of view of human development. The means of development which the individual loses by being prevented from gratifying his inclinations to the injury of others, are chiefly obtained at the expense of the development of other people. And even to himself there is a full equivalent in the better development of the social part of his nature, rendered possible by the restraint put upon the selfish part.[79]

The aim of society is the development of the capacities of its members. Because of the organic nature of society, each person's development is, in Mill's words, "valuable" to others. We are partially dependent upon each other for the development of our own capacities.

The metaphysical principles of process philosophy render it sympathetic with this "mutual stimulation" argument.[80] Types of order are to be rated "according to their success in magnifying the individual actualities . . . " (AI 376). An individual, on the other hand, is rated on a double basis, "partly on the intrinsic strength of its own experience, and partly on its influence in the promotion of a high-grade type of order. These two grounds in part coalesce. For a weak individual exerts a weak influence."[81] An individual is rated, not only on the basis of the strength of his or her *individual* experience, but also on that individual's contribution to the development of *society as a whole*. If, therefore, there is a danger that an individual will develop his or her own capacities without regard for the rights of others to develop their potentialities, the state is justified in coercing that individual for the sake of the common good. Lopsided development gained at the expense of others is as undesirable as its consequential by-product, namely, underdevelopment. Yet we will recall that if the restraints are just *and* are recognized by the individual as such, then they need not, in Mill's view, have pathological consequences. This would be an example of what Whitehead terms control by "reasonable persuasion." In this instance legal restraints are not perceived as coercive because the individual acknowledges their propriety. Indeed, as we see, the individual gains in the development of the social part of his nature. The loss of "minor intensities," which would have been enjoyed by pursuing one's own development at the expense of others, is compensated for by a "finer composition" of feeling that results from the harmonious development of the whole.

## V. THE COERCIVE USE OF FORCE IN INTERNATIONAL RELATIONS

In this chapter we have seen that both Hartshorne and Whitehead supported the circumspect use of coercive power within a society so as to maintain an ordered environment in which opportunities for self-development are maximized. Any use of force that exceeds that necessary for the maintenance of such an order is counterproductive and ultimately destructive of civilization because the good that society seeks to further can only be the product of self-creativity. We now must proceed to the question of the use of force *between* societies. In particular we want to discover whether coercion is acceptable within international relations and, if so, under what circumstances.

In "A Philosophy of Democratic Defense" Hartshorne presents his most detailed argument for the use of military force in defense of democratic freedoms. The object of political action, according to Hartshorne, is "to bring about results of general welfare and of justice."[82] This is as true in international relations as it is for domestic policy. How are such results to be achieved? In this article Hartshorne's concern is to argue against isolationism and to demonstrate the futility of the pacifist option. We have already seen that the use of force to prevent injustice between individuals is in practice unavoidable. Now we are informed that metaphysical considerations make it even more likely that the use of force between groups will be necessary.

> [I]ndividuals can be restrained largely by their own sense of decency, as reinforced by the approval and disapproval of those immediately around them and by the knowledge that they can hardly fight the whole community. But large groups are com-

paratively cut off from intimate contact with other groups, the opinions of the "others" concerned are not so obvious or so easily understood, and the sense of decency . . . is apt to be pretty well exhausted in personal matters and in devotion to the group, which devotion tends to appear in so brilliant a light that devotion to masses of far away strangers appears pale and intermittent, a luxury among virtues, to be cast aside in times of stress.[83]

Hartshorne concludes that "[t]hese disadvantages belong to group relations, not merely temporarily or accidentally or due to corrigible faults of education, but in some degree inherently and by virtue of the nature of man."[84] Thus one of the reasons offered as a metaphysical justification of democracy, namely, that all human beings are basically equal in their limited power of participation, or sympathy, also explains why coercion is unavoidable. We are directly sympathetic with the cells of our own bodies, and only indirectly sensitive to the feelings of other people. Furthermore, those individuals we are most sensitive to tend to be those nearest to us, that is, family, friends, and neighbors. The more removed we are from other people, be it culturally, ideologically, or geographically, the less likely it is that we will be able to sympathize with their needs. As a result, we are more inclined to use force against other nations without due consideration of their needs and interests than we are against those closer to us: "[T]he final result may be that one man causes another man to be starved to death, without any appreciable feeling of how the other feels about this" (DR 155).

In his discussion of international relations Hartshorne wants to avoid an undue emphasis on either national self-interest or international altruism. Both interventionists and noninterventionists often think that a nation will fight only out of self-interest. This line of reasoning, Hartshorne explicitly notes, parallels the claim that an individual's motives all reduce to self-interest.[85] As we saw in chapter four, process philosophy rejects this claim, arguing that the aim of an occasion of experience is always twofold: at intensity of experience in the present *and* at intensity of experience in the future. The future at which one aims is not necessarily one's own or that of one's nation; there is no reason to limit people's interest rigidly to their country anymore than to themselves.

What consequences for international relations did Hartshorne perceive to follow from this metaphysical exclusion of simple egoism and altruism? Since no nation is completely uninfluenced by sympathy for other people, nationalistic sentiments must be modified by feelings of international community. "To make self-interest absolute," writes Hartshorne, "means that national sovereignty can never suffer any diminution in favor of world integration, and is, in effect, to admit the very principle of irresponsibility, which the declared foes of democracy profess."[86] Writing during the Second World War, Hartshorne has in mind the idolatrous nationalism of Nazi Germany which equates "the Good" ultimately with "the good of my nation." The ethically correct approach to balancing national interests is to hold that a nation ought to be influenced by sympathies for other peoples "to whatever extent action in the interest of other nations can be effective without sacrifice of equally important interests in the nation's own welfare."[87] When considering international relations Hartshorne's approach is basically the same as when discussing relationships between individuals within a particular society. Each nation should be free to pursue its own interests to the extent that they do not unduly infringe the interests of other nations. "[E]ven a very tyrannous regime probably has some claim to be let alone, provided this tyranny does not imply . . . a tendency to express itself also in foreign policy."[88] Moreover, national decisions should accommodate the interests of other nations as long as they do not conflict with its own pursuit of equally important interests.

If national policy decisions are to take into consideration the interests of other nations, it becomes apparent that we must be able to discern and evaluate each other's interests. Hartshorne does not assume that everyone is equal in their power of discernment. "[W]hile no man is so wise or good that he can ascribe infallibility to his own view of the true welfare of others," he writes, "it does not follow that all men are equally capable or incapable of wisdom, and that the good man should allow bad or mediocre men to settle things by force to suit their own badness or mediocrity. The vicious claim to superhuman insight can be escaped by a less desperate measure than that of declaring that those who apparently are not even trying to execute disinterested justice, but something admittedly very different, are as likely to be wise and benevolent as ourselves.[89] Earlier we saw that human beings are equal in their common inequality to God and the rest of creation. However this does not mean that everyone is strictly equal in participatory power. In fact there are differences, but apart from extreme cases they are too uncertain to be of practical significance. What we find when we turn to international relations is a parallel argument. Groups, even more than individuals, are lacking in participatory power. "It would be a contradiction in terms for groups to be as intimate with each other as individuals can be, to understand each other as easily and to sympathize with each other as thoroughly."[90] Not every group is equal in its ability to discern the interests of others; however, in general, the differences are too uncertain to be of practical significance. How, then, do we arbitrate between differences in opinion concerning the interests of other nations? I suggest that Hartshorne would appeal again to experience. We cannot determine beforehand which nations are better able to discern the interests of others; but experience will show that there are extreme cases in which a nation is woefully lacking in sympathy for other nations and must be denied equal liberty to determine the course of events. Nazi Germany and Japan are examples of such extreme insensitivity because of their failure to "execute disinterested justice" and because of the opposition to the "New Order" by those upon which it had been imposed. Therefore the Allies were justified in their efforts to defend what they perceived to be the interests of other nations by forcibly resisting Germany and Japan.

Pacifists, according to Hartshorne, will argue that nonviolent activity alone is morally acceptable. The use of military action in defense of democracy is impossible, they claim, because military action is in essence antidemocratic.[91] Again, to kill a man is morally reprehensible and never to be condoned under any circumstances— the end can never justify the means. Hartshorne and Whitehead would agree that persuasion is the preferred way of dealing with individuals and groups who are disruptive of the social order; however, coercion is in some instances unavoidable. Whether we like it or not, "we are bound to coerce one another more or less unsympathetically; and there are those who will do so in an egregious and intolerable fashion if they are not themselves coerced into moderation" (BH 27). Against such arguments Hartshorne makes the following points: First, if any group has a right to defend itself it is a democratic group since "[i]t practices toward its own members those principles of self-determination and the like to which it appeals in order to condemn its foreign aggressor."[92] Hartshorne is not claiming that the use of force in self-defense is the peculiar right of democratic nations for, as we noted earlier, even a very tyrannous regime has a claim to be let alone as long as this tyranny is not expressed in foreign policy. However, in the case of a democracy, such defense of its right to self-determination is in harmony with its own internal policy. Even as citizens are allowed the liberty to pursue their own interests so long as they do not unduly restrict the rights of others, so too nations should be left at liberty to pursue their interests in harmony with other nations.

Second, Hartshorne argues that pacifism leaves the unscrupulous with a monopoly on the use of the power to take life. But such power belongs in the hands of the scrupulous. "To insist that 'moral means,' that is, in this usage, persuasion, must alone be used by good men in dealing with other men, however bad, is to hold that the worst men are more open to influence by 'moral' means than the average man is by the fear of death and torture and the denial of a livelihood."[93]

Hartshorne also claims that it is "better that many should die prematurely than that nearly all men should live in a permanent state of hostility or slavery" (MVG 173). The evils of war are not necessarily greater than those that may result from submission. Hartshorne warns,

> We must remember that men can be killed in other ways and worse ways than on the battlefield—in concentration camps, subjected to every indignity such as soldiers in general do not know, or through slow starvation and disease produced by economic exploitation for the benefit of the conquering nation.[94]

Death is not an ultimate evil.

> The killing of a man is certainly the production of a great evil, and only if a greater evil be thereby prevented, can the killing be justified. But it is an error to suppose that killing is the greatest possible, or an absolute, evil, so that nothing could justify it. For all men die, and killing a man is not the creation of an absolute difference between dying and not dying, but the creation of a relative difference between dying earlier and dying later.[95]

There are numerous ways in which people shorten one another's lives besides killing them in a war. For example, Hartshorne says that to purchase an automobile rather than donating the money to charity "may very well amount in its effects to deciding that someone will die sooner than he or she would have otherwise. . . . "[96]

Against the moral argument that a bad means cannot be justified by the end, Hartshorne, as we would expect, responds by asserting that only ends, by definition, count. This is in keeping with his teleological ethical theory which defines right action as that which maximizes value. Therefore, "a means is bad only if it is unadapted to attain its end or if its use prevents the attainment of some other important end."[97] Although the use of military force will conflict with some important ends, and therefore, like all forms of coercion, should be avoided where possible, it is possible that the consequences of submission may be worse than those incurred by fighting. As we saw when discussing state intervention in the economy, the failure to intervene may result in greater disharmony and ugliness than would the judicious use of force.

Perhaps the most important argument, from our perspective, is his claim that pacifism is contrary to theism. How do we answer the pacifist who argues that love is the essence of God and mankind's ideal, and therefore the coercion of other people by military means is without exception wrong? Hartshorne replies that the pacifist misunderstands the nature of divine love. Love means the "appreciation of the feelings, needs and interests of others, *and action based on such appreciation. It is social realization, taking others as seriously 'as ourselves.'* "[98] On those occasions in which the interests of those you love conflict, if they cannot be harmonized it may be necessary to forcibly restrain an individual in the interests of the greater good. "What love does mean is that, in killing A, one destroys or defeats a part of oneself, as it were, but with the sole alternative of seeing an even larger part of oneself doomed to frustration."[99] Hartshorne is appealing to his idea that tragedy is an unavoidable element in the world, that no one, not even God, is untouched by it, and that God responds to tragic situations by acting in such a way so as to maximize whatever possibilities for good they contain. Such action involves the use of coercive force:

> Proud, willful, uncooperative men will never understand the gentle passivity of God, as weak and flabby men will never understand the energy of his resistance to the excesses of creaturely will at the point where these excesses threaten the destruction of creaturely vitality. The best expression of belief in God is an attitude of social awareness which treats all problems in the spirit of mutuality except where others insist upon treating them in another spirit, at which point we must in our local way, like God in his cosmic way, set limits by constraint to the destruction of mutuality.

A few lines later he concludes that

> [t]he divine love is social awareness and action from social awareness. Such action seems clearly to include the refusal to provide the unsocial with a monopoly upon the use of coercion. Coercion to prevent the use of coercion to destroy freedom generally is in no way action without social awareness but one of its crucial expressions. Freedom must not be free to destroy freedom. (MVG 173)

It is clear that in his defense of the use of coercive force in international relations Hartshorne is employing the same basic arguments that we detected earlier in our discussion of liberty, equality, and development.

Process thought is well known for its rejection of the tyrant conception of deity. This carries with it a rejection of tyrannical politital systems that feed upon the delusion that unsympathetic power is divine. But it is less frequently noted that pacifism, which appears to be the opposite extreme, as also held to result from a neglect of the relative aspect of God's nature. One would have expected that pacifism failed to perceive the active, coercive nature of God. But in *The Divine Relativity* Hartshorne asserts that one of the numerous deficiencies of classical theism is its optimism, that is, "the denial that tragedy is fundamental in the nature of existence and God; an example being what one may call the pacifism of magical politics; let us . . . renounce force and there will be neither war nor any very terrible tyranny."[100] The pacifist delusion follows from classical metaphysics because of its neglect of divine relativity: "A wholly absolute God is totally beyond tragedy, and his power operates uninfluenced by human freedom, hence presumably as infallibly determinative of all events, and therefore, it seems, there need be no tragedy" (DR 150). The pacifist's argument from religion, according to Hartshorne, maintains that God so controls events that he can ensure that individuals never use their freedom in such a way as to threaten the vital interests of other people.

I believe that Hartshorne has misrepresented the pacifist's position. First, pacifists do not necessarily deny the tragic elements in life nor their inevitability; indeed, they may be all too aware of them. Nor need they deny the relative aspect of deity. Moreover, and perhaps most importantly, it is improper to deduce from the pacifist's refusal to kill other human beings in defense of values he or she holds dear the conclusion that he or she believes God is the controlling power that infallibly determines all events. The implicit charge is that pacifists actually support the status quo. Only by a fallacious argument can one conclude that pacifists do not desire to change the situation by *any* means from the premise that pacifists do not desire to change the world by *military* means. Pacifists may be as anxious as anyone else to change the situation they find themselves in; what they reject is that killing other human beings is an acceptable means for accomplishing this. Belief in the ethical impropriety of military power as a means of dealing with fellow human beings does not easily follow from a conception of God as the cosmic despot; a more likely source is the vision of a God who suffers at the hands of men.

Under what conditions should the use of military force be contemplated? When is an attack on a foreign nation a threat to one's own interests? Hartshorne gives the following extended list of criteria:

> A war is more than merely local in proportion as one or more of these conditions are realized:(a) the implied or not improbable outcome of the war is a radical shift in the control of the oceans, in the identity and nature of the dominant sea powers; (b) the war is calculated to establish a precedent of world-wide influence as to the chances of successful aggression; (c) the world is economically interdependent; (d) the communication of information about the causes and progress of the war is sufficiently extensive so that the peoples of neutral nations will live through the affair with such vividness that their political conceptions will be powerfully affected, their sympathies vitally aroused, the face of things intimately changed for them; (e) one of the contestants is likely, in case of victory, to have the will and the power to do far more than the other to promote rather than retard the development of world-democracy, the spread of self-government, national and international, as devoted to the basic human rights.[101]

Should any of the above conditions prevail, which seems virtually certain in any future time of conflict, then any nation is justified in contemplating military intervention in defense of its interests. However, the final decision would have to rest on whether or not the best outcome is likely to be achieved through the use of force. It is only ends that count; therefore, one must calculate whether the use of force is more likely to produce a superior outcome than any other course of action.

When contemplating military intervention in international affairs Whitehead's guidelines are less specific than Hartshorne's. In the article "An Appeal to Sanity" Whitehead wrestles with the question of tolerance and force. Written in 1939 it is concerned with the issue of national isolation. "What is the justification of 'isolation' on the part of a powerful nation," asks Whitehead, "when evil is turbulent in any part of the world?" (ESP 44). First it must be borne in mind that a nation's duty is to foster some particular type of civilization in some specific area. Unless the evils of the world threaten this supreme duty or these evils can be put right without indirectly defeating its performance of this duty, it should remain isolated. Furthermore, war is a "throw-back from civilization for victors and vanquished, whatever be the initial objects of these crusades" (ESP 44) and therefore should be avoided if at all possible. Even if one should win the loses might exceed the gains. Yet he admits that "[w]ar may be necessary to guard world civilization" (ESP 46). Tolerance has its limits, and the preservation of society might finally depend upon the judicious use of force. Whitehead gives three conditions, presumably all of which need to be met, for intervening militarily in the affairs of other nations:

1. When she is violently interfering with the development of other states, without the justification of establishing any principle of social co-ordination, acknowledged as of prime importance.
2. When the consequences of an attempt at forcible prevention will not be worse than the consequences of acquiescence.
3. When such an attempt can secure its direct object.[102]

These conditions are certainly not peculiar to Whitehead. Similar criteria were stipulated by Bentham to aid in determining when a crime should be punished.[103] There are four cases in which Bentham says punishment should not be inflicted: First, where it is "groundless," that is, "where there is no mischief for it to prevent."[104] Such cases include not only those where there has never been any mischief, but also where the mischief has been outweighed by a greater benefit obtained thereby or when the injured party is assured of compensation. This condition, that an individual should be punished only for an action that has caused mischief, is reflected in Whitehead's first criterion for intervention, namely, that the nation to be punished has actually violently interfered in the affairs of other states *without* justification. This qualification is important, for like Bentham, Whitehead appears to perceive violent intervention as being justified by the greater good that it accomplishes, in this instance by the establishment of a principle of social coordination acknowledged as of prime importance. Second, punishment should not be inflicted when it is "unprofitable." By this Bentham means that when the evil of the punishment outweighs by comparison the evil of the offense, then it should not, under ordinary circumstances, be pursued.[105] Similarly, in good consequentialist fashion, Whitehead stipulates that military intervention should only be undertaken when the consequences of such action are not worse than the action it seeks to prevent. Third, when the punishment is "inefficacious" it should be avoided. All punishment is mischief and is in itself evil; therefore, on the basis of the principle of utility, "if it ought at all to be admitted, it ought only to be admitted in as far as it promises to exclude some greater evil."[106] Bentham's point is that if the infliction of punishment is unable to accomplish its ends, namely, "to prevent the mischief,"[107] then it is improper to use it. This condition is paralleled by Whitehead's assertion that a policy of military intervention can be pursued only if it can secure its direct object. Finally, Bentham suggests when it is "needless," when the mischief can be prevented without it, punishment is similarly unwarranted.

What is apparent from this comparison is that the same principles Bentham uses with reference to the exercise of force *within* society are used by Whitehead with reference to the exercise of force *between* societies. Whitehead, like Bentham, is employing consequentialist considerations in determining when it is proper to use force. Both writers view the use of coercive power as something which should, if at all possible, be avoided. Bentham says that "all punishment is mischief; all punishment in itself is evil"[108] Whitehead, in a similar vein, speaks of war as a "throw-back from civilization." Whether or not a situation calls for the use of coercive force is to be determined by comparing the probable outcomes of the various actions. If mischief has been unjustifiably perpetrated upon another, if the use of coercive force in opposition to that evil will result in a net gain in value, and if such action is likely to secure its aim, then it is a proper course of action to take.

## VI. CONCLUSION

The positive contribution that coercion can make to society stems from the social nature of reality in general, and of human beings in particular. When people were considered to be atomic individuals each of whom possessed a fully formed nature it was easy to attribute personal or moral failures wholly to the individual. Character development could be brought about simply by exercising one's will autonomously. Social progress was then seen to be dependent upon each person's improvement of his or her own character. But with the advent of a social conception of human nature the importance of the environment for the development of character became a prominent theme of social reformers. "[T]he misleading juxtaposition of character versus environment made way for the improvement of environment *and* will power as means to character."[109] The ideological struggle now was over "the priority and relative weight of environmental factors in individual and social life. . . . "[110] The Charity Organisation Society, for instance, stressed the individual responsibility whereas liberals like Hobhouse and Ritchie emphasized the social conditions.

Process social philosophy reflects the same tension between environmental factors and individual will. No doubt Hartshorne and Whitehead, like liberals generally, stress the importance of self-reliance and individual character. Society can provide us with a good environment but in the end we are free to decide what we will be within the limits imposed upon us. A civilized society cannot be built upon coercion alone. This is because the good of the individual is not simply development, but *self*-development. Every individual is in part self-created or *causa sui*. An excess of coercion will suppress individuality which is an essential element in an intense and harmonious experience.

However, there is a danger of overemphasizing process philosophy's stress on persuasion. While both philosophers view persuasion as the preferable means of social intercourse, because it is consistent with the meaning of good as self-activity, they recognize that the use of coercive power is an unavoidable feature of social life. Every occasion of experience emerges from its actual world and bears in its own nature the effects of its birth. As Whitehead writes: "[A] species of subject requires a species of data as its preliminary phase of concrescence. But such data are nothing but the social environment under the abstraction effected by objectification" (PR 203[309–10]).

Like actual occasions, "man is a social animal" (PR 204[311]). Therefore if we desire to see a particular type of person emerge within human history this will require the provision of an environment appropriate for such development. This is the metaphysical justification of the social reformer. It is also an apologetic for the reformer's use of coercive power. Coercion is necessary in order to prevent individuals from using their freedom in a way that impedes the (positive) freedom of others. "Coercion to prevent the use of coercion to destroy freedom" (MVG 173) is a "crucial expression" of the divine love. Because we are influenced by our environment it is appropriate that we structure that environment so that it furthers our ideals. Coercion is, therefore, justified by the increased opportunity it brings to individuals for the full and free realization of their capacities. The sole legitimate aim of both state intervention and military action alike is finally the optimization of the promise of freedom. In doing this we are, at least on Hartshorne's analysis, only doing on the local level what God does in his governance of the cosmos.

Our analysis has also brought to light an interesting tension within Hartshorne's social and political thought. On the one hand, the "relative dualism" that he holds to exist between fully organic and quasi-organic wholes allows him to introduce a more individualistic element into his social thought than we typically find among modern liberals. His emphasis upon the tragic and competitive aspects of human social life—an emphasis that operates as a defense of the classical liberal ideals of liberty and equality expounded by people like the Friedmans—is explicable because a human society lacks the unity of a fully organic whole. Thus Hartshorne's understanding of the *social* nature of reality actually leads him to defend an *individualistic* social and political theory. Yet, on the other hand, it is his social conception of deity that saves him from an ethic of pure self-interest and that tempers his acceptance of competitive individualism. Only a supremely relative deity can, in Hartshorne's estimation, provide human beings with a good that is truly common to all. This is because there are no fully organic wholes inclusive of persons apart from God. Our motivation to love other people, which for Hartshorne includes our tolerance of their zestful assertion of personal preferences at odds with our own good, is the fact that the values that they realize contribute to the experience of God. Thus there is a tension in Hartshorne's thought created by his metaphysical distinction between two levels of social unity. To the extent that the quasi-organic nature of human societies is stressed Hartshorne leans toward a classical liberal position of competitive individualism; however, when he emphasizes the fully organic nature of the cosmic society, that is, God, he defends values more clearly identified with modern liberalism. This tension is not as prominent in Whitehead's social and political thought because like most modern liberals he adopts a fully organic theory of human society which admits of a noncompetitive common good on the human level.

# 7

# Process Philosophy and
# Social Development

Whitehead claims that there are four factors that decisively govern the fate of social groups: "the inexorable law that apart from some transcendent aim the civilized life either wallows in pleasure or relapses slowly into a barren repetition with waning intensities of feeling"; the "iron compulsion of nature"; "the compulsory dominion of men over men"; and persuasion (AI 108). The second factor, which Whitehead accepts in modified form from Malthus and links with the "economic interpretation of history," concerns the principle that there is no society in isolation. Every society depends upon a background environment of actual entities which must not only be permissive of that society's continued existence, they must also contribute those characters that the more special character of the society presupposes for its members. Thus, just as a certain type of individual presupposes a certain type of social environment, so too a particular social ideal requires an environment conducive to its realization.[1] As for the third factor, this was dealt with earlier when we considered state intervention and the use of force in international relations. My concern in this chapter is with those aspects of process metaphysics that relate to the first and fourth factors as they affect the historical process.

## I. THE CONCEPT OF ADVENTURE

While an Apostle at Cambridge in 1886, Whitehead attended a meeting at which Goldsworthy Dickinson read a paper on the topic of progress. Following the discussion the question put for the division was "Have we a criterion of progress?" Whitehead voted no.[2] That the Apostles would have debated the issue of progress should hardly surprise anyone given the significance that the idea had during the last half of the nineteenth century. With some justification progress has been described as "the central, most characteristic belief of the Victorians."[3] What is interesting about this episode is Whitehead's negative vote, for the idea of progress—including the criterion of progress—was an important element in his later philosophy. At this point in his life, however, Whitehead rejected, if not progress itself, at least the belief that we have an adequate criterion of progress. And yet, despite this rejection, the records of the Apostles' meetings suggest that Whitehead's general outlook at this time was character-ized by a positive attitude toward change. It appears that Whitehead advocated change while remaining uncertain about progress.

The importance that the notion of change held for Whitehead during his early years at Cambridge remained with him and became the focal point of his mature metaphysics. The relationship between permanence and flux is, in Whitehead's opinion, the "complete problem of metaphysics" (PR 209[318]). Whitehead's attempted solution to this problem resides in his analysis of actuality as process. This analysis is set in opposition to the static notion of reality, which he claims Western society derived from Plato and Aristotle. Change-less perfection is not, as it was for Plato, the metaphysical ideal. For Whitehead eternal objects are changeless, but as abstractions they are void of intrinsic value. Only concrete reality possesses intrinsic value. And since the essence of reality is process, life is conceived as an offensive, as the creation of new values, and not as the defense of some static ideal. The significance that the new metaphysics has for sociology is pointed out by Whitehead himself. He asserts,

> The foundation of all understanding of sociological theory . . . is that no static maintenance of perfection is possible. This axiom is rooted in the nature of things. Advance or Decadence are the only choices offered to mankind. The pure conservative is fighting against the essence of the Universe. (AI 353–54)

The failure of society to advance inevitably leads to social decline as the old values lose their freshness and captivating power.

The fact that the essence of reality is process is not the only reason Whitehead offers in support of his claim that no static maintenance of perfection is possible. He also appeals to the metaphysical principle that all actualization is finite and finitude involves the exclusion of alternative possibilities. "There is no totality," writes Whitehead, "which is the harmony of all perfections" (AI 356). In the process of actualization every occasion necessarily excludes from realization "the unbounded welter of contrary possibilities."[4] In his discussion of Beauty Whitehead says: "There are perfections beyond perfections. All realization is finite, and there is no perfection which is the infinitude of all perfections. Perfections of diverse types are among themselves discordant" (AI 330). It is by means of process that the universe escapes from the limitations of the finite. "No specific finitude is an ultimate shackle upon the universe. In process the finite possibilities of the universe travel towards their infinitude of realization" (MT 75).

This fact, which is "a commonplace in the fine arts," should also be a commonplace of political philosophy and theology (AI 356). Concerning the former he says that history is "the theatre of diverse groups of idealists respectively urging ideals incompatible for conjoint realization. You cannot form any historical judgment of right or wrong by considering each group separately. The evil lies in the attempted conjunction" (AI 356-57). In other words, there is no single ideal that every society should realize, for example, specific economic system. Whitehead rejects the notion that there is a single ideal perfection of beauty.[5]

Because process is a fundamental characteristic of our world the conception of culture as "the knowledge of the best that has been said and done" (ESP 148) is dismissed by Whitehead as defective. Such an attitude is too static, too backward looking. It omits from consideration the profound flux that characterizes the world. The problem that Whitehead finds with the Renaissance movement, a movement that aimed to reproduce the excellencies of Greek and Roman civilization, is that it was based upon the notion of imitation. One particular, historically relative ideal was erected as the standard of civilization. The result of such an approach is "static, repressive, and promotes a decadent habit of mind" (AI 353).

For Whitehead then a sympathetic attitude toward the idea of change was a constant feature of his thought. He expressly states that an adequate social or political theory must recognize the processive nature of the universe. In addition, by the time he produced his cosmology he had come to hold that process is not without purpose. Rather, it is a teleological process and its aim is the maximization of beauty. The achievement of this general purpose pervading nature, with its aim at intensity and variety, requires the emergence of forms of social order that will enable the multiplicity of components in a nexus to be felt as contrasts rather than dismissed as incompatibilities (PR 83[128]). Consequently, whereas the contrast between flux and permanence establishes process as an essential feature of reality, a further contrast, that between order and novelty, is necessary to transform mere process into progress. "[T]here can be no excellence," writes Whitehead, "except upon some basis of order. Mere disorder results in a nonentity of achievement."[6] This same point was stated earlier in *Religion in the Making:* "Depth of value is only possible if the antecedent facts conspire in unison. Thus a measure of harmony in the ground is requisite for the perpetuation of depth into the future. But harmony is limitation. Thus rightness of limitation is essential for growth of reality." (RM 136–37). This passage shows that beauty is partly dependent upon the limitation which is an unavoidable feature of social order. As Hartshorne says, "[E]very society has its routine, its laws or customary ways of behaving. Without such routine . . . there would not be cooperation or mutual understanding, but only mutual frustration or absolute indifference, in other words, no society" (RSP 31). Since the achievement of valuable experience requires social organization, social development involves the evolution of forms of order that promote experiences of greater value. The "rightness of limitation" is determined by the consequences which that social order has for its members.

Although a condition for intensity of satisfaction, it is not true that in proportion to the orderliness of a society there is depth of satisfaction (PR 111[169]). Order can also stifle the "freshness of living." "Order is not sufficient. What is required, is something much more complex. It is order entering upon novelty; so that the massiveness of order does not degenerate into mere repetition; and so that the novelty is always reflected upon a background of system" (PR 339[515]). What is required for progress, as opposed to mere process, is the proper balance between order and novelty. An excess of either "system" or "freshness" leads to the diminution of present experience. What Whitehead is advocating is the Aristotelian doctrine of the golden mean (PR 339[515]). Without the emergence of new ideals, which act as a lure to adventure, a staleness sets in society. The result of this "tedium of indefinite repetition" (AI 332) is a loss of intensity and slow decay. Novelty preserves society from decay. At the same time social order preserves society from anarchy by providing the necessary structure to enable novelty to be creatively appropriated by its members. Novelty is "reflected upon a background of system" rather than dismissed as a moment of irrelevant anarchy.[7]

Order and novelty are both elements of progress that must be held together: "The art of progress is to preserve order amid change, and to preserve change amid order" (PR 339[515]). Consequently established forms of social order should display tolerance toward those discordant elements that herald the dawning of a new age. Similarly, the bearers of novelty within society must avoid dismissing into irrelevance the social order that gave it birth and upon which it is grounded. "The old dominance," writes Whitehead, "should be transformed into the firm foundations, upon which new feelings arise, drawing their intensities from delicacies of contrast between system and freshness."[8] This being the case it is evident that in the transition from social ideal to social ideal the past is not radically negated by the present. Rather it is negated and yet preserved while being raised up to a new level. In Hegelian terminology, forms of social order are *aufgehoben* in the dialectical advance of history.

This brings us to the heart of Whitehead's theory of social development, namely, the idea of adventure. At its culmination every society realizes a certain type of perfection. However, no finite social order is able to retain its intensity of feeling throughout an indefinite number of repetitions. Either there will be a slow growth of anaesthesia, "whereby that social group is gradually sinking towards nothingness" (AI 368) or the society will embark upon an adventure after new ideals. This adventure is what changes chaos into history: "History is the drama of effort. The full understanding of it requires an insight into human toiling after its aim. In the absence of some common direction of aim adequately magnificent, there can be no history. The spectacle is then mere chaos" (ESP 150).

Whitehead distinguishes between two types of adventure. First, there is the adventure that acts within limits. After a particular type of perfection has been reached, a particular form of beauty attained, there is the type of adventure that explores the possible variations within this type of perfection. Such adventures involve acting within limits; they are "the ripples of change within one type of civilization, by which an epoch of a given type preserves its freshness" (AI 359–60). The infinitude of the universe is neglected because this initial type of adventure is the exploration of possible variations that do not introduce discord that would disturb the form of beauty realized.[9]

In addition to this "safe advance of dogmatic spirits" (MT 80) Whitehead conceives of a second type of adventure—the adventure of ideas. The variations within a given type of perfection are eventually exhausted and the society must either advance further or decay. If the society lacks imaginative force then "speculation" will give way to "scholarship": "Perfection was attained, and with the attainment inspiration withered" (AI 331). Zest is lost and decadence sets in leading to a slow decline as the defining characteristics lose their importance. If, however, a race has not exhausted its zest for adventure then a period of transition can set in as the society is grasped by a common aim at a new ideal. Unlike the previous form of adventure, the adventure of ideas involves the introduction of discordances: "Thus the contribution to Beauty which can be supplied by Discord—in itself destructive and evil—is the positive feeling of a quick shift of aim from the tameness of outworn perfection to some other ideal with its freshness still upon it" (AI 330-31). The service that ideas render to a society is the provision of ideals of new perfections that can serve as a program for reform: "The ideal of a new society derived from a new defining characteristic is introduced" (AI 333).

I believe that Whitehead's concept of adventure, together with his understanding of order and novelty, provides us with a dialectical philosophy of history. Here I find myself in disagreement with Cobb who distinguishes between three models of social change: (1) a conflict model according to which one ideal is replaced by, or merely juxtaposed to, another ideal; (2) the Hegelian dialectical model "in which the displacement of one view by another is followed by a new view which is the creative and original synthesis of both . . . "[10]; and (3) a contrast model that seeks to convert diversity into contrast through mental originality. This last model, which Cobb believes Whitehead adopted, "is the fundamental model of growth in distinction from mere change or even quantitative addition."[11] The emphasis that Whitehead placed upon the ideal of harmony cannot be overestimated; however, I do not believe that this places him at odds with the Hegelian dialectic. An examination of Hegel's philosophy of history does not bear out Cobb's assertion that "it seems to justify radical rejection of what is for the sake of its opposite in the confidence that in the end this will necessarily lead to creative synthesis."[12]

Hegel maintains that the progress of the World Spirit *(Weltgeist)* is reflected in the succession of national spirits *(Volksgeister)*: each national spirit represents a stage in the "conquering march of the world spirit as it wins its way to consciousness and freedom."[13] In this progression history displays a dialectical movement. In his analysis of Hegel, Charles Taylor distinguishes between two forms of dialectics.[14] First, there is what he terms the historical dialectic. In this instance the various historical forms of life are subject to an inner contradiction between the purpose they are meant to fulfill and their failure to realize this purpose in the objective world. In this instance existing reality will necessarily be negated as the purpose achieves more adequate realization. The historical dialectic describes the period of cultural development in the life of a particular *Volksgeist:* "The spirit of a nation should thus be seen as the development of a principle; this principle is at first bound up with an indistinct impulse which gradually works its way out and seeks to attain objective reality."[15] It is during this period of cultural development that the essence of the *Volksgeist* and its existence are not identical; the nation is still creating itself. However, when this dichotomy has been overcome the spirit "ceases to respect its immediate existence, for it realises that the principle behind it is a particular one; and as a result, the subjective spirit becomes divorced from the universal spirit."[16] The Idea of the particular *Volksgeist* is fully developed and its inadequacy is now fully apparent. This contradiction between the purpose as presently conceived and its full realization lies beneath the second form of dialectics distinguished by Taylor, the ontological dialectic. In this instance the inadequacy of the purpose is exposed with its realization. As a consequence the spirit destroys the determinate aspect of its being and comprehends its universal aspect resulting in the emergence of a new and higher principle. This is the period of rejuvenation; death is followed by new life. In the spiritual world the internal principle of change is one of progress in which the spirit, like a phoenix rising from its ashes, is not only rejuvenated, but also enhanced and transfigured.[17] At each stage in its development, when the opposition between the essence of the particular *Volksgeist* and its objective existence has been overcome, the spirit once again becomes divided against itself and forsakes its earlier inadequate expression for a new principle that both conserves and transfigures its previous form.

I believe that Whitehead's philosophy of history exhibits the same general pattern. The rise, culmination, and decay of enduring societies are devices whereby order and novelty are combined (AI 369). Each society has before it an ideal which it strives to realize. This is the period of 'cultural development' during which there is a dichotomy between the society's ideal (essence) and its reality (existence). It is this difference that drives history forward. When realized the ideal becomes part of the society's defining characteristics. What once was new is now part of the established order of the society inherited by its members. The ideal has become actualized and therefore is no longer a lure to adventure. However, owing to the finiteness of every manifestation of value in the world, the Eros of the Universe cannot rest content with any level that is attained. When the ideal is realized its limitations as an expression of beauty necessitates that it go under either by way of decay or through new adventure. If the society does not acquire a new aim, then decadence and decay set in. If, on the other hand, new ideals are introduced into the society, and if these ideas capture the imagination of the people so as to become a common vision directing the efforts of the society, then a period of transition ensues. Should there be new adventure, then the society is "rejuvenated": the society is preserved, yet it has been transfigured.[18] Thus the historical life of a society involves the dialectical movement in which its order undergoes a separation and return. Order becomes alienated by the generation of novelty and then returns to itself via the coordination of the new ideal with the previous order.

Support for this interpretation of Whitehead's philosophy of history can be found in *Science and the Modern World* where this pattern of historical life is rehearsed. Whitehead says explicitly that his purpose in those lectures was to "give a record of a great adventure in the region of thought" (SMW 299). He goes on to say that this tale

> tells how a particular direction of reason emerges in a race by the long preparation of antecedent epochs, how after its birth its subject-matter gradually unfolds itself, how it attains its triumphs, how its influence moulds the very springs of action of mankind, and finally how at its moment of supreme success its limitations disclose themselves and call for a renewed exercise of the creative imagination. (SMW 299)

Whitehead has in mind here the development of an ideal within history. Just like the Hegelian *Volksgeist* this ideal "blossoms, grows strong, then fades away and dies." [19] In the very process of realization the inadequacies of the ideal become apparent and the creative advance necessarily pushes forward, transcending whatever finite realizations have been attained in pursuit of a new ideal.

## II. THE "SPIRIT OF LIBERTY" AND SOCIAL PROGRESS

In 1925, almost forty years after he voted against the notion that we have a criterion of progress, Whitehead concluded his Lowell Lectures with a statement concerning the requisites *for* social progress. Having outlined certain key ideas concerning progress and social development contained in his metaphysics, I want to examine the concepts of "uniformity" and "force" which Whitehead identifies as the main threats to progress. As we shall see, these dangers are not only related to the principles of order and novelty in process metaphysics, but also correspond closely to the concern of the new liberals with individuality and sociability.

In his conclusion to *Science and the Modern World* Whitehead refers to the danger posed to social progress by what he terms the "Gospel of Uniformity" (SMW 297). The reason for this danger is clear when viewed in the context of his theory of adventure. The "art of life" is described by Whitehead as the urge "to live, to live well, to live better" (FR 14). Each particular society seeks to realize this purpose in its own way. This constitutes that society's ideal of itself. These ideals find incarnation in various associations, for example, business associations, churches, governments, which make up the concrete sociological structure (FR 65). However, when the social ideal is realized satisfaction withers. "Fatigue" sets in and the society faces an alternative; either it will relapse into mere repetitive life, concerned with mere living, or it will enter upon the adventure of living better. No static maintenance of perfection is possible.

The impetus to new adventure is derived from the introduction of novelty. Conformation to the established ideals leads to static repetition and the slow relapse toward minor forms of experience. Progress can be saved only by grasping a new ideal that can lure society onward. The importance of ideas for Whitehead's theory of history cannot be overestimated. "The key to history," he exclaims, "lies in this fact—as we think we live" (ESP 148). Without the introduction of new ideals the path to further progress is closed. "Mental experience is the organ of novelty, the urge beyond. It seeks to vivify the massive physical fact, which is repetitive, with the novelties which beckon" (FR 26-27). The relationship of ideas to history is brought out forcibly in the following passage from *The Function of Reason*: "Abstract speculation has been the salvation of the world—speculations which made systems and then transcended them, speculations which ventured to the furthest limit of abstraction. To set limits to speculation is treason to the future" (FR 60). The importance of ideas for progress is coupled with an emphasis on individual freedom.[20] Earlier societies were held to be unprogressive because they suppressed individuality. Primitive social groups possess an "instinctive" solidarity. While all societies are based upon "routine" or "communal custom," in primitive societies this feature attains a radical dominance. "Action and mood," he writes, "both spring from an instinct based upon ancestral co-ordination. In such societies, whatever is not the outcome of inherited relativity, imposing co-ordination of action, is sheer destructive chaos. Alien groups are then evil groups" (AI 61-2). Order thus predominates over novelty. On the microscopic level, when the novelty originating in the mental pole of an actual occasion is largely absent, the power of efficient causation escapes modification by conceptual ideals. The same metaphysical principle is operative in human societies in which instinct is dominant. Owing to the dominance of the society's defining characteristic, that is, its definite pattern of structural interrelations, the ancestral pattern of social coordination is repeatedly reproduced by members of the society. Novelty is viewed as destructive chaos and is instinctively repressed by society.[21]

Social progress depends upon the freedom to wander. When man ceases to wander "he will cease to ascend in the scale of being" (SMW 298). Of primary importance here is not physical wandering but mankind's "spiritual adventures—adventures of thought, adventures of passionate feeling, adventures of aesthetic experience" (SMW 298). What is being pleaded for is the freedom to be an individual. "The Gospel of Uniformity" preaches conformity; but differences among nations, races and individuals are required "to preserve the conditions under which higher development is possible."[22] In a well-known passage Whitehead says, "Progress is founded upon the experience of discordant feelings.

The social value of liberty lies in its production of discords" (AI 330). Social progress requires tolerance of diversity. Whitehead admits that mental experience contains in itself a factor of anarchy (FR 27). There is a sense, therefore, in which progress is made only through struggle, through the introduction of discord into an established social order provoking it to new adventure.[23] Yet although in itself destructive and evil, such discord is sometimes to be preferred to the stale repetition of an outworn ideal.[24] Better an imperfection that has as its aim a higher type than the waning intensities of feeling brought about by a worn-out perfection.

This emphasis upon the importance of ideas and individuality for human progress is a feature of Whitehead's thought that he shared with the new liberals. In *A System of Logic* Mill identifies "the speculative faculties of mankind" as the primary agent of social progress:

> Every considerable advance in material civilization has been preceded by an advance in knowledge: and when any great social change has come to pass, either in the way of gradual development or of sudden conflict, it has had for its precursor a great change in the opinions and modes of thinking of society.[25]

Mill, like Whitehead, elevates intellectual forces above economic ones to explain social progress: "It is what men think, that determines how they act. . . ."[26] Similarly, Hobhouse asserts that "[g]reat changes are not caused by ideas alone; but they are not effected without ideas. The passions of men must be aroused if the frost of custom is to be broken or the chains of authority burst. . . ."[27] Ideals are as necessary to the reformer as established traditions are to the conservative.[28]

Because social progress requires the emergence of new ideals that can function as a program for reform, the new liberals staunchly defended individual freedom. "The foundation of liberty is the idea of growth,"[29] says Hobhouse. Progress depends upon the preservation of liberty and therefore society must be careful to ensure that the immediate necessities of order do not "crush the spirit of independence."[30] In a passage that is strikingly reminiscent of Whitehead's theory of adventure Hobhouse asserts:

> What is spontaneous in a people, be it in the movement of an individual, a class, or a nation, is always the source of life, the

well-spring of the fresh forces which recruit jaded civilisation. In proportion as the weight of government succeeds in crushing this spontaneity, in that proportion . . . it tends inevitably to arrest development and inaugurate a period of decay.[31]

Of course, the price of freedom is the possibility of evil. To be free to do good requires that one be free to reject the best,

> and those who seem to suggest the contrary are . . . trying to get the best of two incompatible worlds. We may make a man conform outwardly to what we consider the best standard or we can let him decide for himself. But we cannot at once leave the decision to him and be certain that he will conform.[32]

However, Hobhouse believes that the price is worth paying:

> In the end we get nearer to the truth by letting error develop its fallacies than by stifling it at birth. . . . [T]hose things which we ourselves hold true and right and socially just we know for partial truths which will gain in the end by the contest with their rivals in the open. But these considerations have weight only when we conceive the social order as a stage or a process of development, and that a development of a spiritual or rational kind. If it were merely a question of realizing immediate good as it appears to us, coercion would always be in place. Liberty has its value only in a far longer game.[33]

One of the staunchest defenders of individuality in the nineteenth century was Mill. In the treatise *On Liberty* he sought to combat the "tyranny of opinion," which was his way of referring to the "Gospel of Uniformity." Protection against the tyranny of the magistrate" is insufficient; it is also necessary that there be protection against

> the tyranny of the prevailing opinion and feeling; against the tendency of society to impose . . . its own ideas and practices as rules of conduct on those who dissent from them; to fetter the development, and, if possible, prevent the formation, of any individuality not in harmony with its ways, and compel all characters to fashion themselves upon the model of its own.[34]

He goes on to say: "The despotism of custom is everywhere the standing hindrance to human advancement, being in unceasing antagonism to that disposition to aim at something better than customary, which is called, according to circumstances, the spirit of liberty, or that of progress or improvement."[35] The tyranny of opinion robs society by impeding the exercise of individuality which is so necessary for human progress. The danger that faces society is "not the excess, but the deficiency, of personal impulses and preferences.[36] Individuals are "cramped and dwarfed" like trees that have been "clipped into pollards. . . . "[37] Their minds having been "bowed to the yoke" of custom, individuals "exercise choice only among things commonly done: peculiarity of taste, eccentricity of conduct, are shunned equally with crimes: until by dint of not following their own nature, they have no nature to follow: their human capacities are withered and starved. . . . "[38]

Like Hobhouse, Mill believes that we are better off suffering each others' eccentricities than we would be if everyone was compelled to conform to the opinion of the masses.[39] By silencing unorthodox opinions we lose at the very least the benefit of "the clearer perception and livelier impression of the truth" we now hold, and perhaps even the opportunity of "exchanging error for truth."[40] Similarly, just as the value of diversity of opinions stems from mankind's imperfection, so also "there should be different experiments of living; that free scope should be given to varieties of character, short of injury to others; and that the worth of different modes of life should be proved practically. . . . "[41] Mill admits that there are few persons whose experiments of living would, if adopted by everyone, lead to the improvement of mankind; but it is generally true that such improvement that does occur begins with an individual. "The initiation of all wise or noble things comes and must come from individuals; generally at first from some one individual."[42] Therefore if the masses are ever to rise above their mediocrity it is necessary that they "give the freest scope possible to uncustomary things, in order that it may in time appear which of these are fit to be converted into customs."[43]

It is the "honour and glory of the average man" that he is capable of following the initiative of his superior.[44] In contrast to Hegel's world-historical individuals who compel the rest to follow, Mill's exceptional individuals can only claim the "freedom to point out the way. The power of compelling others into it is not only inconsistent with the freedom and development of all the rest, but corrupting to the strong man himself."[45] The exceptional person contributes to human progress by the example he or she sets. Progress is brought about through *persuasion* and not through compulsion.[46]

Whitehead agrees with both Mill and Hobhouse that overall we are better off suffering each to live as seems good to themselves than by compelling each to live as seems good to the rest: "Error is the price which we pay for progress."[47] Such tolerance, indeed encouragement, of social diversity is evident throughout his academic career. The records of the Apostles show that when asked "What shall we do with social experiments, encourage, make, discourage?" he voted to encourage them. Again, he rejected the proposition that we "accept Morrison's Pill for all stomachs," and voted that the world should not agree about tastes, nor that we should "be normal." Finally, when asked, "Does the devil exist, or is he merely loathsome?" Whitehead said yes and then added, "He is the Homogeneous." As Victor Lowe points out, homogeneity, or uniformity, is the victory of "the devil" over life. Lowe concludes with the assessment that throughout his Apostolic years Whitehead "took a position on the side of diversity and adventure whenever the question concerned their contrast with uniformity and the status quo."[48]

In later years Whitehead continued to hold that the achievement of high civilization requires tolerance of individuality. For example, in his criticisms of the effects of mass production on society one can hear an unmistakable echo of Mill's earlier repudiation of "prevailing opinion and feeling." "We are witnessing a determined attempt to canalize the aesthetic enjoyments of the population," he declares.

> [A]ll intensity of enjoyment, sustained with the strength of individual character, arises from the individual taste diversifying the stream of uniformity. Destroy individuality, and you are left with a vacancy of aesthetic feeling, drifting this way and that, with vague satisfactions and vague discontents. (ESP 118)

Just as Mill wrote in 1859 of the deficiency of "personal impulses and preferences" within British society, Whitehead argues in 1933 that modern methods of production, by forcing standardized products upon consumers, are causing a "gradual vanishing of aesthetic preferences as effective factors in social behaviours. The aesthetic capacities of the producers and the aesthetic cravings of the buyers are losing any real effectiveness" (ESP 119). An efficient system of mass production requires that consumers conform to a standard fashion. "The result" concludes Whitehead, "must be the creation of a public with feeble individual tastes. There is nothing that they really want to buy, unless the world around them is also buying" (ESP 118). The very capacity of human beings for aesthetic experience is being destroyed; and with the loss of individuality we are left with only "generalized mass emotion" (ESP 119).

In addition to these obvious parallels to Mill's arguments in *On Liberty* we can observe Whitehead employing a further argument in defense of the liberal ideal of tolerance. Referring to Plato he says:

His Dialogues are permeated with a sense of the variousness of the Universe, not to be fathomed by our intellects, and in his Seventh Epistle he expressly disclaims the possibility of an adequate philosophic system. The moral of his writings is that all points of view, reasonably coherent and in some sense with an application, have something to contribute to our understanding of the universe, and also involve omissions whereby they fail to include the totality of evident fact. The duty of tolerance is our finite homage to the abundance of inexhaustible novelty which is awaiting the future, and to the complexity of accomplished fact which exceeds our stretch of insight. (AI 65)

The value of diversity of opinion lies, for Whitehead as for Mill, in the imperfection of human knowledge. No one has a perfect grasp of reality and therefore everyone has the duty to tolerate diversity of opinion in order that the progress of human knowledge might be facilitated (FR 65). In both the history of thought and the history of practice we find that "one idea after another is tried out, its limitations defined, and its core of truth elicited." The proper test of both intellectual and social systems "is not that of finality, but of progress" (PR 14 [21]).

Whitehead's concern for the tyranny of the majority is also evident in his discussion of professional groups. A profession is defined as "an avocation whose activities are subjected to theoretical analysis, and are modified by theoretical conclusions derived from that analysis" (AI 72). Intellect is essential to a profession. This is in contrast to a craft, which is predominantly based upon "customary

activities and modified by the trial and error of individual practice"
(AI 73). The importance of these professional groups stems from the
fact that each profession is given its "liberty" from the state to
supervise the "standards of individual professional competence and
of professional practice" (AI 77). In other words, the limits to
individual freedom in certain matters are determined, not by the state
or by the uninformed opinion of the masses who are "intellectually
quiescent" (AI 85), but by the general professional opinion.[49] As with
Mill's intellectual elite, the professionals provide the masses with
"objective information as to the sort of weight to be attached to
individuals and as to the sort of freedom of action which may safely
be granted."[50] According to Mill, the masses should accept the
authority of the more cultivated minds and in normal circumstances
"there exists a large body of received doctrine . . . which no one
thinks of questioning, backed as it is by the authority of all, or nearly
all, persons, supposed to possess knowledge enough to qualify them
for giving an opinion on the subject."[51] Similarly for Whitehead the
freedom of the nonprofessional is secured because the dangers of
extravagant notions should have been demonstrated by the profession.

## III. EVOLUTION AND SOCIAL PROGRESS

In his support for individuality and the importance of ideas for
progress Whitehead was defending the traditional liberal value of
liberty. However, this value was significantly modified by both
Whitehead and the new liberals through their substitution of a
socially rooted individuality for the abstract or atomic individualism
of classical liberalism. As Freeden has demonstrated, this modification among the new liberals can be explained by the link that they
forged between biological and socio-political theory.[52] While not
wishing to claim that Whitehead was influenced directly by any
particular evolutionist theory, I suggest that his use of biological and
evolutionary ideas, especially when discussing the conditions for
social progress, closely parallels arguments made by the new
liberals.[53]

Late Victorian thought was greatly influenced by scientific
developments in the area of biology. Darwin's theory of evolution
was particularly significant in that its application by Herbert Spencer
to human society offered the Social Darwinists the "public authority

of science by which they could attempt to legitimatize their private vision of human progress."[54] Competition due to population pressure on resources and the consequent elimination of weaker individuals was viewed as the means by which social progress was achieved. By coupling the Malthusian theory of the struggle for existence with Darwin's conclusions concerning biological progress Spencer and the Social Darwinists defended laissez-faire against the growing call for social reform. From their perspective such reforms, although presented as humanitarian, were in fact counterproductive. By securing the continued existence of the "unfit," misguided social reformers were weakening the common stock and ultimately preventing the race from progressing.

The new liberals responded to the challenge of Social Darwinism by seeking to demonstrate the extent to which biological theory supported their social and political program. Consequently, increasing weight was given in progressive social thought to the "co-operative-altruistic version of Darwinism."[55]

> The socio-biological argument opposed to Social Darwinism maintained that natural processes of development were leading to increased co-operation which replaced the evolutionary mechanism of competition. That this could be proved by Darwinian methods was of immense importance in legitimizing the new direction liberal thought was taking.[56]

This cooperative version of Darwinism was championed by Hobhouse. In *Democracy and Reaction* he is concerned to repudiate the conservative reaction to the humanitarian social ideals of Liberalism. The primary intellectual cause of this reaction, he argues, is the belief that "human progress depends upon the forces which condition all biological evolution. . . . " He continues: "Just as the doctrine of Malthus was the main theoretical obstacle to all schemes of social progress through the first two-thirds of the century, so the doctrine derived in part from Malthus by Darwin has provided a philosophy for the reaction of the last third."[57] However, the blame for this lies not in the theory of evolution per se, but in its misunderstanding by others. "A just conception of evolution," he writes, "does not support the view that the struggle for existence is the condition of progress. It therefore lends no sanction to the prevailing worship of force."[58] Hobhouse claims that Darwin was aware that the development of the moral consciousness involves a suspension of the blind struggle for existence.[59] Unfortunately what has "filtered through into social and political thought of the time has been the belief that the time-honoured doctrine 'Might is Right' has a scientific foundation in the laws of biology. Progress comes about through a conflict in which the fittest survives. It must, therefore, be unwise in the long run—however urgent it seems for the sake of the present generation—to interfere with the struggle."[60]

The "worship of force" by the Social Darwinists was also identified by Whitehead as a main obstacle to progress. In particular he objected to the "Gospel of Force" preached by classical liberals in the last century. Like Hobhouse, Whitehead observed that the application of the Malthusian doctrine and of biological science to human society posed a challenge to the "whole humanitarian movement" (AI 44). By fixing their attention on the feature of environmental limitations contained in these theories some sociologists were led to conclude that competition was the engine of social progress. "From this point of view, there is a given amount of material, and only a limited number of organisms can take advantage of it. The givenness of the environment dominates everything. Accordingly, the last words of science appeared to be the Struggle for Existence, and Natural Selection" (SMW 163). The exclusive attention paid by many liberals to the competitive aspect of life was denounced as a "disaster of the first magnitude" (SMW 295).

We should be clear that Whitehead did not simply reject the theories of Malthus and Darwin. To a large extent, although not entirely, the environment is fixed. "The massive habits of physical nature, its iron laws, determine the scene for the sufferings of men" (AI 84). The struggle for existence is real and must not be ignored. Equally real is the fact that in this struggle the fittest to survive eliminate the less fit. Yet while Social Darwinists treated natural selection as the sole agency of social progress, Whitehead held that it was but one agency among others. The truth that it contains is that the environment places restrictions upon organisms to which they must adapt or perish. This is one side to "the machinery involved in the development of nature" (SMW 163).

There is, however, another side to social development. Like Hobhouse and the new liberals, Whitehead considered the "full conclusion to be drawn from a philosophy of evolution" to be of a "more balanced character" than that adopted by classical liberalism.[61] Spencer's doctrine of the survival of the fittest can explain neither how complex organisms with deficient survival power ever evolved nor why the trend of evolution has been upward.[62] This upward trend has been accompanied by a growth of the converse relation: not only do species adapt to their environment, but the higher animals progressively undertake to adapt the environment to themselves (FR 4). This is the other side to the "evolutionary machinery" which Whitehead terms "creativeness" (SMW 163; emphasis deleted). Organisms are to a limited extent able to create their own environment. This requires cooperation. "Those organisms are successful which modify their environments so as to assist each other" (SMW 296). Whitehead identified the key to the progressiveness of the European races as compared to the North American Indians in the way they cooperated so as to modify their environment. "In the history of the world," concludes Whitehead, "the prize has not gone to those species which specialised in methods of violence . . . " (SMW 297). This is because the use of force defeats its own object. Progress requires cooperation.

The evolutionary fallacy suggested by the phrase "survival of the fittest" is "the belief that fitness for survival is identical with the best exemplification of the Art of Life."[63] In like manner Hobhouse argues that the conception of the survival of the fittest "gives no guarantee of progress in any sense which is of interest to man. . . . "[64] While it is true that rivalry and competition will secure the survival of those fittest to survive by that method, Hobhouse argues that it is incompatible with organization in social life. Social progress at the very least "involves a fuller and more many-sided life."[65] To speak of progress is to make a value judgment. Therefore, if we are to discuss the relation of evolution to progress we must have a "clearly formed conception of the standard of value by which we judge what progress is."[66]

What does Hobhouse understand this standard of value to be? The final standard and the supreme object of human activity is the ideal of collective humanity. The full realization of human potentialities, which Hobhouse also speaks of as the evolution of mind or "orthogenic evolution," is the *telos* of human activity. The higher life is one that is inclusive of others. "Their interests and hopes and feelings are a part of its own, incorporated in its own scheme, and bound up with its own happiness."[67] Hobhouse concludes that the true line of social progress is "the development of that rational organization of life in which men freely recognize their interdependence, and the best life for each is understood to be that which is best for those around him."[68]

As with Whitehead's aesthetic theory of value this realization
of human capacities requires the advance of organization, and this
in turn depends upon the two principles of unity and differentiation. On the sociological level these principles take the form of
order and liberty. Primitive societies display the kind of unity that
Hobhouse calls "solidarity."[69] This is a mechanistic form of
organization and is based upon the forceful suppression of individual personality. As an alternative to this mechanistic unity, "a
higher order may be sought within which individuality has full
play, . . . in which, though no right is made absolute to the
prejudice of others, none is ignored in the synthesis achieved."[70]
This is the ideal of an organic harmony which allows for the
many-sided development of its members. The higher form of
organization characteristic of modern societies is "that in which a
richer, fuller, more differentiated structure is knitted together in a
deeper, more thoroughgoing unity."[71] Such organization necessitates the mutual cooperation of individual members.

Whitehead's discussion of types of beauty in *Adventures of Ideas*
not only offers a striking parallel to Hobhouse's idea of harmony and
his distinction between types of social unity, but also highlights the
way in which historical progress is understood in terms of the
emergence of more adequate types of social order. The "minor form
of beauty," we are told, is "the absence of mutual inhibition among
the various prehensions" (AI 324). There are two meanings of
inhibition which must be carefully distinguished. Complete inhibition
through negative prehension involves the total exclusion of a feeling
as a component of a given occasion's subjective form. Such inhibi-
tions are necessary for a finite occasion to realize a determinate
satisfaction, that is, to be "this" and not "that." This type of
inhibition does not derogate from "perfection" for there is " 'perfection' in its kind—that is to say, in its type of finiteness with
such-and-such exclusions" (AI 329). Whitehead terms this type of
inhibition "anaesthesia" (AI 329). I suggest that the unity of a
primitive or traditional society displays such a minor form of beauty.
The power of the society's defining characteristics is such that
individuality is almost completely inhibited thus suppressing discordant elements. The harmony attained in such a society is a "mere
qualitative Harmony within an experience comparatively barren of
objects of high significance . . . " (AI 339). Such a harmony is,
Whitehead continues, "a debased type of Harmony, tame, vague,
deficient in outline and intention" (AI 339).

There is, however, a second meaning of inhibition that does derogate from perfection. Unlike "anaesthesia," this type of inhibition, which Whitehead terms "aesthetic destruction," involves the positive prehension of conflicting feelings. This gives rise to a third feeling, a discordant feeling of "mutual destructiveness . . . " (AI 329). In other words, incompatible prehensions are both felt in such a way as to prevent either component feeling from realizing the strength proper to it. This condition is a peculiarly apt expression of nineteenth-century industrial society as portrayed by Whitehead. The demise of the Middle Ages saw individualism replace coordination as the keynote of sociological theory (AI 37–38). "What the notions of 'form' and 'harmony' were to Plato, that the notions of 'individuality' and 'competition' were to the nineteenth century" (AI 39). Its watchwords were "struggle for existence, competition, class warfare, commercial antagonism between nations, military warfare" (SMW 295). While the classical economists believed that individual self-interest worked to promote the public interest in the present, and while Social Darwinists maintained that individual competition was the means by which the ideal society would be realized in the future, Whitehead viewed competitive individualism as a "painful clash," as a period of "vulgarity" (AI 324) in human history. Far from realizing the social ideal, radical individualism derogates from perfection and actually prevents individuals from fully realizing their personality.

The liberal faith of the nineteenth century was rejected as a "*compromise* between the individualistic, competitive doctrine of strife and the optimistic doctrine of harmony" (AI 41; emphasis added). Instead of a compromise what is needed is an understanding that "elucidates the *interfusion* of strife and harmony" (AI 40; emphasis added). In other words, what is required is an organic conception of society in which the competing aims of the individual parts achieves a higher synthesis in a common good. This appears to be what Whitehead has in mind when he speaks of the "perfection of Beauty." The minor form of beauty is the absence of conflict that is achieved through negative prehension. The major form of beauty "presupposes the first form, and adds to it the condition that the conjunction in one synthesis of the various prehensions introduces new contrasts of objective content with objective content" (AI 324). As a consequence of this synthesis the conformal feeling in the component feelings is intensified. Thus, Whitehead concludes, "the parts contribute to the massive feeling of the whole, and the whole contributes to the intensity of feeling of the parts" (AI 324). What he is describing, he claims, is the "metaphysical doctrine of the inter-weaving of absoluteness upon relativity" (AI 339). When applied to a work of art, "the relativity becomes the harmony of the composition, and the absoluteness is the claim for separate individuality advanced by component factors" (AI 339–40). I suggest that the applicability of this metaphysical principle extends beyond art to include sociology as well. The "interweaving" of absoluteness upon relativity in art is paralleled by his call for the "interfusion" of strife and harmony in sociology. When the metaphysical principle is applied to human social arrangements the relativity becomes the harmony of the social organism, and the absoluteness is the claim for individuality advanced by the members. Thus a society exhibits the major form of beauty when the the interrelation of the members is such that the individuality of every member is stimulated and intensified as each contributes to the common good.

I suggest then that Whitehead held to a theory of social progress like that advanced by modern liberal political theorists such as Hobhouse and Mill. Progress requires, broadly speaking, cooperation and individuality. Force and uniformity, on the other hand, are perceived as posing special dangers to social development. The "Gospel of Uniformity" neglects the element of individuality operative in the world whereas the "Gospel of Force" neglects the contrasting element of harmony or sociability. These two features, which might appear to be in tension, come together in the the modern liberal notions of an organic harmony and the common good.

## IV. THE ADVENTURE OF THE UNIVERSE AS ONE

Any discussion of social development in Whitehead's thought would be incomplete without examining the operation of deity in the creative process. A complete understanding of history from the perspective of process philosophy requires that we perceive God as the ultimate *telos* of history and the world as the vehicle by which this *telos* is being achieved. The principle of intrinsic incompatibility of values, which we referred to earlier in our discussion of flux and permanence, needs to be reflected in our understanding of the divine nature. "We must conceive the Divine Eros," he writes, "as the active entertainment of all ideals, with the urge to their finite realization, each in its due season. Thus a process must be inherent in God's nature, whereby his infinity is acquiring realization" (AI 357).

As we have seen, this was a relatively late development in White-head's thought, a development that brought him closer to the concept of God entertained by Hegel. What they shared was a belief in the incompleteness of God. Consequently the creation of the world becomes necessary as a means by which deity completes its own being. In Whitehead's earlier metaphysics, the creation of the world is also necessary, but in a different sense. As an attribute of Creativity, its "Concept" so to speak, God qualifies the creative process, but is not in turn qualified by the world. The unity of the divine primordial vision achieves actuality in the many temporal occasions. This is the *telos* of history and explains the necessity of creation. The world is necessary in this first instance because it is the medium in which Creativity instantiates the conceptual vision (Concept) of God.[72] With the development in Whitehead's metaphysics the *telos* of history is no longer the realization in the world of an expression adequate to God's vision; now the *telos* is God's own depth of experience. The world remains an end in that the primordial nature still has an urge toward realization; however, this end is itself turned into a means for the achievement of the ultimate end of history, namely, the completion of God. The consequent nature of God is the "final end of creation" (PR 349[530]). The world achieves its own satisfaction in part from the sense of its contribution to God's life.

As I mentioned in the opening chapter of this study, the similarities between Whitehead's philosophy of history and that of Hegel are surprising given his claim to have read only a single page of Hegel's writings. Given the extent to which features of Idealism and new liberalism coincided during this period I believe it is entirely feasible that the influence of Hegel's ideas on Whitehead was due in part to Whitehead's acquaintance with political views of such new liberal Idealists as Haldane and Green. In this respect it is interesting to observe how Whitehead's understanding of God and history parallels that of Green, for in both instances Hegelian ideas are employed to support a modern liberal theory of society and social development.

Like Hegel before him and process thinkers after him, Green adopted a theory of history according to which the deity realizes itself within the process of world history. The progressive self-realization of God is the *telos* of history.[73] Consequently, Green regards the orthodox Christian conception of God as utterly transcendent to be a mistake and to have had a deleterious impact on society. In place of a conception of faith as a "certain condition of the spiritual consciousness,"[74] Green argues that orthodox theologians had set the notion of an assent to authoritative proclamations and to historical propositions.[75] As a result God is "externalized" and treated as an object transcending the believer's own life. "Such terms as forgiveness, reconciliation, and salvation," he writes,

> instead of representing experiences of the believer, processes of his spiritual life, came to represent certain divine transactions, in which the believer had no personal part, though through faith he had the benefit of them in the acquisition of final happiness. The death and resurrection of Christ ceased to be looked upon as perpetually re-enacted in the surrender of the fleshly self and the substitution for it of a new man in the moral life.[76]

In orthodox Christianity the religious life of the believer is privatized leading to a dislocation between the believer and the community. Salvation is regarded as an objective transaction by a transcendent deity which the believer will participate in after death, rather than as an immanent historical process finding realization within society through the believer's own personal efforts. Moreover, Green considers the orthodox Christian emphasis upon a God who utterly transcends the created order to have resulted in a negative estimation of the world as inherently inferior to some transcendent divine existence. That which is ultimately real and genuinely good is not to be found or realized in this life but awaits us in the next.

Green's response is evident in his lay sermons where, for example, he claims the essence of Christianity to be

> the thought of God, not as 'far off' but 'nigh,' not as a master but as a father, not as a terrible outward power, forcing us we know not whither, but as one of whom we may say that we are reason of his reason and spirit of his spirit; who lives in our moral life, and for whom we live in living for the brethren, even as in so living we live freely, because in obedience to a spirit which is our self. . . .[77]

In place of the tyrannous and transcendent God of classical theism Green follows the lead of Hegel and posits a God who is immanent within human history. God is not presented as an "external lawgiving power" but as one who is present and working in us, enabling us to fulfill the law through love.[78] Green identifies God with the "possible self" which is the *telos* of moral action. As such God is "the final cause of the moral life, the ideal self which no one, as a moral agent, is, but which everyone, as such an agent, is however blindly seeking to become. . . ."[79]

It is this process in which a person seeks to realize his or her full potentialities as a moral being that constitutes for Green the reconciliation of the world to God. The reconciliation of the world through Christ is not a transaction in the heavens but something realized through the efforts of people here and now. In a revealing passage Green says that Christ is imagined to be "a man in whom that which seems to be the end of moral discipline and progress has been fully attained, viz., the union of the will with God, perfect unselfishness, the direction of desire to ends which one rational being can consciously share with all other rational beings."[80] Notice that Green brings together in his discussion of religion the ideas of progress and the common good. The divinity of Christ lies in his pursuit of that ultimate end that can be shared with all others, that is, an end that is noncompetitive. Progress is understood in terms of the realization of such a condition. Yet how can Christ be thought to have achieved salvation apart from the rest of the world? Does not the salvation of one entail the salvation of all in an organic conception of the world? Green therefore continues:

> Such a 'man' would not be man as we know man, because the conditions of human existence in this world are such that this end can never be completely attained. Thus the religious imagination of God as Christ has to become the imagination of him as a 'glorified' Christ; a Christ such as Jesus of Nazareth was potentially, not actually; a Christ 'put to death in the flesh,' but alive and giving life in the spirit.[81]

It is not possible that the ideal that is God should find full representation or expression in the world we see.[82] Instead, what the believer sees in Jesus is the pattern of moral life. The essence of the divine nature was revealed in the cross and resurrection of Jesus. "A death unto life, a life out of death" is the eternal act of God himself, and therefore one which is reenacted by mankind.[83] We are to put off the old man, the man of flesh, and put on the new man, which is Christ, the wisdom of God.[84] This constitutes a "new intellectual consciousness, which transforms the will, and is the source of a new moral life."[85]

The social implications of Green's philosophical theology are not hard to identify. Here he would be in full agreement with Bosanquet's assertion that "The *duties of religion are the same as the duties of morality.* If we speak of duties to God, we mean the same duties as duties to man."[86] The ideal of religion is the ideal of a *social* or common good; therefore, Green is able to consider the political action of citizenship as well as the individual act of faith as religious.[87] Deity realizes itself in the particularities of moral life, in the customs, institutions and laws of human social life. God is reason "as taking a body from, and giving life to, the whole system of experience which makes the history of man."[88] It is the consciousness of God, which is being progressively realized in history, that is the formative principle of society. Under its influence the desire to satisfy momentary and individual wants becomes

> an impulse of improvement which forms, enlarges, and recasts societies; always keeping before man in various guise, according to the degree of his development, an unrealised ideal of a best which is his God, and giving divine authority to the customs or laws by which some likeness of this ideal is wrought into the actuality of life.[89]

In other words, the ideal of personal development, an individual's higher self, is a *telos* that is achieved only through social institutions and customs. One's duty becomes the pursuit of that course of action that furthers this common good. Sin, then, consists in "the individual's making his own self his object, not in the possible expansion in which it becomes that true will of humanity which is also God's, but under the limitation of momentary appetite or interest. . . ."[90]

Turning again to Whitehead's theory of history we can detect a number of interesting areas of contact with Green's philosophy. First, in a manner similar to Green, Whitehead stresses the function of God as the source of novel ideals that persuade individuals toward greater beauty. Green held that God is not a "terrible outward power, forcing us we know not whither," but exists within us as an ideal of what we can become, persuading us toward the realization of an ideal aim, which is the common good. This is not to make God an "impotent abstraction" because "all moral action begins from ideas."[91] As we saw earlier, moral action cannot be coerced; therefore, the power of God can only be the power of persuasion since God aims at the moral ideal. Whitehead similarly understands one of

God's cosmological functions to be the Eros of the universe, persuading actual entities toward ideal aims derived from the primordial nature. This ideal aim is toward the maximum intensity of feeling for the individuals as part of the larger social whole. To that extent God's ideal aim is always the moral ideal (pace Green). But does this account of divine causality leave God without concrete power? This is the question raised by Daniel Day Williams and I suspect that Whitehead's answer would be like Green's, namely, that moral action cannot be coerced.[92] As Williams himself notes, part of Whitehead's moral critique of the divine despot conception of God is that persuasion and not coercion "is seen to be the mode of achievement of all high values."[93] This is a perspective shared by all modern liberals.

Thus we see that for Whitehead God is "that power in history which implants into the form of process, belonging to each historic epoch, the character of a drive towards some ideal, to be realized within that period. This ideal is never realized, it is beyond realization, and yet it moulds the form of what is realized" (MT 164–65). He goes on to give the example of the American Constitution, which is an "ideal of human liberty, activity, and cooperation."

> It has never been realized in its perfection; and by its lack of characterization of the variety of possibilities open for humanity, it is limited and imperfect. And yet, such as it is, the Constitution vaguely discloses the immanence in this epoch of that one energy of idealization, whereby bare process is transformed into glowing history. (MT 165)

As with Green, Whitehead rejects any notion that there can be a full realization of the general ideal that governs the social development of an historical epoch. Moreover, there is no general ideal that would exhaust the "variety of possibilities" open for humanity. There can be no end to history. What these possibilities are is the subject of endless discovery. It is a goal that gets defined only in the process of its realization.

It is also interesting to note the way in which Whitehead relates religion to historical development in *Adventures of Ideas*. There he expressly locates the value of religion in the moral ideals that it expresses (AI 19). Ethical ideals are themselves "the supreme example of consciously formulated ideas acting as a driving force effecting transitions from social state to social state" (AI 21). What Christianity provides humanity is its "impracticable ethics" which constitute mankind's "most precious instrument of progress" (AI 20). The essence of Christianity is "the appeal to the life of Christ as a revelation of the nature of God and of his agency in the world" (AI 214). However, as with Green, what is important in this appeal is not, in Whitehead's opinion, the reconstruction of the historical details surrounding that life, but the power of the images to evoke a positive response from us today. Its value lies in its ability to lure individuals to higher levels of life. The life of Jesus is "primarily an exhibition in life of moral intuition . . . " (AI 213). It is the ethics of Christianity as pictured in the life of Jesus that supplies a gauge by which to evaluate social structures. "The progress of humanity," concludes Whitehead in a statement strongly reminiscent of Green's philosophy, "can be defined as the process of transforming society so as to make the original Christian ideals increasingly practicable for its individual members" (AI 18).

For both philosophers it is the religious/moral ideals that provide the criteria by which human social arrangements are evaluated and progress assessed. "You cannot consider wisdom or folly, progress or decadence, except in relation to some standard of judgment, some end in view," says Whitehead. "Such standards, such ends, when widely diffused, constitute the driving force of ideas in the history of mankind" (AI 5). For Green the standard is the ideal of human development. Although humanity does not fully know what its ultimate well-being consists in, an examination of history reveals that it must involve the complete fulfillment of human capacities. This idea is the "guiding idea of our lives" and enables us to say of particular forms of life and action that they are better, or contribute more to true well-being than others.[94] Earlier he says that "we know enough of ultimate moral good to guide our conduct; enough to judge whether the prevailing interests which make our character are or are not in the direction which tends further to realise the capabilities of the human spirit."[95] The ideal for Green is therefore of a common good, a social good in which every individual is able to realize his or her own capacities. This is what Green understands to be the *telos* of history, and it is a goal shared by modern liberals generally.[96]

While Whitehead would agree with Green that the ultimate *telos* of history is the self-realization of God, he rejects the simple identification of God with mankind. Green is following Hegel for whom the world spirit is "the spirit of the world as it reveals itself through the human consciousness; the relationship of men to it is that of single parts to the whole which is their substance. And this world spirit corresponds to the divine spirit, which is the absolute spirit."[97] The process philosophy of Whitehead and Hartshorne sees the world as the vehicle of God's self-realization in a different sense. There is an ontological pluralism lacking in the Hegelian philosophy of history. For process metaphysics, history is not, as G. A. Cohen says of Hegel, "spirit's biography."[98] There is a history of the Universe as One, but this does not result in an identification of God and the world, only in deity's inclusion of the world as the datum for its own life.

What consequences follow from this difference between Green and process philosophy? Hartshorne argues that humanity cannot be that good which "can command innermost loyalty while measuring by its own transcendence the relativity of all human achievements, purposes, and powers." He continues in a lengthy but important passage:

> Insist upon reducing this transcendence to the mere ideal potentialities of man himself, and you throw everything into doubt, vagueness, and confusion: doubt, for man appears ultimately doomed upon this planet, so that, if he is the ultimate value, the ultimate value is apparently the value of doom; vagueness, for only by thinking of God as the maximal value of all variables can we see clearly the direction in which man must move to reach higher values of these variables; confusion, for if man is the measure of value, then the line between opinion and verity, preference and right, becomes too subtle for ordinary people to see. . . . (BH 36–37)

Hartshorne believes that only the idea of God as supremely relative can provide an adequate criterion of good and bad, fortunate and unfortunate. God alone is perfect love and therefore God alone provides us with a cause worthy of our devotion. Failure to recognize that our true unity resides in a superhuman organism leads to the placement of final value in something not worthy of such devotion and the inevitable falsification of human relations either in the direction of a "vicious individualism," an ethics of enlightened self-interest, or toward a "vicious state-worship" (BH 32).

What are we to make of what is in effect an implicit criticism of modern liberalism? The suggestion that treating man as the measure of value necessarily leads to confusion is of questionable force. As we saw in chapter four, Hartshorne does not admit to the reality of a common good on the level of human society; therefore, the question of God becomes central to his ethical and social theory. He assumes that without a "mighty mediator" to adjudicate between conflicting claims we will be left to the mercy of opinion and preference. Elsewhere he says that without metaphysics "we must admit that we have no objective intelligible standard by reference to which we can decide between conflicting human ideals, including Hitler's ideal of ruthless power."[99] It is metaphysics that indicates the absolute value that is the measure of all relative values. For example, he argues that because the cosmic being cannot be egoistic, the will to power cannot be ultimate. The problem with Hartshorne's argument is that modern liberals like Green would find no difficulty agreeing fully with the claim that metaphysics—and perhaps also God—is necessary and yet still hold that humanity is the measure of value. This is because modern liberals generally adopt as a metaphysical premise the belief that human beings are by nature social and therefore one's own good is bound up with the good of everyone else. It is not the preferences and opinions of atomic individuals that determine what is right or what human capacities represent a true line of development, but the ideal of a common good. Hence the distinction that is often made between what a person prefers and his or her true good. By bringing a dipolar deity that transcends humanity into the equation are we being provided with an "objective intelligible standard" superior to that of modern liberalism? I believe not. The fact that Whitehead and Hartshorne's process metaphysics leads to a social and political theory closely paralleling that of modern liberalism suggests that the practical significance of dipolar theism for human affairs is not that very different from modern liberalism's aim at the common good. An example can be found in the way Hartshorne appeals to God in order to justify tolerance—a key liberal value. "What is needed," he writes, "is a metaphysical basis, at least for the principle of tolerance. This basis is that none of us is God, and yet there is a God."[100] This same argument, which is essentially an argument from human ignorance, can also be expressed along modern liberal lines. Green would hold that we need to be tolerant because there is an ideal of human fulfillment, but no one completely knows what that fulfillment consists of.

Hartshorne's claim that without the idea of God as the "maximal value of all variables" humanity will be left bereft of a clear guide to progress is also unfair to modern liberalism. Green and Hobhouse would claim that the ideal of a common good provides us with clear direction for future human progress. Such progress consists in the reform of society in ways that lead to a greater organic harmony of the individual members. I believe that Hartshorne seriously underestimates the value that the "ideal of human potentialities" has as a guide to progress. Yet to say that the modern liberal ideal has value is not to claim that it is wholly adequate. The ideal of a supremely relative deity is superior because it takes into consideration mankind's relationship to the wider environment.[101] The metaphysics of dipolar theism provides grounds for including the value of natural world within one's determination of the moral ideal. Process philosophy thus goes beyond the anthropocentrism of modern liberal thought by extending the notion of the common good to include the natural environment as well as human ideals within its scope.

The strongest argument against treating humanity as the ultimate *telos* of history is the probability that the human species will eventually pass out of existence. Green, like Hegel, understands mankind to be the vehicle of divine realization in a strong sense not shared by process theology. For example, we find him making claims such as the following: "God is not to be sought in nature, nor in any beginning or end of nature, but in man himself."[102] The *telos* of history is being actualized *within* human history. God is coming to self-consciousness *in* humanity; God is the ideal possibilities of *human* life. But if the value of the historical process resides in the realization by humanity of its innate capacities, then either the human species must exist forever or the historical process is ultimately futile.[103] Green appears to opt for the former alternative, holding that the ideal will never find adequate exemplification in history and therefore history will never end. Process metaphysics, on the contrary, does not identify God and humanity in this way and therefore does not face the problem posed by the transitory nature of human existence. God is supremely relative and therefore preserves in the divine life the values achieved within creation. Human beings, along with the rest of the created order, contribute value to the everlasting and all-inclusive life of God. The world is thus a vehicle of divine realization in the weak sense that it provides data for the fulfillment of the being of God.

The difficulty with viewing humanity as the final locus of divine self-realization is that it cannot deal with the problem posed by human finitude. The fact that "the past fades, that time is a 'perpetual perishing' " is, in Whitehead's opinion, the "ultimate evil" of the temporal world, an evil that objective immortality in the temporal world is unable satisfactorily to deal with.[104] What is required is "everlastingness" (PR 347[527]). Peace is the religious intuition of "another order, where there is no unrest, no travel, no shipwreck: 'There shall be no more sea' " (PR 340[516]). This is expressly brought out in AI 368-69:

> Decay, Transition, Loss, Displacement belong to the essence of the Creative Advance. The new direction of aim is initiated by Spontaneity, an element of confusion. The enduring Societies with their rise, culmination, and decay, are devices to combine the necessities of Harmony and Freshness. . . . Amid the passing of so much beauty, so much heroism, so much daring, peace is then the intuition of permanence.

Here we need to recall Whitehead's understanding of the creative process. The primordial nature of God constitutes the first moment in that process. God as primordial is the Divine Eros, "the active entertainment of all ideals, with the urge to their finite realization, each in its due season" (AI 357). These ideals find incarnation in the finite world which constitutes the second moment of the creative process. However, the incompatibility of finite values necessitates that they go under. This is what Whitehead means by the evil of transitoriness. This evil is overcome in the third moment of the creative process which is a synthesis of the first two moments. In God as consequent and fully actual the finite values of the world are *aufgehoben;* the temporality of the finite entity is negated as the value achieved is preserved everlastingly in God. The values attained by each individual are saved and yet they are also elevated and transformed by their incorporation in the "eternal order which is the final absolute 'wisdom' " (PR 347[527]). Peace is the intuition of this third moment, the "kingdom of heaven."

It is at the end of his study of civilization that Whitehead introduces the notion of peace. The reason for this, I suggest, is his desire to set the history of Western civilization within the larger framework of the adventure of the Universe as One.

> The Unity of Adventure includes among its components all individual realities, each with the importance of the personal or social fact to which it belongs. Such individual importance in the components belongs to the essence of Beauty. In this Supreme

Adventure, the Reality which the Adventure transmutes into its Unity of Appearance requires the real occasions of the advancing world each claiming its due share of attention. This Appearance, thus enjoyed, is the final Beauty with which the Universe achieves its justification. (AI 381)

Whitehead is describing God's own transcendent beauty in which the universe finds its justification. Here we find the heart of Whitehead's theodicy. It is by the inclusion of the finite in the infinite that the evil of history receives its justification. Hegel similarly believes that evil is overcome through its inclusion in the infinite. Thus he depicts the study of history as a theodicy. Philosophy is concerned with "the glory of the Idea mirroring itself in the History of the World," that history being the "process of development which the Idea has passed through in realizing itself. . . . "[105] By justifying the ways of God to man the individual can be reconciled with the world, and this reconciliation is achieved when finite subjectivity comes to see itself as the vehicle of the spirit in which the *necessary* development of the spirit takes place. The plan of history is that of the Idea; therefore "the dialectic of history is to be understood as reflecting the conceptually necessary stages in the self-unfolding of the Idea."[106] Because of the ontological identity of God and the world in Hegel's system, because the finite world is the product of self-positing spirit, the stages of history reflect the divine plan, or providence. "[P]hilosophy should help us to understand," writes Hegel, "that the actual world is as it ought to be. It shows us that the rational will, the concrete good is indeed all-powerful, and that this absolute power translates itself into reality."[107] The overall content of world history has been determined by God; consequently, we become reconciled to the world, to our destinies, when we see ourselves as part of a larger life, as a moment in the life of the spirit.

For Whitehead the evil of perpetual perishing is overcome by the realization that the finite values achieved in this world are not simply nullified, but are preserved everlastingly in God. We are part of a larger life that tenderly saves everything that can be preserved. But for Whitehead, the universe receives its justification not because the course of history has been determined, but because God shares in the suffering of the world. "The Adventure of the Universe starts with the dream and reaps tragic Beauty. This is the secret of the union of Zest with Peace—That the suffering attains its end in a Harmony of Harmonies" (AI 381). For Whitehead, the course of history is not determined. The absence of necessity lies in the ontological pluralism of his system. The eternal objects, which God orders, and the actual entities in which the primordial values find incarnation and through which God's aim at intensity of experience is realized, are not the product of divine self-differentiation. Hence, even though the primordial nature, like the Hegelian Idea, guides the adventure of the universe (the warp of history), and even though both philosophers perceive human passions as a means by which the divine *telos* is being realized (the weft of history), in Whitehead's philosophy of history there is "an element of incompleteness and divine suffering in the ultimate outcome"[108] For Hegel, God's incompleteness is part of his completeness; it is only a stage, a moment, in the life of God. Hegel claims,

> This is the explication of reconciliation: that God is reconciled with the world, or rather that God has shown himself to be reconciled with the world, that even the human is not something alien to him, but rather that this otherness, this self-distinguishing, finitude as it is expressed, is a moment in God himself, although, to be sure, it is a disappearing moment.[109]

But for Whitehead, there is a real openness about God's completion because there is not an ultimate identity of God and the world; therefore, what the world creates in God is not necessary. Consequently, while the experience of peace is the result of an intuition that one is part of a larger life, and while this experience enables one to be reconciled to one's finitude, to the tragedy, pain, and loss experienced in life, it does not lead one to acquiesce to present circumstances. Peace is not the negative conception of anaesthesia; "it preserves the springs of energy."[110] It stimulates adventure while removing the narrowness of self-interest.

Since Green was interested in social reform, in motivating individuals to strive after an ideal of the common good that lay before them, he could not accept, anymore than Whitehead could, a deterministic theory of history that might produce quietism or complacency. This he perceived to be the danger of Hegel's philosophy of history. Hegel's theodicy justified God whereas Green wanted to justify the social reformer. Green was able to avoid the negative implications of Hegel's philosophy of history because in his metaphysics God is identified with the ideal self which is never perfectly realized in human history. There is no actual state in which God is actually identical with human life. The reason for this is not simply because the ideal is always developing. It is also because passion and selfishness are inevitably combined with moral motives in our actions. Since, according to Green, from good comes only good and from evil only evil, it follows that a full realization of the ideal self is impossible; for the ideal self is the *telos* of moral endeavor, and as such it can be realized only through moral actions. Green therefore emphasizes the struggle of mankind toward perfection. As Melvin Richter says:

> At the very heart of his metaphysics, there is the pathos of the imperfect. God realises himself gradually, but never perfectly in human customs, laws, institutions. Man must struggle to attain perfection, but never can quite do so. This Faustian motif links virtue with the incessant attempt to attain what by its nature is unattainable.[111]

Whitehead similarly rejects any notion that there can be a full realization of the general ideal that governs the social development of an historical epoch: "[T]he aim is always beyond the attained fact" (AI 102). The adventure of the universe begins with a dream and reaps tragic beauty; struggle and tragedy are unavoidable features of the historical advance.

Peace is for Whitehead the religious dimension at the base of a great civilization. As such it operates in a way similar to the element of "God-consciousness"[112] in Green's philosophy and "harmony" in the thought of Hobhouse. Green argued that our consciousness of mankind's ideal possibilities (God-consciousness) was the source of that adventure wherein we endeavor to realize a good common to all. This involves the rejection of our own narrowly selfish interests for the good of humanity as such. It is in this process of self-transcendence that true freedom lies. We die in order to live. Similarly we find Whitehead claiming that peace is the "harmony of the soul's activities with ideal aims that lie beyond any personal satisfaction" (AI 371). The sense that the world contributes to the everlasting life of God leads to an inversion of relative values (AI 367). One's field of attention is enlarged and one moves away from a selfish concern for particulars to a concern for the whole. Peace is thus a barrier against narrowness, the removal of inhibition, and it results in a love of mankind as such. Our intuition of God, our God-consciousness, "constitutes the zest of self-forgetful transcendence belonging to Civilization at its height" (AI 381). With this sense of participation in God comes the freedom for adventure. It secures that "liberty of thought and action, required for the upward adventure of life on this Earth" (AI 109). Again, we are told that it is through the immediate experience of the "final Fact" that the world "receives its persuasion towards such perfections as are possible for its diverse individual occasions" (AI 381; see AI 86). Peace frees us from ourselves and for others; we experience the "personal gratification" that "arises from aim beyond personality" (AI 371; see AI 373).

Yet this similarity of function must not blind us to the significant difference that exists between Green's notion of God-consciousness and that advocated by process philosophy. For Whitehead and Hartshorne God-consciousness cannot be equated with a consciousness of our ideal possibilities as human beings apart from the rest of the universe. Rather, it is a consciousness of the value inherent in reality as a whole. While the values attained by human persons are a significant part of the values realized in the world we know, they remain only a part. The sense of peace therefore leads us beyond an anthropocentric view of history and compels us to include the natural world in the universal process of salvation. Humanity cannot be the ultimate *telos* of history because it is unable to preserve everlastingly all of the values realized in the world. It is this reinterpretation of the *telos* of history that provides process philosophy with an important contribution to modern liberal thought. By removing this *telos* from humanity and locating it within a dipolar God Whitehead and Hartshorne seek to overcome the problems posed by human finitude while retaining the religious dimension at the base of society. God continues to operate as an inspiration to "self-forgetful transcendence," as a motivation for political action, yet without limiting the scope of the common good to human values.[113]

# 8

## Conclusion: Toward a
## Political Theology

> *Wherefore men say that the Gods have a king,*
> *because they themselves either are or were in*
> *ancient times under the rule of a king. For they*
> *imagine, not only the forms of the Gods, but their*
> *ways of life to be like their own.*
>
> Aristotle, Politics

Modern liberalism—as represented by Mill, Green, Hobhouse, and Bosanquet—is a diffuse movement within an even broader, dynamic liberal tradition; yet all its proponents share a common aim to reconcile individuality and sociability through an organic conception of human nature and society. Of course, as Gaus notes, if this is all we can say about modern liberalism then we will be hard pressed to identify it as a distinct political ideology. There are other traditions, most notably Marxism, that share a similar interest. Gaus responds by asserting that modern liberalism is not characterized simply by the attempt to achieve a reconciliation between individuals and society but, in addition, "by (i) the form that reconciliation takes and (ii) the way in which the theory of human nature is used to justify liberal-democratic institutions."[1] Thus it is the new understanding of what it is to be a human person that lies at the root of modern liberalism's divergence from classical liberalism, and at the same time it is the use of that new understanding in defense of traditional liberal values and institutions, including capitalism, that helps to differentiate modern liberalism from Marxism. This effort to unite features of both the liberal and socialist traditions led Hobhouse to describe the new liberal creed as "Liberal Socialism."[2]

On the basis of our exposition and analysis of Whitehead's and Hartshorne's social and political thought I believe we are justified in concluding that they share not only modern liberalism's concern to reconcile the individual and society through an organic theory of reality, but are also committed to the wider perspective and class interests that characterize a modern liberal ideology. We have seen, for example, how Hartshorne employs the notion of organic sympathy (of which the preeminent example is God) to defend liberal interpretations of equality and the democratic idea of rule. And Whitehead is able to develop a theory of human society that transcends the means/ends distinction characteristic of earlier utilitarian thought because of his theory of organic mechanism. Given the social nature of reality, true self-realization involves the self-realization of others. While salvation is something we achieve as individuals, at the same time it is something we only realize together. The antithesis between individual interest and the common good is shown to be a false antithesis owing to the essential relatedness of actual occasions. I suggest, therefore, that Whitehead and Hartshorne expressly relate the social conception of reality advanced by their respective metaphysics to their more specific social and political prescriptions.

Whitehead and Hartshorne share the basic perspectives of modern liberalism; yet they also diverge from one another on a number of issues. Where differences do occur Hartshorne consistently leans toward a more classical liberal position. This is particularly evident in their interpretations of the common good. According to Whitehead a human society can properly be said to have its own *telos* or perfection which is a harmony of detail and final synthesis. The "perfection of Beauty" for human society is exhibited when social arrangements are such that the individuality of each person is maximized as each contributes to the common good. In other words, the social ideal is of an organic unity and a common good on the level of human societies. This ideal of a noncompetitive good common to all is typical of modern liberal thinkers. Hartshorne, on the other hand, rejects the notion that human societies can realize a fully organic unity; therefore, they do not possess a common good in the modern liberal sense of the term. According to his social theory of reality a human society is not a "well-unified" whole; it is a "collection" and not a unity of individuals. In keeping with the classical liberal tradition Hartshorne considers the value of human social structures to be purely instrumental.

The consequences of Hartshorne's rejection of the ideal of a common good on the level of human society are felt elsewhere in his social and political theory. They are evident, for example, in the stress he lays on the tragic and competitive aspects of social life as opposed to life's cooperative and harmonious elements. Hartshorne also emphasizes a negative conception of freedom and defends democracy and equality before the law on the grounds of our *lack* of organic sympathy, whereas modern liberals generally defended positive freedom and stressed the fully social nature of human life. Yet, despite this tension in Hartshorne's thought, I do not believe that it disqualifies the claim that he, like Whitehead, is a representative of modern liberalism. It simply means that he is a modern liberal in the vein of Mill or Bosanquet whereas Whitehead is more akin to Green and Hobhouse.

Not only are Whitehead and Hartshorne personally committed to modern liberalism, but their metaphysics function to legitimate that ideology. Process metaphysics, in other words, did not originate as a neutral, value-free system of thought, but one that reflects the interests, aspirations, and characteristics of its founders. Hartshorne claims to possess a metaphysics of freedom,[3] a metaphysics of democracy,[4] and a metaphysics of individualism[5]—not to mention a metaphysics of capitalism—which will provide the "Free World" with the intellectual weaponry necessary to resist the standing threat posed by Marxism. However, Hartshorne's opposition to Marxism is not simply philosophical. "The point is not that unless we know Marxism to be philosophically mistaken we shall lack grounds for opposing totalitarianism. On the practical points of freedom and sovereignty we know well, nearly all of us, that present-day communism ought to be opposed" (CAP 8)." Hartshorne wants to oppose Marxism on *practical* grounds; fortunately for him, he has discovered a metaphysics that *theoretically* legitimates not only his practical opposition to Marxism but his practical support for liberal democracy as well. Such good fortune, I believe, is hardly coincidental.

Although for different reasons, Hartshorne also sees a connection between the principles underlying liberal democracy and neo-classical metaphysics. He rhetorically asks,

Can faith in the value of freedom have simply no connection with superior insight into its universal metaphysical principle? . . . But suppose the principle is the secularization of the theological idea of creativity, of action that no causal explanation can ever derive from antecedent conditions, or of decision whose possibility can indeed be causally explained but not the realization of precisely this possibility rather than others that would have been equally explicable from the same conditions. (CAP 9)

Likewise he asks whether there is

> really no connection between our faith in the rights of persons
> not to be tyrannized over for the alleged benefit of future
> generations (as this benefit is defined by a ruling clique) and the
> belief that only one, namely God, has an unconditioned right to
> prefer His wisdom to that of the rest of us? Has the definition of
> a liberal, one "who knows that he is not God," really been
> superseded? (CAP 9)

For Hartshorne the connection between the a priori truths of neoclassical metaphysics and the practical ideals of liberalism is that the latter are "secularized" versions of the former; dipolar theism, in other words, provides a model or paradigm that should be imitated in the vastly more restricted domain of human social and political life. The clearest example of this is found in the analogy that Hartshorne constructs between civil law and natural law, between the use of coercive power by the state and divine providence. And even God's monarchical rule of the universe offers us a model to be imitated; however, far from supplying a divine right of kings, divine governance of the universe is the preeminent example of the "democratic idea of rule," according to which power should be proportionate to one's ability to sympathize with others. Owing to our extremely limited and roughly equal participatory power, our secularized version of the divine model will take the form of democracy. And while Hartshorne occasionally points out that what we get from the metaphysics are socio-political principles rather than codes (CAP 12, 13), the fact is that as long as human beings remain limited and equal in participatory power, which is virtually certain for the indefinite future, then the democratic form of government is the only legitimate expression of the democratic idea of rule.

Hartshorne's understanding of the relationship between metaphysics and politics is idealist in nature; he treats his neoclassical system as a "heavenly Jerusalem" which is to be duplicated in a secularized form here on earth. The state and society are copies and shadows of the "city of God," each exemplifying in its local providence the principles that govern the cosmos at large. However, having uncovered Hartshorne's ideological commitment and having demonstrated the ways in which his philosophy functions to legitimate that ideology, I contend that there are sufficient grounds for suspecting that his metaphysics is a theologized expression of the secular, or more precisely liberal, ideas of freedom, equality, and democracy. Behind Hartshorne's "metaphysics of democracy" lies his "political idealism," his lifelong commitment to a liberal democratic political program, a program that receives its ultimate validation from his "most enlightened view of deity" (CAP 9). When weighed in the balance against the absolute value of metaphysics, all political options other than liberal democracy are found wanting.

> Without metaphysics, we must admit that we have no objective intelligible standard by reference to which we can decide between conflicting human ideals, including Hitler's ideal of ruthless power. The rational answer to Hitler is a metaphysical one, namely, that his ideal does not lend itself to the construction of an adequate metaphysics. The cosmic Being cannot possibly be egoistic; for all beings must be dear to the inclusive Being by virtue of this inclusiveness. . . . I believe that in the end the most effective basis of self-criticism man can have, the best weapon against overindulgence in merely personal preferences and prejudices, as against those of others, the final resort of a democratic attitude, is to force oneself to make the experiment of asking: "Can this principle of mine reasonably generalize itself into a metaphysics, in competition with the other possible principles?"[6]

Metaphysical principles are, on Hartshorne's own admission, generalized human ideals. Yet he also regards such principles to be necessarily true. As a result, those ideals that can be generalized into a metaphysics acquire thereby a necessary validity of their own. Hartshorne contends that the human ideals that underlay liberalism are capable of generalization in a way that Marxist and fascist ideals are not; therefore, the political and economic institutions that safeguard those ideals can be defended with the necessary truths of metaphysics.

It would appear that, in the end, the relationship between Whitehead's and Hartshorne's process philosophies and their political beliefs is circular in nature. Even though Hartshorne attempts to derive practical principles from his metaphysics in such a way that the human social and political spheres become ideally a microcosm of the universe, the metaphysics is itself a generalization of human experience. Lewis Feuer puts his finger on the issue when, in his reflections on Whitehead, he concludes:

A metaphysics is a perspective toward the universe that has been shaped by one's formative experiences, and which fills the unknowns and gaps in our understanding with "realities" that are projected, with as much logic as can be distilled from, or superimposed upon, our underlying hopes, desires, dislikes.[7]

For both philosophers, their flights into the "thin air of imaginative generalization" (PR 5[7]) started from their own experiences, including their own deep-rooted commitments to a liberal ideology. Their metaphysics are perspectives shaped by these experiences and reflective of their personal hopes, desires, and dislikes. Kleinbach's assertion that Whitehead's "images of 'civilization' are more reflective of a liberal gentleman than they are of a rigorous application of his philosophy of organism to social theory"[8] is misguided. The antithesis he perceives between Whitehead's personal reflections and a rigorous application of process metaphysics to social theory simply does not exist. Quite the opposite is the case. The application of Whitehead's metaphysics to social theory leads one in the direction of Marxism only as far as the "Liberal Socialism" of the new liberals. Yet, as we have seen, this is still farther than Hartshorne is willing to go. His process metaphysics will not take one in the direction of Marxism much beyond the liberalism of Henry Simons or even the Friedmans.

By uncovering Whitehead's and Hartshorne's ideological commitments and the possible connections between these commitments and their metaphysical speculations, this study can make a contribution to the task of constructing a process political theology. From our analysis I believe that we have substantial grounds for questioning the validity of Cobb's assertion that "[t]here is nothing in process categories that is inherently white, North American, or middle class."[9] Cobb accepts that process thinkers, like everyone else, must become critically aware of their social location; otherwise, their work is likely to be ideological. I contend that the same issue needs to be addressed to the work of Whitehead and Hartshorne. If, as it appears, their metaphysics are generalizations of their social locations and if their philosophies function in turn to legitimate liberal democratic institutions—including a reformed capitalism and the social inequalities which that still entails—then a process political theology constructed from the perspective of process metaphysics could unconsciously legitimate this ideology.

In addressing the issue of ideology Cobb is responding to a forceful challenge posed by liberation theologians to theologians in Europe and North America. As part of their methodological presuppositions liberation theologians such as Juan L. Segundo and Jose Miguez Bonino argue that ideology is inseparable from theology. They reject as naive that type of academicism "which posits ideological neutrality as the ultimate criterion; which levels down and relativizes all claims to absoluteness and all evaluations of some ideas over others."[10] Theological reflection cannot be done in a vacuum; it cannot be immunized against contemporary ideological struggles. "The sociology of knowledge," writes Bonino, "makes abundantly clear that we think always out of a definite context of relations and action, out of a given praxis."[11] Therefore theology cannot be above politics. Every theology is political because it necessarily presupposes a "unified perception of the world, i.e., an ideology."[12] The ideological option that a person makes consciously or unconsciously informs his or her subsequent theological reflection. Part of the theologian's task therefore is to "understand and appreciate the ideological mechanisms of established society" in order that theology can "take the word of God and convert it from a vague outline to a clearly worked out message. Otherwise theology will become and remain the unwitting spokesman of the experiences and ideas of the ruling factions and classes."[13]

Theology inevitably involves a prior commitment to a particular praxis. This praxis is ideological and reflects a commitment made "not on the basis of theological criteria . . . but on the basis of human criteria."[14] Elsewhere Segundo speaks of the "pretheological human commitment to change and improve the world"[15] made by liberation theologians. Theology cannot be done apart from some prior commitment, without a partiality that conditions and relativizes one's faith. Traditional theology often sees faith as an absolute that preserves us from the relativities of history. On this view revelation becomes an absolute criterion from which we can deduce our proper response to every concrete situation. The eternal message of the gospel is then an infallible and immutable guide to historical human praxis. Liberation theologians reject this approach to faith. God's revelation, they claim, never comes to us in "pure form" but is always "fleshed out in historical ideologies. . . ."[16]

Liberation theology thus denies that there is an unmediated access to divine revelation; therefore, we are compelled to commit ourselves to a relative human ideology. The theologian does not begin with an absolute theological criterion from which he can derive his political commitment, but begins to theologize having already made an ideological commitment on other human, as opposed to divine, criteria. These ideological mediations must be recognized, analyzed, and accepted critically. Bonino is clear that when liberation theologians adopt a Marxist analysis of society there is no "sacralization" of an ideology.

> We move totally and solely in the area of human rationality—in the realm where God has invited man to be *on his own*. The only legitimate question is therefore whether this analysis and this projection do in fact correspond to the facts of human history. If they do, or to the extent that they do, they become *the unavoidable historical mediation* of Christian obedience.[17]

We must therefore employ the critical tools provided by social sciences, we must as Mannheim would say employ a fully evaluative method of ideological investigation, in order to determine what ideological option is truest to the facts of human history.

Ideological criteria are therefore "logically *prior*, but in no way *alien* to theology."[18] Theology presupposes a contextual option that gives it meaning. It is at this point that European and North American theologians, including those who are specifically involved in political theology, are deemed to fail. Whereas liberation theology consciously accepts theology's relationship with politics and incorporates into its methodology the task of ideological analysis, political theologians in Europe have in the past stopped short of making the required commitment. In Bonino's words: "[T]hey want to remain at some neutral or intermediate level in which there is no need to opt for this or that concrete political praxis, i.e., to assume a particular analysis and a particular ideological projection."[19] For example we find Johann Baptist Metz speaking of the church as an "institution of critical liberty."[20]

> In the pluralistic society it cannot be the socio-critical attitude of the Church to proclaim one positive societal order as an absolute norm. It can only consist in effecting within this society a critical, liberating freedom. The Church's task here is not the elaboration of a system of social doctrine, but of social criticism. The Church is a particular institution in

society, yet presents a universal claim; if this claim is not to be an ideology, it can only be formulated and urged as *criticism*.[21]

The basis of this critical task is the "eschatological dimension" of the Church's self-understanding. God's "eschatological proviso" reveals the "provisional nature of every stage that society has attained. . . . "[22] It is the eschatological kingdom of God that is absolute in Metz's theology and that relativizes every social option. The Church, therefore, is to remain above ideologies, which are relative, for the sake of the coming kingdom, which is absolute. Its function in society is purely critical. Liberation theologians respond by claiming that this refusal to make a choice is itself a choice. In arguing for the "critical freedom" of the Church that stands over and against all political movements which tend to universalize themselves, First World theologians are in the eyes of liberation theologians the unwitting spokesmen of the status quo. "When they conceive critical freedom as the form in which God's eschatological Kingdom impinges on the political realm, they are simply opting for *one* particular ideology, that of liberalism."[23]

Here we must emphasize that the *primary* criticism that Bonino in particular is levelling at North Atlantic theologians is not that they adopt a liberal ideology. First and foremost what is being criticized is the belief that theology can somehow transcend politics and retain a critical freedom vis-à-vis every ideology. It is this belief that leads them to neglect the important task of identifying and evaluating the ideology underlying any given religious praxis *including their own*. As a result, they are not sufficiently self-critical and are blinded to the ideological functioning of their own praxis which, as it happens, is liberal. The fact that it is liberal, however, is only a secondary criticism. "[I]t is important to recognize," writes Bonino in a lengthy but significant passage,

> that this identification of the ideology implicit in a given historical praxis does not as such disqualify it. Any course of action which keeps a certain coherence implies a unified perspective on reality, an explicit or implicit project. Ideology, in this sense, has also a positive meaning; it is the instrument through which our Christian obedience gains coherence and unity. It is so, though, provided that it be always brought to consciousness and critically examined both in terms of the gospel and of the scientific analysis of reality.[24]

European and North American theologians need to bring to consciousness and critically examine the ideology implicit within their theology. What Bonino claims will emerge is a particular liberal democratic project which must then be defended. "They may be totally justified in this choice. The only point is that it should not be camouflaged as 'the critical freedom of the gospel' but analytically and ideologically presented and justified. . . . "[25] If a liberal ideology can be justified, if upon evaluation it corresponds to the "facts of human history" then to that extent it will become "the unavoidable historical mediation of Christian obedience."[26]

Like other First World theologians, process theologians have largely failed to acknowledge the essential relationship that theology and philosophy have with politics and consequently have not been self-critical of the ideological significance of process metaphysics. Although by no means alone, an example of the latter can be found in the work of John Cobb. To his credit, Cobb was one of the first process theologians to recognize that "when political theology and liberation theology arose, process theology was subject to their criticisms hardly less than were the dominant theological movements."[27] Much of his recent and very valuable work is concerned with atoning for this earlier neglect. However, when we look closely at his writings, admirable as they are, we find that the issue of ideology in the context of process theology is sidestepped rather than confronted squarely. Without incorporating an ideology-critique as part of his methodology, we are presented with attempts to outline the implications of process philosophy for politics. Such an approach, which liberation theologians would reject as idealist, gives the impression that process philosophy is being treated as an objective system with no ideological significance of its own. On this assumption, the task of a process political theology consists in taking these antiseptic ideas and extrapolating from them a political theory suitable for our present situation.

An illuminating illustration of the possible consequences of ignoring process metaphysics' ideological significance can be found in Cobb's article, "The Political Implications of Whitehead's Philosophy." There he decides, instead of developing a political philosophy, to note some theses that are distinctive to Whitehead's thought although not unique to him. He writes: "The themes I treat are fundamental ones in Whitehead. I believe they could be illuminating in historical analysis and useful foundations for political theory."[28] The first theme concerns the relationship of the individual to society.

Liberal thought, he says, "conceives of people as individuals and of society secondarily as the result of arrangements among individuals. Marxism, on the other hand, views people as members of a class rather than as individuals."[29] Whitehead's view differs from both liberalism and Marxism. With liberalism Whitehead asserts the intrinsic value of the individual person; at the same time he agrees with Marx that individuality is rooted in society. By bringing together valuable insights advanced by Marxism and liberalism Cobb believes that Whitehead's philosophy can make a positive contribution to political theory. What is unfortunate about this discussion is the way in which Cobb seeks to outline various theses that might be useful as foundations for political theory without first addressing the possibility that a political ideology might itself be the foundation of these distinctive theses in Whitehead's thought. Because Cobb has not undertaken an ideology-critique of process philosophy he unwittingly ends up locating process philosophy's contribution to political theory precisely in those areas where modern liberalism made its original contribution almost a century ago. And this is so not only for the notion of individuality and sociability, which is in essence what Cobb is referring to here, but also for the other theses outlined by him, namely, Whitehead's theory of social development and his emphasis upon self-creativity and persuasion. A modern liberal ideology thus becomes for Cobb a deduction based upon universal metaphysical presuppositions. In contrast to the methodology of liberation theology, Cobb is seeking to derive his politics from his theology.

A similar failure to come to terms with the ideological significance of Whitehead's philosophy is evident in Cobb's support for Jürgen Moltmann's approach to politics. While discussing the criticisms levelled by liberation theologians against some European political theologians Cobb notes that Moltmann manages to keep the distinction between theology and politics clear and still provide "powerful images of the society for which we are to work and direction for our present practice."[30] These images are the "symbols" for the liberation of humanity from the "vicious circles of death."[31] Cobb describes Moltmann's analysis as "a beautiful summary of guiding images for practice for which a process theologian can only be grateful" and sees his own work as being in full harmony with these images.[32] Yet he immediately adds, correctly in my opinion, that "[c]ommitment to these symbols must be related more concretely to political theory and practice."[33] He also agrees with Moltmann's approach of "balanced criticism of both liberal capitalism and state socialism in their actual manifestations and practices. . . . "[34] Such an approach is considered to be "appropriate" for the North Atlantic situation. But political theologians must go on to examine the "theories underlying practice in both free market and socialist states."[35] Unfortunately, Cobb does not pursue these further tasks. In particular, he does not show how the symbols *already are* related to political theory. This is surprising given that ten years earlier Bonino concluded that what emerges from them is "one form of the liberal social-democratic project which progressive European theologians seem to cherish particularly."[36] Relating the symbols and political theory is treated as something that yet needs to be done; however, I maintain that such a relationship already exists. Nor does Cobb locate the reason for the harmony between these symbols and process theology. That reason, I suggest, lies in the similar ideologies implicit within them both, ideologies that need to be consciously accepted and defended in competition with other ideologies. However, among process theologians it remains largely latent and unjustified. This is again evident in Cobb's acceptance of Moltmann's program of "mutual criticism." He believes that process thought is able to bring together the positive features of liberalism and socialism alike. Yet Cobb appears unaware that the harmonization of these political theories into a "Liberal Socialism" was a central aim of the new liberals. In other words, modern liberalism is firmly entrenched in the middle ground which is here claimed for Whitehead.

Given the tendency of process philosophy to legitimate liberal political and economic institutions, it should come as no surprise that liberation theologians are not avidly pursuing a process political theology. Even George Pixley, a liberation theologian who explicitly acknowledges his indebtedness to process theology, has reservations concerning the ideological functioning of Whitehead's metaphysics. He speaks, for example, of the "latent counterrevolutionary tendencies of Whitehead's philosophy. . . . "[37] Elsewhere Pixley compares the work of Cobb and Jon Sobrino on Christology. He writes

> I am not capable of making a scientific analysis of the genesis of the ideological elements in process theology. We shall have to be content with this mere description of the ideological consequences of process theology as they appear by contrast with a work which is conscious of its working-class perspective.[38]

He then sums up his comparison by saying that

the fact that the conceptual tools of process thought are of metaphysical abstractness has taken its toll in Cobb's effort to reflect on the history which Christians take as normative. The intermediary steps that would have made such an analysis convincing have not been taken. Perhaps they are not possible from a process starting point. With their lack, the direct application of abstractions leads to ideological concealment, the inability to transcend a dominant-class perspective.[39]

Thus process theology will likely be suspected by liberation theologians of being yet one more "religious accompaniment of free enterprise, liberal, capitalist democracy."[40] This liberal ideology has supported structures that have kept Third World nations in positions of dependence and it is perceived to function today as an instrument of neocolonial domination. From their perspective, therefore, the findings of our investigation are negative—our study unmasks the implicit bourgeois ideology that is camouflaged as a universal metaphysics.

From the perspective of a process theologian, however, the findings of our investigation may be viewed as a positive contribution toward the development of a process political theology. This study provides process theologians with an important prolegomenon to the full development of a political theology, namely, a critical reflection upon the ideological commitment that informs Whitehead's and Hartshorne's metaphysics. Up to this point process thinkers have been generally blind to the ideology inherent within their philosophical tradition. If they are to develop successfully a fully critical political theology then the modern liberal ideology that informs process philosophy must be confronted. Process theologians can no longer allow a modern liberal democratic project to masquerade as the logical consequence of an objective metaphysical system.

# Notes

## CHAPTER 1

1. David L. Hall, *The Civilization of Experience: A Whiteheadian Theory of Culture* (New York: Fordham University Press, 1973), xiii.

2. Ibid., ix.

3. John B. Cobb, Jr., "The Political Implications of Whitehead's Philosophy," in *Process Philosophy and Social Thought*, ed. John B. Cobb, Jr., and W. Widick Schroeder (Chicago: Center for the Scientific Study of Religion, 1981), 12.

4. Robert W. Hoffert, "A Political Vision for the Organic Model," *Process Studies* 5/3 (1976): 176.

5. W. Widick Schroeder, "Structure and Context in Process Political Theory: A Constructive Formulation," in *Process Philosophy and Social Thought*, ed. John B. Cobb, Jr., and W. Widick Schroeder (Chicago: Center for the Scientific Study of Religion, 1981), 73.

6. Cobb, "The Political Implications of Whitehead's Philosophy," 12.

7. Douglas Sturm, "Process Thought and Political Theory: Implications of a Principle of Internal Relations," *The Review of Politics* 41/3 (1979): 375–76. Other scholars who employ process ideas without wedding themselves to them include David Hall, Robert Neville, and Delwin Brown to name a few.

8. Joseph Needham, "A Biologist's View of Whitehead," in *The Philosophy of Alfred North Whitehead*, ed. Paul Arthur Schilpp (Evanston: Northwestern University, 1941), 267.

9. Ibid., 268.

10. Although restricted in scope, a valuable contribution has been made by George Allan in "The Metaphysical Axioms and Ethics of Charles Hartshorne," *The Review of Metaphysics* 40/2 (1986): 271–304.

11. A. H. Johnson, *Whitehead's Philosophy of Civilization* (New York: Dover Publications, 1962). The material on social philosophy is a revised version of some earlier works including "The Social Philosophy of Alfred North Whitehead," *The Journal of Philosophy* 40/10 (1943): 261–71; "Whitehead and the Making of Tomorrow" *Philosophy and Phenomenological Research* 5 (1945): 398–406; and "A Philosophical Foundation for Democracy," *Ethics* 68/4 (July 1958): 281–85.

12. Hall, *Civilization of Experience*, x–xi.

13. Ibid., x.

14. Peter Clarke, *Liberals and Social Democrats* (Cambridge: Cambridge University Press, 1978), 109.

15. See Victor Lowe, *Alfred North Whitehead: The Man and His Work*, vol. 1 (Baltimore: The Johns Hopkins University Press, 1985), 161–63.

16. Andrew Vincent and Raymond Plant, *Philosophy, Politics and Citizenship: The Life and Thought of the British Idealists* (Oxford: Basil Blackwell, 1984), 135–36.

17. For example, the MP Sir John Gorst, an early supporter of the settlements, spoke of them as a fulfillment of "the obligation which the classes which possess culture and leisure have towards those who are less highly endowed" (Quotation taken from Vincent and Plant, *Philosophy, Politics and Citizenship*, 133.) See Whitehead's essay "The Rhythmic Claims of Freedom and Discipline" in *The Aims of Education* (New York: Macmillan Publishing Co., 1929): 29–41.

18. Lowe, *Alfred North Whitehead*, 313–14. Extracts from Whitehead's speech were published as a pamphlet entitled "Liberty and the Enfranchisement of Women," which has been republished in *Process Studies* 7/1 (1977): 37–38.

19. In addition to the books by Peter Clarke and by Vincent and Plant referred to earlier see Michael Freeden, *The New Liberalism: An Ideology of Social Reform* (Oxford: Clarendon Press, 1978); Stefan Collini, *Liberalism and Sociology: L.T. Hobhouse and Political Argument in England, 1880–1914* (Cambridge: Cambridge University Press, 1979); John Allett, *New Liberalism:. The Political Economy of J. A. Hobson* (Toronto: Toronto University Press, 1981); H. V. Emy, *Liberals, Radicals and Social Politics, 1892–1914* (Cambridge: Cambridge University Press, 1973).

20. A. Toynbee, "Are Radicals Socialists?" *Industrial Revolution* (London: Rivington, 1884). Found in Vincent and Plant, *Philosophy, Politics and Citizenship*, 35.

21. For a defense of the terms "collectivism" and "individualism" as organizational categories see Collini, *Liberalism and Sociology*, 13–50.

22. Gerald F. Gaus, *The Modern Liberal Theory of Man* (London: Croom Helm, 1983), 2–3.

23. We do know, however, that he was involved with the Liberal Club at Harvard which he helped found. See Eugene Peters, *Hartshorne and Neoclassical Metaphysics* (Lincoln: University of Nebraska Press, 1970), 6.

24. Charles Hartshorne, "An Economic Program for Religious Liberalism," *The Christian Century*, 5 June 1935, 762.

25. Hobhouse's philosophical views might be described more accurately as a blending of realist and idealist strands into an organic theory. As Collini says: "[H]e was most frequently described by his contemporaries as a 'Realist' in epistemology . . . whilst his metaphysical views came increasingly to be dominated by an organic concept of rationality which he recognized as Idealist in origin . . . " (Stefan Collini, "Hobhouse, Bosanquet and the State: Philosophical Idealism and Political Argument in England 1880–1918," *Past and Present* 72 [1976], 90, n. 16).

26. Gaus notes that in addition to their theory of human nature further arguments are necessary in order to connect this theory to practical social and political issues. It is the variety of ways in which this theory of human nature is linked to political prescriptions that explains the diversity among modern liberal political theories. (See Gaus, *Modern Liberal Theory*, 4.)

27. See L.T. Hobhouse, *Democracy and Reaction* (London: T. Fisher Unwin, 1904), 77.

28. Vincent and Plant, *Politics, Philosophy and Citizenship*, 44.

29. Lowe, *Alfred North Whitehead*, 130.

30. Collini, "Hobhouse, Bosanquet and the State," 110.

31. Hobhouse, *Liberalism* (New York: Oxford University Press, 1944 [1911]), 110.

32. L. T. Hobhouse, *The Metaphysical Theory Of the State* (London: George Allen and Unwin, 1918), 24.

33. L. T. Hobhouse, *The Rational Good* (London: Watts and Co., 1947), 137. There is, as Collini notes, a "historiographical dispute about the comparative strength of Hobhouse's affinities with Mill and with Green" (*Liberalism and Sociology*, 125). Collini concludes that "Hobhouse is much closer to Green. His account of the 'organic' conception of society, of the primacy of the common good, and of the basis of rights in the fulfillment of

functions often amount to little more than a restatement of the relevant sections from *The Principles of Political Obligation*" (Ibid., 126).

34. Collini, *Liberalism and Sociology*, 242.

35. For recent contributions to the comparative study of Whitehead and Hegel see George R. Lucas, Jr., ed., *Hegel and Whitehead: Contemporary Perspectives on Systematic Philosophy* (Albany: State University of New York Press, 1986); Joseph Bracken, "Spirit and Society: A Study of Two Concepts," *Process Studies* 15/4 (1986): 244–55; George R. Lucas, Jr., *Two Views of Freedom in Process Thought: A Study of Hegel and Whitehead* (Missoula: Scholars Press, 1979).

36. Vincent and Plant, *Politics, Philosophy, and Citizenship*, 48.

37. For discussions of both McTaggart and Dickinson see Lowe, *Alfred North Whitehead*, 126–32.

38. See Antoon Braeckman, "Whitehead and German Idealism: A Poetic Heritage," *Process Studies* 14/4 (1985): 265–86.

39. Lucas, *Two Views of Freedom*, 8.

40. Ibid.

41. For a discussion of the concept of ideology and its history see Jorge Larrain, *The Concept of Ideology* (Athens: The University of Georgia Press, 1979); Jorge Larrain, *Marxism and Ideology* (London: The Macmillan Press, 1983); David McLellan, *Ideology* (Minneapolis: University of Minnesota Press, 1986).

42. Karl Marx, *Preface to A Critique of Political Economy*, in *Karl Marx: Selected Writings*, ed. David McLellan (Oxford: Oxford University Press, 1977), 389.

43. Larrain, *The Concept of Ideology*, 46.

44. Karl Mannheim, *Ideology and Utopia* (New York: Harcourt, Brace & Company, 1936), 69.

45. Ibid.

46. Ibid., 239.

47. Ibid., 70

48. Ibid., 70–71.

49. Here I am borrowing some of the ideas of Colwyn Williamson as organizational principles for my own understanding of ideology. See Colwyn Williamson, "Ideology and the Problem of Knowledge," *Inquiry* 10 (1967): 121-38.

50. Williamson, "Ideology and the Problem of Knowledge," 135.

51. Larrain, *The Concept of Ideology*, 112.

52. C. B. Macpherson, *Democratic Theory: Essays in Retrieval* (Oxford: Clarendon Press, 1973), 157.

53. This idea is taken from Williamson who distinguishes between ideologies "which contain more or less direct recommendations as to political action," and bodies of thought which do not. He gives as an example Darwin's theory of the struggle for existence concerning which Marx says, " . . . it is splendid that Darwin again discovers among plants and animals his English society with its division of labour, competition, opening of new markets, 'inventions' and Malthusian struggle for existence." Williamson contends that Darwin's theory is not an ideology, but has ideological significance. See Williamson, "Ideology and the Problem of Knowledge," 134.

54. Hans Lenk, "Ideology, Technocracy and Knowledge Utilization" (unpublished paper, 1989), 8. This comment was made about ideologies in general, but it is a clear statement of what I have termed the ideological significance of a body of thought.

55. Williamson, "Ideology and the Problem of Knowledge," 131.

56. John B. Cobb, Jr., "Points of Contact Between Process Theology and Liberation Theology in Matters of Faith and Justice," *Process Studies* 14/2 (1985): 125.

57. Ibid., 127.

58. Ibid., 134.

# CHAPTER 2

1. Those who are interested in a more thorough introduction to the philosophy of Whitehead are encouraged to consult the following standard works: William A. Christian, *An Interpretation of Whitehead's Metaphysics* (New Haven: Yale University Press, 1959); Elizabeth M. Kraus, *The Metaphysics of Experience: A Companion to Whitehead's Process and Reality* (New York: Fordham University Press, 1979); Ivor Leclerc, *Whitehead's Metaphysics: An Introductory Exposition* (New Jersey: Humanities Press, 1958); John B. Cobb, Jr., *A Christian Natural Theology Based on the Thought of Alfred North Whitehead*

(London: Lutterworth Press, 1966); and Victor Lowe, *Understanding Whitehead* (Baltimore: The Johns Hopkins University Press, 1959).

2. John B. Cobb, Jr., and David Ray Griffin, *Process Theology: An Introductory Exposition* (Belfast: Christian Journals Limited, 1977), 14.

3. Leclerc, *Whitehead's Metaphysics*, 116.

4. It should be pointed out that this internal relatedness is what Hartshorne terms "asymmetrical." L. Ford writes:

> This is the freedom of the universe: the past does not entail the present, although the present entails the past out of which it grows. The relation between past and present is external with respect to the past, and internal with respect to the present. This doctrine of asymmetrical relatedness . . . preserves Whitehead's . . . commitment to pluralism and freedom.

(Lewis Ford, "An Appraisal of Whiteheadian Nontheism," in *Southern Journal of Philosophy*, 15/1 [Spring, 1977]: 32).

5. There are also more complex types of feelings, that is, comparative feelings such as propositional feelings (PR 164[249]) but these are actually made up of the two basic types.

6. PR 44(70). See PR 22(32), 23(34), 149(226). The doctrine of eternal objects has been one aspect of Whitehead's thought that has come in for particularly heavy criticism. Hartshorne, for example, wants to restrict the eternal to the categorical universals which God always envisages and somehow applies. Specific qualities, however, are not eternally distinct, fully determinate entities. (See Charles Hartshorne, "Whitehead's Idea of God," in *The Philosophy of Alfred North Whitehead*, ed. Paul Arthur Schlipp [Evanston: Northwestern University, 1941], 557–58). Other criticisms can be found in Victor Lowe, *Understanding Whitehead*, 317–21, and Edward Pols, *Whitehead's Metaphysics: A Critical Examination of Process and Reality* (Carbondale: Southern Illinois University Press, 1967), 143–58.

7. Christian, *An Interpretation of Whitehead's Metaphysics*, 204.

8. A fuller discussion of the differences between the Platonic forms and Whitehead's eternal objects can be found in Christian, *An Interpretation of Whitehead's Metaphysics*, 196–200.

9. PR 46(73). See PR 32(48). The dipolar nature of God and his mode of activity in the world will be discussed more fully below.

10. Russell L. Kleinbach, *Marx Via Process: Whitehead's Potential Contribution to Marxian Social Theory* (Washington: University Press of America, 1982), 23. See Dermot A. Lane, *Foundations for a Social Theology: Praxis, Process and Salvation* (Dublin: Gill and Macmillan, 1984), 108.

11. D. D. Raphael, *Hobbes: Morals and Politics* (London: George Allen and Unwin, 1977), 66.

12. Lucas, *Two Views of Freedom in Process Thought: A Study of Hegel and Whitehead* (Missoula: Scholars Press, 1979), 17.

13. For a criticism of Whitehead's philosophy precisely on the grounds that it cannot provide for true freedom see Pols's *Whitehead's Metaphysics: A Critical Examination of Process and Reality.* For a response to Pols's criticisms see Lucas, *Two Views of Freedom,* 36–40.

14. We might ask in what sense an actual occasion is genuinely creative. Clearly Whitehead allows for the freedom to *choose* from a finite selection of possibilities for self-realization, but is this the same thing as genuine creativity? This problem arises because of Whitehead's theory of eternal objects. Hartshorne may be better equipped to account for the genuine creativity of finite agents because of his rejection of eternal objects and his identification of possibility with indeterminateness.

15. Cobb, *A Christian Natural Theology,* 96.

16. Lucas attempts to deal with this situation by insisting that "while initially 'conformal,' the actual occasion is *not* entirely passive. Instead, *it actively prehends* . . . the ideal envisagement of possibilities in God's Primordial Nature, resulting in the individual subjective aim governing that concrescence" (*Two Views of Freedom,* 28). He thus concludes: "As an individual instance of the generic activity of creativity, every actual occasion would begin, *not* passively, but *actively,* as instinctive "grasping" both for data and for design. . . . 'Creativity' . . . itself serves as a sufficient 'reason' or explanation for concrescence" (29). Although Lucas himself does not apply his interpretation in this way, I suggest that he could explain the development of the subjective aim by a similar reference to the power of creativity which originates every occasion.

17. Cobb, *A Christian Natural Theology,* 154.

18. With fully determinate ideal possibilities there would appear to be no reason for God not providing an occasion with a particular ideal aim. This would not be the case, however, if we were to abandon Whitehead's theory of eternal objects. Hartshorne has in fact done just this and, as we shall see in the following chapter, his conception of divine agency can be understood in a way similar to that suggested here.

19. See Delwin Brown, *To Set at Liberty: Christian Faith and Human Freedom* (Maryknoll, New York: Orbis Books, 1981), 32–33, 56.

20. The parallels between Whitehead's conception of God and certain platonic notions are striking. Like the Demiurge, God is not the cause of either the eternal objects (Being) or the actual occasions (Becoming). God is the cause only of order in the "realm of Becoming"; the deity is a

"craftsman" who "operates" upon materials that were not created *ex nihilo*. The divine "operation" consists in supplying ideal consequents to the actual occasions on the basis of God's envisagement of the forms. Again, like the Demiurge, the limitation of God is his goodness (RM 153). Through the divine immanence God's own "unchanged consistency of character" is imposed on every phase of the creative process. Evil is therefore not the consequence of God's activity, but owing to the limitations with which God must operate, namely, the freedom or creative indetermination of the actual occasions. See Laurence F. Wilmot, *Whitehead and God: Prolegomena to Theological Reconstruction* (Waterloo, Ontario: Wilfrid Laurier University Press, 1979) and Ivor Leclerc, "The Problem of God in Whitehead's System," *Process Studies* 14/4 (Winter 1985): 301-15.

21. Unlike those who hold that Whitehead made no substantial changes in his concept of God after *Religion in the Making*, I would argue that *Religion in the Making* is closer in thought to *Science and the Modern World* than it is to *Process and Reality*. Cf. Cobb, *A Christian Natural Theology*, 149. In his study of the development of Whitehead's thought Ford has arrived at a similar conclusion. See Lewis Ford in *The Emergence of Whitehead's Metaphysics: 1925-1929* (Albany: State University of New York Press, 1984), 140-47.

22. Thus I also disagree with Wilmot who maintains that because each occasion "enters into and is transmuted in the nature of God, this ideal or possible consequent as it stands in God's vision is also added to the total situation . . . " (*Whitehead and God*, 28). I find no evidence in *Religion in the Making* that actual occasions "enter into" God's nature. The transmutation of evil occurs primordially in the divine ordering of all possibilities. It is there that it is met with a novel consequent which enters the world because of its relevance to the actual course of events. There is no consequent nature because Whitehead does not yet see God as requiring completion: God is the one systematic, complete fact.

23. There are passages that assert undeniably a parallelism between God's primordial and consequent natures and the mental and physical poles of a finite actual occasion, for example, PR 87-88(134-35), 345(524). Whitehead's language, however, is not consistent. As I shall argue below, there are other passages in which Whitehead offers a more Hegelian analysis of the consequent nature as the synthesis of the primordial nature and the world. Moreover, the objection that my interpretation of Whitehead makes God unique among actual entities loses its force when it is remembered that Whitehead repeatedly treats God as an exception, for example, God is a nontemporal actual entity who originates in a conceptual vision of possibilities and achieves satisfaction without perishing.

24. Although the first summary explicitly refers to the "threefold creative act" which is repeated in the first three phases of the final summary, Whitehead adds a fourth phase in which the "perfected actuality passes back into the temporal world . . . " (PR 351[532]). The idea that God's consequent nature affects the world, though hinted at here and elsewhere, was left

undeveloped by Whitehead himself. Throughout the vast majority of *Process and Reality* and *Adventures of Ideas* he restricts the divine activity to the provision of an initial aim on the basis of the primordial envisagement of possibilities. It has been later process thinkers who, in trying to deal with the ambiguities in Whitehead's thought, have developed a theory of divine activity through the consequent nature of God (often accompanied by a reformulation of the idea of God along the lines of a living person as opposed to an actual entity). It is my estimation that with this notion Whitehead has introduced a red herring into his system which is best eliminated. It is an ambiguity in his thought which stems from his uncertain development of a dipolar conception of deity.

25. Kraus, *The Metaphysics of Experience*, 65.

26. Franklin Gamwell makes a similar claim: "[T]he coordinated life of an individual may, for the most part, be considered analogous to a concrete experience or activity" (Franklin I. Gamwell, *Beyond Preference: Liberal Theories of Independent Associations* [Chicago: University of Chicago Press, 1984], 138). A. H. Johnson, in his writings on Whitehead and civilization, also employs (but I believe much too carelessly) a form of argument from analogy. See Johnson, "The Social Philosophy of Alfred North Whitehead," *The Journal of Philosophy* 40/10 (1943): 266–70; "A Philosophical Foundation for Democracy," *Ethics* 68/4 (July 1958): 283–84.

27. George Allan, "Process Social Philosophy: The Continuing Conversation," *Process Studies* 15/4 (1986): 241.

28. Lowe, *Understanding Whitehead*, 245. A few pages later he adds: "I suggest that thinking about the patterns discernible equally in—to take one example—the conditions of the growth of human individuals or societies, and the conditions of the growth of forests, is at the bottom of Whitehead's whole constructive effort" (p. 249).

## CHAPTER 3

1. Charles Hartshorne, "Contingency and the New Era in Metaphysics (II)," *The Journal of Philosophy* 29 (18 Aug. 1932): 465.

2. Ibid.

3. Charles Hartshorne, "Causal Necessities: An Alternative to Hume," *The Philosophical Review* 63 (Oct. 1954): 491.

4. Ibid., 485.

5. Ibid., 484.

6. Charles Hartshorne, "Contingency and the New Era in Metaphysics (I)," *The Journal of Philosophy* 29 (4 Aug. 1932): 423.

7. See CSPM 59. A useful analysis of the differences between Hartshorne and Whitehead on the nature of possibility can be found in the articles by David Griffin and Lewis Ford in *Two Process Philosophers: Hartshorne's Encounter with Whitehead* (Tallahassee, Florida: American Academy of Religion, 1973).

8. For a critique of Hartshorne's conception of possibility and omniscience see Richard E. Creel, *Divine Impassibility: An Essay in Philosophical Theology* (Cambridge: Cambridge University Press, 1986), 35–63. While agreeing with Hartshorne that a thing cannot be known as actual before it becomes actual (p.45), Creel holds that

> there is no reason to think that he [God] would not know in advance of every actualization of an individual every property and relation that any individual might instantiate. This is possible because God knows possibilities in the mode of continua, and to know a continuum perfectly . . . is to know exhaustively and simultaneously an infinite range of possibilities of a certain type. . . . (p.47)

9. Charles Hartshorne, "Whitehead's Idea of God," in *The Philosophy of Alfred North Whitehead*, ed. Paul Arthur Schilpp (Evanston: Northwestern University, 1941): 558.

10. See Hartshorne, "Whitehead's Idea of God," 556: "If all the 'forms of definiteness,' each perfectly definite in itself, are eternally given to God, it is not altogether clear to me what actualization accomplishes."

11. While Hartshorne's identification of actuality with definiteness appears innocuous enough, Eugene Peters argues that it "actually imperils the philosophy of process" (Eugene Peters, "Hartshorne on Actuality," *Process Studies* 7/3 [Fall 1977]: 202). As we have seen, actuality is determinate and possibility is determinable. Given this, Peters asks where the process of transition is to be found and whose decision leads to the realization of new definiteness. The past, being fully determinate, is incapable of action, and yet there is in the present "*no actuality* which is coming to be or developing, none by whose decision-making new definiteness is being realized" (Ibid., 201). Hartshorne rejects Whitehead's theory of genetic succession within an actual occasion. For Whitehead it is the actual occasion that is the locus of decision by which the multitude of feelings in incomplete phases are united in a single feeling of satisfaction. "If there is no such succession," writes Ford, "of indeterminate phases contrasting with the final determinate satisfaction, it is difficult to see how becoming can be understood as the creation of determinate being, or be that which must perish in order for being to be" (Ford, "Whitehead's Differences from Hartshorne," *Two Process Philosophers* [Tallahassee, Florida: American Academy of Religion, 1973], 74). It is just such an

explanation of the transition from possibility to actuality that Hartshorne's metaphysic does not appear to provide.

12. Hartshorne, "Causal Necessities: An Alternative to Hume," 497.

13. It is generally held that for Whitehead the divine dipolarity is that of an actual entity: the primordial nature is analogous to its conceptual pole and the consequent nature is analogous to its physical pole. There is good textual support for this interpretation. I have argued that it remains possible to bring Whitehead closer to Hartshorne by holding that the consequent nature is God as concrete and fully actual and as such inclusive of the abstract primordial nature.

14. Charles Hartshorne, "Whitehead's Novel Intuition," in *Alfred North Whitehead: Essays on His Philosophy*, ed. George L. Kline (Englewood Cliffs: Prentice Hall, 1963), 23.

15. See Charles Hartshorne, "Ideal Knowledge Defines Reality: What Was True in Idealism," *Journal of Philosophy* 43/21 (10 Oct. 1946): 577.

16. Griffin, "Hartshorne's Differences from Whitehead," *Two Process Philosophers* (Tallahassee, Florida: American Academy of Religion, 1973), 51.

17. In CSPM 119 Hartshorne specifically says that "There are not subjects *and* objects but only objects in subjects, . . . not God and the world but the world in God. . . . " The first clause is perfectly correct, but the additional claim overlooks the fact that there is the class of finite subjects that are not yet objects of divine knowledge. (See Santiago Sia, *God in Process Thought* [Dordrecht: Martinus Nijhoff, 1985], 90, n.40.) The problem appears to stem from the pluralistic nature of process theology. This might preserve the freedom of the individual, but perhaps at the cost of making God less than the Whole. As we shall see later, Hegel grasped the other horn of the dilemma through his identification of God and the world.

18. William Lad Sessions, "Hartshorne's Early Philosophy," in *Two Process Philosophers: Hartshorne's Encounter with Whitehead*, ed. Lewis Ford (Tallahassee: American Academy of Religion, 1972), 24.

19. Charles Hartshorne, "The Social Theory of Feelings," *The Southern Journal of Philosophy* 3 (Summer 1965): 87.

20. Ibid.

21. Ibid., 88. This is explained elsewhere in terms of the absence of negative prehensions in God's experience. "[S]uch prehensions are all that prevent ordinary prehending from capturing the complete immediacy of past entities" (Charles Hartshorne, "The Dipolar Conception of Deity," *Review of Metaphysics* 21/2 [December 1967]: 287). Hartshorne mistakenly takes "negative prehensions" to mean "inadequate" prehensions (Ibid.). This is understandable given his rejection of eternal objects, for in Whitehead's

theory a negative prehension is the exclusion of an eternal object from effectiveness. Negative prehensions are being confused with the necessity for abstraction by finite subjects. Yet, as I hope to show on another occasion, there are good reasons for believing that Whitehead advocated an identity of subjective form between subject and object.

22. Eugene Peters, *Hartshorne and Neoclassical Metaphysics* (Lincoln: University of Nebraska Press, 1970), 120.

23. Hartshorne explicitly says that "God does not 'suffer' simply as we do; but no more does He rejoice simply as we do. He does not suffer from fear of his own destruction or degradation. . . . I devoutly believe that God suffers, as he also rejoices, through sheer 'sympathy' with us in our sorrows and joys. No doubt this is analogical language" (Charles Hartshorne, "Tillich's Doctrine of God,"in *The Theology of Paul Tillich*, ed. Charles W. Kegley and Robert Bretall [New York: The Macmillan Co., 1952], 191). How does this claim that he is using analogical language fit with his belief that God's omniscience entails his *complete* knowledge of the world?

24. Peters, "Hartshorne on Actuality," 204.

25. Creel raises an interesting and related problem when he questions whether Hartshorne's conception of qualities allows for God to experience the same feeling that a finite occasion experiences. As Hartshorne says in CSPM 64: "[T]he precise qualities of particulars are themselves particular and *unrepeatable*. Only abstract, more or less generalized traits are repeatable" (emphasis added). Four pages earlier he also asserts that prehension is "a theory of *literal identity*, the same entities entering over and over again into subsequent entities" (emphasis added). It would seem that if God has the same qualitative experience then this calls into question the uniqueness of qualities; but if God only experiences a similar experience, then his claim that God's knowledge defines reality is jeopardized. See Creel, *Divine Impassibility*, 60; Ford, "Whitehead's Differences from Hartshorne," 64.

26. Sia, *God in Process Thought*, 78.

27. For a defense of Aquinas against the charge that he presents a tyrant conception of deity see Hugo Meynell, "The Theology of Hartshorne," *Journal of Theological Studies* 24 (1973): 155.

28. Hartshorne, "Tillich's Doctrine of God," 183.

29. Charles Hartshorne, "A Philosopher's Assessment of Christianity," in *Religion and Culture: Essays in Honor of Paul Tillich*, ed. Walter Leibrecht (New York: Harper and Brothers, 1959), 174.

30. Charles Hartshorne, "Whitehead and Berdyaev: Is There Tragedy in God?" *The Journal of Religion* 37 (April 1957): 74.

31. Cf. Schubert M. Ogden, *The Reality of God and Other Essays* (London: SCM Press, 1967), 180.

32. There appears to be a problem with the idea that God imposes natural laws on the universe, and that is, how can Hartshorne at the same time hold that natural laws are *statistical* in nature? By the divine action God determines a particular range of real possibilities. This would appear to be a fairly definite limit even though within the range there is scope for further determination. If this limitation is then thought to be the laws of nature, why are not the laws inviolable rather than statistical? It seems absurd to say that some individuals, the occasional atomic particle, can disobey the laws of nature if those laws prescribe what is possible.

33. Charles Hartshorne, "Efficient Causality in Aristotle and St. Thomas," *Journal of Religion* 25 (1945): 30.

34. Charles Hartshorne, "Politics and the Metaphysics of Freedom," in *Enquête sur la liberté, Fédération internationale des sociétés de philosophie*. Publié avec le concours de l'u.n.e.s.c.o. (Hermann and Cie, Editeurs, Paris, 1953), 79.

# CHAPTER 4

1. Lewis S. Ford, *The Emergence of Whitehead's Metaphysics 1925–1929* (Albany: State University of New York Press, 1984), 23.

2. Ivor Leclerc, "Individual and Society in Metaphysical Perspective" in *Person and Society*, ed. George F. McLean (Lanham: University Press of America, 1988), 40. In an interesting argument Leclerc claims that the metaphysics that underlay the new conception of nature which emerged in the seventeenth century was "founded in the renaissance resuscitation of Neoplatonism, in opposition to the antecedent domination of Scholastic Aristotelianism" (Ibid., 39). Yet we should not overlook the importance of the Greek atomists, Democritus and Epicurus, to the budding metaphysics. In his book *Seventeenth Century Metaphysics*, W. von Leyden argues that the process that led to the new scientific cosmology included the replacement of an organic conception of nature with the view that natural phenomena should be understood on analogy with a machine. "Accordingly, on this view, causes were antecedent motions and, as such efficient causes: all physical change was explained as the effect of the motions and impacts of matter in space and time" (p.5). This, coupled with the fact that efficient rather than final causation was found to be compatible with Bacon's "instrumental" conception of science (p.202), led to a revival of the materialist doctrines of Democritus and Epicurus who "explained natural processes as the effect of the locomotion of unchanging and indivisible particles of matter" (p.6).

3. Leyden, *Seventeenth Century Metaphysics: An Examination of Some Main Concepts and Themes* (London: Gerald Duckworth and Co., 1968), 133.

4. C. B. Macpherson, *The Political Theory of Possessive Individualism: Hobbes to Locke* (Oxford: Oxford University Press, 1962), 30. Macpherson notes that the resolutive element of Hobbes's methodology is often over-looked by readers of *Leviathan*. This is understandable given that Hobbes begins *Leviathan* with the result of that initial process and only takes the reader through the compositive part. Macpherson argues that the whole construction of Hobbes's theory had its source in his thinking about civilized man (Ibid., 31). He concludes that "Hobbes's theory of the social motion of man requires the assumption of a certain kind of society . . . " (Ibid., 16), namely, the possessive market society of seventeenth-century England. In other words, Hobbes did not simply appropriate seventeenth-century metaphysics and then construct a political theory that cohered with it; he made prior assumptions about human nature based upon his perceptions and experiences of contemporary English society which were important premises in the compositive part of his work.

5. Thomas Hobbes, *Leviathan* (Oxford: Basil Blackwell, 1946), 82.

6. Ibid. 112. Emphasis removed.

7. Quotation of Hobbes found in R. S. Peters, "Hobbes, Thomas," in *The Encyclopedia of Philosophy* (New York: Macmillan Publishing Co., 1967) ed. Paul Edwards, Vol. 6, 40.

8. Charles Birch and John B. Cobb, Jr., *The Liberation of Life* (Cambridge: Cambridge University Press, 1981), 88.

9. Ford, *Emergence*, 31.

10. See F.H. Bradley, *Appearance and Reality* (Oxford: The Clarendon Press, 1959), 513–19.

11. D. C. Phillips, *Holistic Thought and Social Science* (London: The Macmillan Press, 1977), 8–9.

12. Ford argues that in his early metaphysical writings Whitehead subscribed to a doctrine of mutual internal relatedness among simultaneous events (*Emergence*, 27–31). It is clear that in his mature metaphysics he adopts a theory of asymmetrical relations. Contemporary occasions are not able to prehend one another, and while present occasions are internally related to the past, the past is externally related to the present.

13. George Lucas, *Two Views of Freedom in Process Thought* (Chico, Calif.: Scholars Press, 1979), 156–57.

14. John B. Cobb, Jr., *Process Theology as Political Theology* (Manchester: Manchester University Press, 1982), 98. See also the discussion of process theology and privatization in Lane, *Foundations for a Social Theology*, 104–105.

15. Lucas, *Two Views of Freedom*, 34. Nancy Frankenberry makes a similar assessment: "The significance of the doctrine of asymmetrical relatedness is its demonstration of the way in which real internal relations among the 'parts' within the 'whole' do not compromise freedom. It is thus a doctrine which offers holism without determinism" (Nancy Frankenberry, "The Emergent Paradigm and Divine Causation," *Process Studies* 13/2 [1983]: 204).

16. On Whitehead's use of microscopic/macroscopic and microcosmic/macrocosmic see the editors' note in PR 401–402.

17. A parallel discussion is found in AI 273–74: "The discipline of a regiment inheres in the regiment in a different mode from its inherence in the individual soldiers" (p. 74). This is another way of saying that the effect is greater than the sum of the causes.

18. Frankenberry, "The Emergent Paradigm," 203. Leclerc likewise says that "there is a whole constituted by the interacting which is something more than, and thus not adequately analyzable as the mere arithmetical sum of the interacting subjects. Moreover, that whole has a character or definiteness which is analyzable as the definiteness of the relational interacting" (Leclerc, "Individual and Society," 47).

19. Frankenberry, "The Emergent Paradigm," 204.

20. Phillips, *Holistic Thought*, 16.

21. Cf. David L. Hall, *The Civilization of Experience: A Whiteheadian Theory of Culture* (New York: Fordam University Press, 1973), 68: "The Whiteheadian conception of society agrees with Hegel's organic view in that it holds that human society expresses a natural *telos*, but it conflicts with the Hegelian view in holding that this *telos* has its locus in the individual human beings of the society, not in the society itself." This conclusion depends upon the "ontological distinction" he asserts exists between a human individual and a society of such individuals. However, in making this contrast Hall commits the fallacy of misplaced concreteness. A human being is as much a society of occasions exemplifying a particular complex social order as is a group of such "individuals." Hall also appears to believe that if a society had a *telos* not identical with that of the parts this would lead to each individual citizen being treated as "an instrument with a purpose to be defined wholly in terms of the *telos* of the state" (Ibid.). This overlooks the fact that organic or collectivist theories of society are not all the same as we shall see below.

22. Ford, *Emergence*, 32.

23. Charles Hartshorne, "Organic and Inorganic Wholes," *Philosophy and Phenomenological Research* 3/2 (December 1942): 127.

24. See RSP 55–56 for a defense of this claim.

25. In a passage that closely resembles an argument of Hartshorne's in LP 193, Whitehead says that the bodies of higher animals have some resemblances to the complex societies of some insects (MT 35–36). However, whereas the individual insect has a greater capacity for adaptation than does the whole community, an animal has more power of adaptation than its bodily parts. Hartshorne argues that because the parts of the insect community display a more unified existence than does the community itself, the community is not a true organism. Whitehead makes no such deduction.

26. Gerald F. Gaus, *The Modern Liberal Theory of Man* (London: Croom Helm, 1983), 7. Hobhouse is particularly keen to argue that such changes are true developments within the liberal tradition rather than deviations from liberalism. See L. T. Hobhouse, *Democracy and Reaction* (London: T. Fisher Unwin, 1904), 204–44.

27. Michael Freeden, *The New Liberalism: An Ideology of Social Reform* (Oxford: Clarenden Press, 1978), 4.

28. See Michael Freeden, "Biological and Evolutionary Roots of the New Liberalism in England," *Political Theory* 4/4 (1976): 471–90.

29. Stefan Collini, *Liberalism and Sociology: L. T. Hobhouse and Political Argument in England 1880–1914* (Cambridge: Cambridge University Press, 1979), 154. See James Allen Rogers, "Darwinism and Social Darwinism," *Journal of the History of Ideas* 33 (1972): 265–80.

30. Ibid., 155.

31. Gaus, *Modern Liberal Theory*, 73.

32. L. T. Hobhouse *Social Development: Its Nature and Conditions* (London: George Allen and Unwin, 1966 [1924]), 65.

33. L. T. Hobhouse, *Liberalism* (Oxford: Oxford University Press, 1944 [1911]), 125.

34. L. T. Hobhouse, *Social Development*, 65. See PR 90–91 (139).

35. L. T. Hobhouse, *The Elements of Social Justice* (London: George Allen and Unwin, 1922), 28. Emile Durkheim provides an example of a sociologist who held that "social facts" are "external" to the substratum of individuals, and which have an objective existence as an "independent organic reality with its own laws, its own development and its own life" (Tom Campbell, *Seven Theories of Human Society*, [Oxford: Clarendon Press, 1981], 144). This comes out clearly in *The Rules of Sociological Method*: "If . . . the synthesis *sui*

*generis* which every society constitutes yields new phenomena, differing from those which take place in the individual consciousness, we must also admit that these facts reside exclusively in the very society itself which produces them, and not in its parts—that is, its members" (Found in Anthony Giddens, *Emile Durkheim: Selected Writings*, [Cambridge: Cambridge University Press, 1972], 69).

36. L. T. Hobhouse, *Social Evolution and Political Theory* (Port Washington, N.Y.: Kennikat Press, 1968 [1911]), 96. Freeden argues that the failure by Hobhouse to posit a social mind and to grant society an autonomous existence limited his ability to develop fully the new liberal vision. This distinction was left to J. A. Hobson who criticizes Hobhouse because he "does not carry his central organic mind quite far enough, as, for instance, when he says that 'there is no thought except in the mind of an individual thinker'"(Hobson, Review of Hobhouse's *Social Evolution and Political Theory*. Found in Freeden, *New Liberalism*, 105). This highlights the fact that organicism is a broad term capable of bearing a variety of connotations.

37. Hobhouse, *Elements of Social Justice*, 29.

38. T. H. Green, *Prolegomena to Ethics*, ed. A. C. Bradley (Oxford: The Clarendon Press, 1890), 193.

39. Hobhouse, *Elements of Social Justice*, 30.

40. Green, *Prolegomena*, 193.

41. Hobhouse, *Elements of Social Justice*, 31.

42. Hobhouse, *Democracy and Reaction*, 132.

43. Hobhouse, *Liberalism*, 126; *Elements of Social Justice*, 37. For a discussion of Green's theory of rights see John Roberts, "T. H. Green," in *Conceptions of Liberty in Political Philosophy*, ed. Zbigniew Pelczynski and John Gray (London: Athlone Press, 1984), 243–59; A. J. M. Milne, *The Social Philosophy of English Idealism* (London: George Allen and Unwin, 1962), 127–30.

44. Hobhouse, *Elements of Social Justice*, 39. Collini points out that Hobhouse makes a significant distinction between what has been called "negative" and "positive" rights. Negative rights guarantee an individual protection against interference from others in one's freedom to do something ("forbearance"), while positive rights guarantee a person the receipt of certain benefits from others ("aid"). The former are usually emphasized by Individualists, the latter by Collectivists. Hobhouse uses the latter to argue for welfare measures which would provide each person with the necessary conditions for full self-development. See Collini, *Liberalism and Sociology*, 125. According to Peter Weiler, this view of rights as a positive power for

self-development was a restatement of the position advanced previously by T. H. Green. See Peter Weiler, "The New Liberalism of L. T. Hobhouse," *Victorian Studies* 16/2 (1972): 150.

45. L. T. Hobhouse, *Development and Purpose: An Essay Towards a Philosophy of Evolution*, rev. ed. (London: Macmillan, 1927), 179.

46. Hobhouse, *Social Development*, 68–69.

47. Freeden emphasizes that this notion of the common good, which is Hobhouse's brand of collectivism, "never implied more than harmony and co-ordination between individual and social claims" (Freeden, *New Liberalism*, 93).

48. Hobhouse, *Democracy and Reaction*, 126–27.

49. Hobhouse, *Elements of Social Justice*, 30.

50. Hobhouse, *Democracy and Reaction*, 119.

51. Hobhouse, *Elements of Social Justice*, 24.

52. Ibid., 23.

53. Ibid.

54. Ibid., 24.

55. Hobhouse, *Democracry and Reaction*, 136. Hobhouse adds: "[T]hough the common morality of mankind does not express final truth, it does express the rough truth which long experience yields" (Ibid., 135–36).

56. Ibid., 137.

57. Hobhouse expressly states that "Politics must be subordinate to Ethics . . . " (*Elements of Social Justice*, 13–14). See also L. T. Hobhouse, "The Ethical Basis of Collectivism," *International Journal of Ethics* 8/2 (1898): 143.

58. Freeden, *New Liberalism*, 49.

59. Hobhouse, *Elements of Social Justice*, 31.

60. Douglas Sturm, "Process Thought and Political Theory: Implications of a Principle of Internal Relations," *The Review of Politics* 41/3 (1979): 399.

61. Hobhouse, *Social Evolution*, 199.

62. See Green, *Prolegomena*, 208.

63. A comparison of Hartshorne and Mill can be found in John C. Moskop, "Mill and Hartshorne," *Process Studies* 10/1–2 (Spring-Summer 1980): 18–33. A challenge to Moskop's comparison has recently been published by Thomas A. Nairn, "Hartshorne and Utilitarianism: A Response to Moskop," *Process Studies* 17/3 (1988): 170–80.

64. Charles Hartshorne, "Beyond Enlightened Self-Interest: A Metaphysics of Ethics," *Ethics* 84 (1973–74): 214.

65. Elsewhere Hartshorne says that in order to ascertain what is good "ethics must lean upon aesthetics. For the only good that is intrinsically good, good in itself, is good experience, and the criteria for this are aesthetic" ("Beyond Enlightened Self-Interest," 214).

66. Although Hobhouse did not use specifically aesthetic concepts to explain his theory of value, he did define "the good" in terms of a harmony of interconnected parts and evil as the experience of disharmony. Thus there are significant points of contact between Hobhouse's social ethics and the value theory of process thought.

67. Like Mill, both Whitehead and Hartshorne claim that a certain kind of experience is the ultimate end of human action. For Mill this was happiness, while for process philosophy it is the experience of intense satisfaction. However, as Moskop points out, whereas Mill defends his principle of utility on the basis of human psychology, "Hartshorne views it as an implication of a Whiteheadian metaphysical system which is held to be valid for all *possible* states of the universe. . . . Unlike Mill, then, Hartshorne does not merely assert the fundamentality of happiness for motivation; rather, he derives this conclusion from a metaphysical system in which the concept of experience figures prominently in the basic structure of reality" (Moskop, "Mill and Hartshorne," 25–26).

68. Hartshorne, "Beyond Enlightened Self-Interest," 214. See "The Dipolar Conception of Deity," *Review of Metaphysics* 21/2 (December 1967): 286. The question that neither Whitehead nor Hartshorne adequately address is whether morality is concerned primarily with consequences or with motives. In RSP 44 Hartshorne explicitly says that "ethics is concerned with consequences or with justice to others. . . . " Similarly, in the passage quoted he specifically states that an ethically good act contributes to harmony in spectators (consequences). But it also implies that an act is good whether or not it enhances the possibilities for intense experiences in the community (motive). This latter consequence further depends on whether the action was "wise and fortunate *as well as good.*" In CSPM 308 he states that the good will "enriches one's own present experience and in its consequences *tends to enrich* future experiences . . . " (emphasis added). Similarly Whitehead can say both that an actual entity is beautiful by reason of its "contribution to the perfection of the subjective form" of another occasion, and that it "may be beautiful by reason of the Beauty that *would be* realized by a fortunate association with other data combined with a fortunate exercise of spontaneity

by the occasion prehending it" (AI 328–29; emphasis added). This issue is discussed by Belaief in "A Whiteheadian Account of Value and Identity," *Process Studies* 5/1 (Spring 1975), and by Gamwell in "Happiness and the Public World: Beyond Political Liberalism," *Process Studies* 8/1 (Spring 1978).

69. I believe this to be the case despite the fact that he explicitly refers to the common good. Having mentioned the need for social change and having denied that the impetus for such change should be expected from those whose positions in life are comfortable he adds: "Yet even they are under obligation . . . to try to understand that their own needs are not the measure of the common good and that some discontent of a vicarious sort would become them" ("Beyond Enlightened Self-Interest," 216). The problem is what meaning he can give to the "common good" on the level of human societies apart from the mere sum of individual goods.

70. See Hartshorne, "Beyond Enlightened Self-Interest," 208–209.

71. Ibid, 209–210.

72. Hobhouse, *Democracy and Reaction,* 119.

73. Notice that social order is rated solely on the basis of its instrumental value in promoting strength of experience in individuals, whereas individuals are held to be both ends and means. Yet what is the end to which individuals are means? That end is a high-grade type of *order*. This implies that in society there is a reciprocal relationship between parts and whole—each promoting the full realization of the other—and that social order is in some sense itself an end.

74. Here I dissent from Beer's claim that "The metaphysics of this [Whitehead's] philosophy is collectivist, but its ethics and politics are strenuously individualist" (Samuel H. Beer, *The City of Reason* [Cambridge, Mass: Harvard University Press, 1949], 201).

75. Hobhouse, *Social Justice*, 30.

76. This point has been persuasively argued by Franklin I. Gamwell in *Beyond Preference: Liberal Theories of Independent Associations* (Chicago: University of Chicago Press, 1984).

77. T. H. Green, "Fragment of an Address on the Text 'The Word is Nigh Thee,' " in *Works*, vol. 3, ed. R. L. Nettleship (London: Longmans, Creen, and Co., 1891), 224.

78. Green, *Prolegomena*, 189.

79. Ibid., 266–67.

80. Ibid., 203, 256.

81. Andrew Vincent and Raymond Plant, *Philosophy, Politics and Citizenship: The Life and Thought of the British Idealists* (Oxford: Basil Blackwell Publishers, 1984), 22.

82. Green, *Prolegomena*, 199.

83. Ibid., 192.

84. Ibid., 200.

85. Ibid., 248, 249, 252. Roberts questions the logicality of Green's conclusion.

> Green seems to be confusing the social good in the sense that each individual's good is social—that is, requires social life as a necessary condition for its existence—with social good in a different sense, that is, the good of society. The fact that I am a social being does not necessarily constitute the good of the community as my good.

(John Roberts, "T. H. Green," in *Conceptions of Liberty in Political Philosophy*, ed. Zbigniew Pelczynski and John Gray [London: Athlone Press, 1984], 256).

86. Green, *Prolegomena*, 257.

87. Roberts, "T. H. Green," 258.

88. Although it is God who presents the subject with its *initial* aim and thereby functions as a final cause *pace* Green, each subject ultimately "presents to itself" its own *subjective* aim that functions as an ideal to be realized by that occasion (PR 87[133]). Whitehead is therefore in agreement with Green's dictum that morality is "an action determined by desire for an object which is not merely presented to the agent, but which he presents to himself as his own end" (T. H. Green, "The Word is Nigh Thee," *Works* 3, 224).

89. Gamwell, "Happiness and the Public World," 27.

90. This is the argument of Gamwell in "Happiness and the public World," 27. Given Whitehead's atomic theory of reality the good done to others does not ever rebound upon the same atomic individual. Gamwell assumes that by treating societies of occasions, for example, a personal society constituting a human being, as itself an individual analogous with an actual entity this solves the problem. While I obviously agree that societies are treated by Whitehead as genuine "wholes," I do not see this as a solution to the problem in question. The problem can only be solved if the pursuit of the good of others is an end in itself rather than a means to our future good.

91. The utilitarians would say that a morally conscientious character has no intrinsic value, but is good simply as a means to an end *different than itself,*

that is, maximum possible pleasure. This quotation from *Modes of Thought* reveals Whitehead's difference from utilitarian ethics and his affinity with Green for whom "the virtuous character is good not as a means to a 'summum bonum' other than itself but as in principle identical with the 'summum bonum' . . . " (*Prolegomena*, 319).

92. See John B. Cobb, Jr., "What Is the Future? A Process Perspective," in *Hope and the Future of Man*, ed. Ewert H. Cousins (London: The Garnstone Press, 1973), 6: " . . . Whitehead's analysis of the role of anticipation in each moment connects the meaning of the moment to the destiny of mankind."

93. There is one passage in *Process and Reality* that explicitly asserts the transcendence of the means/end distinction. "The function of being a means is not disjoined from the function of being an end. The sense of worth beyond itself is immediately enjoyed as an overpowering element in the individual self-attainment. It is in this way that the immediacy of sorrow and pain is transformed into an element of triumph" (PR 350[531]). While written in the context of the individual's inclusion in the life of God, I would argue that Whitehead's general position would permit its application to social ethics.

94. Hobhouse, *Democracy and Reaction*, 124–25.

95. Ibid., 131. The positions of both Whitehead and Hartshorne have found advocates among contemporary process philosophers. W. Widick Schroeder defends a position reminiscent of Hartshorne's when he argues: "Self-interest may be qualified and modified by one's identification of one's self-interest with the common good, but self-interest cannot be eliminated. . . . Because the state can be oppressive and because novelty is often suppressed, the individual also needs some protection from the 'common good' " (Schroeder, "Structure and Context in Process Political Theory," *Process Philosophy and Social Thought*, ed. John B. Cobb, Jr. and W. Widick Schroeder (Chicago: Center for the Scientific Study of Religion, 1981), 74). Whitehead's more communitarian approach is advocated by Sturm: "The individual's political duty is not merely to respect the rights of other individuals. It is to contribute to the common good, the good of the polity. Rights are not ends in themselves. They are requisites to creative symbiosis. To be sure, as requisites, they are abused where suppressed, for their suppression is a denial of human action. But they are also abused if not employed for the common good" ("Process Thought and Political Theory," 399–400).

96. See David Nicholls, "Images of God and the State: Political Analogy and Religious Discourse," *Theological Studies* 42/2 (1981): 195–215; and "Federal Politics & Finite God: Images of God in United States Theology," *Modern Theology* 4/4 (1988): 373–400.

97. Nicholls, "Images of God and the State," 196.

98. Nicholls, "Federal Politics & Finite God," 373.

99. John J. McDermott, ed., *The Writings of William James* (New York: The Modern Library, 1967), 492–93.

100. Schroeder, who treats the antagonism between individual self-interest and the common good as a metaphysical necessity, perceives a connection between process philosophy and the federal system of government: "The separation of executive, legislative, and judicial powers in the organizing center of the society, the development of a multiplicity of initiating centers, and the necessity for public officials to be accountable to an electorate who may remove them all deter inordinate self-interest, provide some enhancement of the vision of the welfare of the broader community, and offer to the individual some protection from the community" ("Structure and Context in Process Political Theory," 74–75). Of course, Schroeder presents this as a normative form of political organization which he derives from a consideration of abstract principles. I contend that the concrete reality of the social and political systems in the United States functioned as an environmental factor conditioning the development of those principles in the first place.

101. Nicholls, "Images of God and the State," 201.

## CHAPTER 5

1. Charles Hartshorne, "Man in Nature," in *Experience, Existence, and the Good: Essays in Honor of Paul Weiss*, ed. Irwin C. Lieb (Carbondale: Southern Illinois University Press, 1961), 99. A detailed discussion of many of the issues contained in this chapter by someone who stands within the Whiteheadian tradition can be found in Robert Neville's *The Cosmology of Freedom* (New Haven: Yale University Press, 1974).

2. Charles Hartshorne, "Politics and the Metaphysics of Freedom," *Enquête sur la liberté, Fédération Internationals des sociétés de philosophie*. (Publié avec le concours de l'u.n.e.s.c:o. (Paris: Hermann and Cie, Editeurs, 1953): 79.

3. A similar conclusion is reached by Johnson when discussing freedom in Europe while under Nazi rule: "Is it not true that many people 'give up the fight' and submit to the hostile environment? To this specific objection Whitehead is able to reply that *the submitting* is in accordance with the unshakable autonomy of the actual entity in question" (A. H. Johnson, "The Social Philosophy of Alfred North Whitehead," *The Journal of Philosophy* 40/10 [May 1943]: 270).

4. Hartshorne, "Politics and the Metaphysics of Freedom," 79.

5. Ibid., 83.

6. Ibid., 79.

7. Ibid.

8. Gerald F. Gaus, *The Modern Liberal Theory of Man* (London: Croom Helm, 1983), 29.

9. Ibid., 49 n.74.

10. Charles Hartshorne, "Born Equal: The Importance and Limitations of an Ideal," *Parables and Problems* (Winona, Minnesota: College of St. Theresa, 1968): 60–61.

11. Charles Hartshorne, "Individual Differences and the Ideal of Equality," *New South* 18 (February 1963): 5.

12. Ibid., 4. See Hartshorne, "Born Equal," 66.

13. Ibid., 5.

14. Charles Hartshorne, "Equality, Freedom, and the Insufficiency of Empiricism," *Southwestern Journal of Philosophy* 1/3 (1970): 21. See Charles Hartshorne, "A Metaphysics of Individualism," *Innocence and Power: Individualism in Twentieth-Century America*, ed. Gordon Mills (Austin: University of Texas Press, 1965), 136.

15. Ibid., 22.

16. Ibid., 25. A similar argument was advanced by the British Idealist David G. Ritchie. Ritchie accepts as a principle of justice that everyone should receive according to his merits, but then asks whether it is of much "practical value." "[H]ow are we to find a standard by which to estimate the 'merits' of individuals? . . . How are we to decide between the competing claims of different sorts of excellence? Proportion may be allowed to the 'justice of the gods,' but human justice has, in many cases, to be the justice of mere equality, simply because of the difficulties of assigning proportionate inequalities fairly" (*Studies in Political and Social Ethics* [London: Swan Sonnenschein, 1902], 33).

17. Although the divine perspective is absolute, it would seem that even God would constantly have to reevaluate an individual's importance in the light of the new developments in the historical process. Thus no historical achievement could ever attain a final value until the end of history.

18. Hartshorne, "Born Equal," 65.

19. Hartshorne, "Politics and the Metaphysics of Freedom," 83.

20. Ibid., 84.

21. Ibid.

22. Ibid.

23. Ibid., 79 (emphasis added).

24. Ibid., 85.

25. Hartshorne, "Born Equal," 71.

26. Hartshorne, "Politics and the Metaphysics of Freedom," 79.

27. Despite the practical problem, it is clear that Hartshorne does feel uneasy about the extent of economic inequality in some societies, including the United States (CSPM 314). He has recently added that "without a substantial measure of economic equality genuine political equality cannot be achieved" (CAP 235).

28. See Michael Freeden, *The New Liberalism: An Idealogy of Social Reform* (Oxford: Clarendon Press, 1978), 170-77; Gaus, *Modern Liberal Theory*, 243-50.

29. Gaus, *Modern Liberal Theory*, 251.

30. Milton and Rose Friedman, *Free to Choose: A Personal Statement* (London: Seeker and Warbury, 1980), 129.

31. Ibid., 132.

32. Ibid., 133.

33. Ibid., 134.

34. Ibid., 148.

35. Ibid., 146.

36. Ibid., 132.

37. Hartshorne, "Individual Differences," 7. Emphasis added.

38. See Gaus, *Modern Liberal Theory*. 187-95.

39. Hartshorne, "Politics and the Metaphysics of Freedom," 84.

40. David Nicholls, "Images of God and the State: Political Analogy and Religious Discourse," *Theological Studies* 42/2 (1981): 199.

41. Ibid., 200.

42. Charles Hartshorne, "A Philosophy of Democratic Defense," *Science, Philosophy, and Religion: Second Symposium* (New York: Conference on Science, Philosophy, and Religion in Their Relation to the Democratic Way of Life, Inc., 1942): 158.

43. Charles Hartshorne, "Whitehead and Berdyaev: Is There Tragedy in God?" *The Journal of Religion* 37 (April 1957): 72.

44. Hartshorne, "Equality, Freedom, and the Insufficiency of Empiricism," 26.

45. Hartshorne, "Individual Differences," 6.

46. A similar line of argument for democracy can be developed from Calvin's theology. Calvin's official doctrine is that any form of government, be it monarchy, aristocracy, or republic is divinely authorized by God and therefore to be endured by the people (For a discussion of Calvin's attitude toward monarchy see Harro Hopfl, *The Christian Polity of John Calvin* [Cambridge: Cambridge University Press, 1982], 152–71; Quentin Skinner, *The Foundations of Modern Political Thought, Vol. 2: The Age of Reformation* [Cambridge: Cambridge University Press, 1978]). Later Calvinists, however, by transposing his anthropology and theory of divine governance of the world from a religious to the secular sphere, were able to employ his theological ideas as a rationale for democratic government. On account of God's predestination of some to eternal life and others to damnation one could argue that there exists a real inequality among people. However, as real as this inequality is, Calvin held that it is not possible to identify the elect on earth. There is, therefore, a practical equality among individuals: we are all equally depraved and equally sinners. Because of our depravity, it is "safer and more bearable for a number to exercise government, so that they may help one another, teach and admonish one another; and, if one asserts himself unfairly, there may be a number of censors and masters to restrain his willfulness" (John Calvin, *Institutes of the Christian Religion*, ed. John T. McNeill [Philadelphia: The Westminster Press, 1960], 2: 1493–4). As Lakoff says, "If all men are fallible and seekers after power, no one ought to have more authority than can be safely entrusted to a man known to be corrupt" (Sanford A. Lakoff, *Equality in Political Philosophy* [Boston: Beacon Press, 1964], 45).

47. Hartshorne, "Equality, Freedom, and the Insufficiency of Empiricism," 26.

48. Our initial concern over such sentiments may be somewhat allayed when we pause to consider the principle of social relatedness: "A 'ruler' is the eminent influence in his society," writes Hartshorne, "but not in any sense the sole influence. And the better the ruler, the more sensitively he responds to significant influences coming to him from the ruled. Ruling is interaction, not mere action" (NTT 97).

49. Merold Westphal, "Temporality and Finitism in Hartshorne's Theism," *The Review of Metaphysics* 19/3 (March 1966): 560-61.

50. Charles Hartshorne, "The Dipolar Conception of Deity," *The Review of Metaphysics* 21/2 (Dec. 1967): 281.

51. Whitehead also held that the value of democracy lies, in part, in its preservation of liberty. We are told that once when Mrs. Whitehead asserted that "the one thing democracy has that is worth saving is the freedom of the individual," A. N. Whitehead replied:

"I would say . . . two: the freedom of the individual is one. But your knowledge of history will remind you that there has always been misery at the bottom of society: in the ancient world, slavery; in the mediaeval world, serfdom; since the development of machine technique, industrial proletariats. Our own age is the first time when, if this machine production is sensibly organized, there need be no material want. Russia has relieved the suffering of the masses at the price of the individual's liberty; the Fascists have destroyed personal liberties without really much alleviating the condition of the masses; the task of democracy is to relieve mass misery and yet preserve the freedom of the individual" (D 91).

Of particular interest is the way this passage resembles Mill's statement that the "social problem of the future we considered to be, how to unite the greatest individual liberty of action, with a common ownership in the raw materials of the globe, and an equal participation of all in the benefits of combined labour" (John Stuart Mill, *Autobiography*, in *The Collected Works of John Stuart Mill*, vol. 1, ed. John M. Robson and Jack Stillinger [Toronto: University of Toronto Press, 1981], 239). Whitehead's understanding of the state's role in relieving mass misery will be discussed in the following chapter.

52. Henry C. Simons, "A Positive Program for Laissez Faire: Some Proposals for a Liberal Economic Policy," in *Economic Policy for a Free Society* (Chicago: University of Chicago Press, 1948), 43.

53. See Charles Hartshorne, "An Economic Program for Religious Liberalism," *The Christian Century* (June 1935): 761-62.

54. Hartshorne, "The Dipolar Conception of Deity," 281.

55. Charles Hartshorne, "A New Look at the Problem of Evil," in *Current Philosophical Issues: Essays in Honor of Curt John Ducasse*, ed. Frederick C. Dommeyer, (Springfield, Illinois: Charles C. Thomas, 1966), 202.

56. C. B. Macpherson, *The Life and Times of Liberal Democracy* (Oxford: Oxford Univesity Press, 1977), 24.

57. Jeremy Bentham, *Constitutional Code, Works,* 143. Found in Macpherson, *The Life and Times of Liberal Democracy,* 36.

58. John Stuart Mill, *Considerations on Representative Government,* in *The Collected Works of John Stuart Mill,* vol. 19, ed. J. M. Robson (Toronto: University of Toronto Press, 1977), 403. Unlike Bentham, for whom this argument was the sole case for democracy, Mill also provides an educative argument which will be discussed below.

59. Ibid., 405.

60. Ibid., 404.

61. Mill, *Representative Government, Works* 19:473.

62. Ibid.

63. Hartshorne, "A Metaphysics of Individualism." 143.

64. Hartshorne, "Politics and the Metaphysics of Freedom," 84.

65. This contrasts with the more elitist positions of Mill and Hobson. "That every man's life is of equal value to Society," writes Hobson, "in the sense that it can yield equal social service, is not only false but absurd; and, if political power rightly varies with the capacity for public service, the case for equality of franchise utterly collapses" (J. A. Hobson, *The Crisis of Liberalism: New Issues of Democracy,* [London: P.S. King and Son, 1909], 78). While adopting with Mill and Hartshorne the basic principle that political power should be proportionate to one's ability to use it for the good, Hobson rejects Hartshorne's belief in a general equality of capability among all people. Also, in place of Mill's theory of plural voting Hobson advocates the centralization of power for certain purposes in the hands of expert legislators as the appropriate way of dealing with the problem of unequal abilities of citizens as agents in social conduct within the social organism (Ibid., 79ff.).

66. Hartshorne, "Individual Differences," 6.

67. Mill, *Representative Government, Works* 19:473.

68. C. B. Macpherson, *Democratic Theory: Essays in Retrieval* (Oxford: Clarendon Press, 1973), 27.

69. Ibid., 32.

70. Ibid., 10.

71. John Stuart Mill, *On Liberty,* in *The Collected Works of John Stuart Mill,* vol. 18, ed. J. M. Robson (Toronto: University of Toronto Press, 1977), 263.

72. John Stuart Mill, *Utilitarianism*, in *The Collected Works of John Stuart Mill*, vol. 10, ed. J. M. Robson (Toronto: University of Toronto Press, 1969), 233.

73. Gaus, *Modern Liberal Theory*, 208.

74. Hartshorne, "The Dipolar Conception of Deity," 281.

75. T. H. Green, *Prolegomena to Ethics*, ed. A. C. Bradley (Oxford: Clarendon Press, 1890), 365.

76. L. T. Hobhouse, *The Elements of Social Justice* (London: George Allen and Unwin, 1922), 68.

77. L. T. Hobhouse, *Liberalism*, (Oxford: Oxford University Press, 1944 [1911]), 143.

78. Ibid., 228. Not every modern liberal was as reticent as Hobhouse when it came to the question of coercion. Hobson, for instance, perhaps because he believed that the general will embodied a higher morality than did individual wills, seemed to view the use of force by the community as an instrument for the good. See John Allett, *New Liberalism: The Political Economy of J. A. Hobson* (Toronto: University of Toronto Press, 1981), 213.

# CHAPTER 6

1. Charles Hartshorne, "Politics and the Metaphysics of Freedom,"in *Enquête sur la liberté, Fédération internationale des sociétés de philosophie*. Publié avec le concours de l'u.n.e.s.c.o. (Herman and Cie, Editeurs, Paris, 1953), 80.

2. Charles Hartshorne, "Organic and Inorganic Wholes," *Philosophy and Phenomenological Research* 3/2 (Dec. 1942): 133.

3. Ibid. In a similar vein Hobhouse declared that "[n]othing short of omniscience could establish a perfect harmony in all social relations at once" (*Social Development*, 69). Hartshorne, of course, denies that even divine omniscience is sufficient to establish a perfect harmony since within the world there are numerous centers of free creativity. See Hartshorne, "A Philosopher's Assessment of Christianity," *Religion and Culture: Essays in Honor of Paul Tillich*, ed. Walter Leibrecht (New York: Harper and Brothers, 1959), 170.

4. Charles Hartshorne, "A New Look at the Problem of Evil," *Current Philosophical Issues: Essays in Honor of Curt John Ducasse*, ed. Frederick C. Dommeyer (Springfield, Ill.: Charles C. Thomas, 1966), 206.

5. DR 50. Similarly Delwin Brown says: "God's love . . . is a commitment to the sustenance and enhancement of finite creativity, to the capacity

of each creature to 'come from itself' in a rich, ennobling context" (Delwin Brown, *To Set at Liberty: Christian Faith and Human Freedom* [Maryknoll, New York: Orbis Books, 1981], 53.

6. Hartshorne, "A Philosopher's Assessment of Christianity," 177.

7. LP 204. It should be noted that God does not act so as to maximize freedom per se, but to maximize the *promise* of freedom. God's interest in maximizing the opportunities for self-realization in the universe, to be fulfilled, requires both freedom and restraint.

8. Hartshorne specifically states that "while the search for a risk-free utopia seems vain," he would "heartily support the search for a better system of risk-opportunity, more appropriate to our technology than we have now." As an example he says that the major dangers of pollution, nuclear war, and unjust extremes of rich and poor can only be effectively counterbalanced by restricting the freedom of each national group to be judge in its own cause (Charles Hartshorne, "Beyond Enlightened Self-Interest: A Metaphysics of Ethics," *Ethics* 84 [1973–74]: 211–12).

9. AI 71. Hobhouse likewise argues that the idea that force is the basis of society rests upon an antisocial view of human nature. On the contrary, he says, by arguing that force is the basis of society one is "taking the exception for the rule, and regarding human nature as unsocial because there are a few men of low social standard, and a few occasions on which better men are tempted to antisocial acts" (L. T. Hobhouse *Social Development: Its Nature and Conditions* [London: George Allen and Unwin, 1966 (1924)], 56). See L. T. Hobhouse, *The Elements of Social Justice* (London: George Allen and Unwin, 1922), 89–90.

10. L. T. Hobhouse, *Democracy and Reaction* (London: T. Fisher Unwin, 1904), 127–28. Whitehead, of course, made a very similar statement with regard to the use of force in international relations. War, he writes, is a "throwback from civilization for victors and vanguished" (ESP 44).

11. Perhaps Whitehead, like Mill, would explain this by saying that self-imposed restraints, limitations that are seen to be just and for the common good, do not produce the same negative results (John Stuart Mill, *On Liberty*, in *The Collected Works of John Stuart Mill*, vol. 18, ed. J. M. Robson [Toronto: University of Toronto Press, 1977], 266).

12. RSP 105. Hartshorne makes this comment in the context of a discussion about the traditional use of the doctrines of heaven and hell as motives for "Christian charity." He adds that it is "the business of the state and other social forms to provide whatever rewards or punishments the deficiencies of love make necessary and to do it so thoroughly that nothing of that sort would be left for any cosmic magistrate" (Ibid.). As we saw in our

initial exposition of his philosophy, Hartshorne views God as acting on a *cosmic* level, leaving it to local powers, such as the state, to set the appropriate limits for action by human agents.

13. L. T. Hobhouse, *Liberalism* (Oxford: Oxford University Press, 1944 [1911]), 23–24. See also pp. 153–54.

14. Andrew Vincent and Raymond Plant, *Philosophy, Politics and Citizenship: The Life and Thought of the British Idealists* (Oxford: Basil Blackwell Publishers, 1984), 73. Green, for example, describes the end of human activity as "a character not a good fortune, as a fulfillment of human capabilities from within not an accession of good things from without, as a function not a possession." The true good is "the perfection of human character" which is achieved through the activity of the individual as he fulfills his capabilities "according to the divine idea or plan of them" (T. H. Green, *Prolegomena to Ethics*, ed. A. C. Bradley [Oxford: Clarendon Press, 1890], 267).

15. T. H. Green, *Lectures on the Principles of Political Obligation*, in *Works*, vol. 2, ed. R. L. Nettleship (London: Longman, Green, and Co., 1891), 345. Green specifically mentions the Poor-law which, in his estimation, "takes away the occasion for the exercise of parental forethought, filial reverence, and neighbourly kindness" (Ibid).

16. Green, *Principles of Political Obligation, Works* 2:345–46 (emphasis added). See LP 204 as well as Hartshorne's strictures against paternalism in "Individual Differences and the Ideal of Equality," *New South* 18 (Feb. 1963): 6.

17. Hobhouse, *Social Development*, 76.

18. Ibid.

19. L. T. Hobhouse, *Social Evolution and Political Theory* (Port Washington, N.Y.: Kennikat Press, 1968 [1911]), 195–96.

20. Hobhouse, *Liberalism*, 59.

21. Hartshorne concludes his discussion of Marxism and metaphysics by quoting (with obvious approval) the following comment by James Devlin: "Marx disbelieves in adventure (since it all ends in a classless fixity) and he utterly disbelieves in freedom. Above all, Marx decides against concrete people and in favor of the aggregate, the body politic. His most radical hatred (implemented by Lenin) was the hatred for idiocy in the Greek sense— privacy" (IOGT 232). Such examples of Hartshorne's naive disapprobation of Marxism are, unfortunately, littered throughout his writings. Still, while they tell us little if anything of value concerning Marxism, they do provide us with an insight into Hartshorne's own disposition and political commitments.

22. Charles Hartshorne, "An Economic Program for Religious Liberalism," *The Christian Century* (June 1935): 762. See BH 36.

254    Notes

23. Ibid.

24. Henry C. Simons, "A Positive Program for Laissez Faire: Some Proposals For A Liberal Economic Policy," *Economic Policy For A Free Society* (Chicago: University of Chicago Press, 1948), 40 (emphasis added).

25. Ibid.

26. Ibid., 41.

27. Ibid., 41-42. Emphasis deleted.

28. Ibid., 43.

29. Ibid., 42.

30. Ibid.

31. Ibid., 51. Emphasis deleted.

32. Hartshorne, "An Economic Program for Religious Liberalism," 762.

33. Gerald F. Gaus, *The Modern Liberal Theory of Man* (London: Croom Helm, 1983), 236.

34. Simons, "Positive Program for Laissez Faire," 42.

35. Hartshorne, "An Economic Program for Religious Liberalism," 761-62.

36. Ibid., 762. Emphasis added.

37. Ibid.

38. John C. Moskop, "Mill and Hartshorne," *Process Studies* 10/1-2 (Spring-Summer 1980): 31. See Thomas A. Nairn, "Hartshorne and Utilitarianism: A Response to Moskop," *Process Studies* 17/3 (1988): 173-76.

39. Hartshorne, "An Economic Program for Religious Liberalism," 762.

40. Hobhouse, *Liberalism*, 86.

41. J. A. Hobson, *The Crisis of Liberalism: New Issues of Democracy* (London: P. S. King and Son, 1909), 3.

42. Ibid., 92.

43. T. H. Green, "Lecture on Liberal Legislation and Freedom of Contract," in *Works*, vol. 3, ed. R. L. Nettleship (London: Longman, Green, and Co., 1891), 366.

44. Ibid., 365. "How often have measures of social reform been opposed on the ground that they weakened individual responsibility—as if men's characters were perfectly isolated phenomena, and not affected at every moment by their antecedents and surroundings" (D. G. Ritchie, *Studies in Political and Social Ethics* [London: Swan Sonnenschein, 1902], 196–97).

45. Charles Taylor, "What's Wrong with Negative Liberty?" *The Idea of Freedom: Essays in Honour of Isaiah Berlin*, ed. Alan Ryan (Oxford: Oxford University Press, 1979), 179.

46. Green, "Liberal Legislation," *Works* 3:370–71.

47. Hobhouse, *Liberalism*, 91.

48. Ibid., 92. Emphasis added.

49. Green, "Liberal Legislation," *Works* 3:372.

50. See Isaiah Berlin, *Four Essays on Liberty* (Oxford: Oxford University Press, 1969), 127.

51. Hobhouse, *Elements of Social Justice*, 59.

52. Hobhouse, *Liberalism*, 92. See Hobhouse, *Development and Purpose: An Essay Toward A Philosophy of Evolution*, rev. ed. (London: Macmillan, 1927), 224.

53. Hobson, *Crisis of Liberalism*, 94.

54. Ritchie, *Political and Social Ethics*, 57–58.

55. Hartshorne, "Politics and the Metaphysics of Freedom," 79. In his discussion of negative freedom Berlin says that Locke and Mill held that a certain minimum of individual freedom must be maintained. "Political liberty in this sense is simply the area within which a man can act unobstructed by others," and coercion is the contraction of this area beyond a certain minimum (Berlin, *Four Essays*, 122).

56. Berlin, *Four Essays*, 161.

57. Ibid.

58. Green, "Liberal Legislation," *Works* 3:371.

59. Hartshorne, "Politics and the Metaphysics of Freedom," 80.

60. Herbert Samuel, *Memoirs*, 25. Found in Vincent and Plant, *Philosophy, Politics and Citizenship*, 73.

61. Peter Weiler, "The New Liberalism of L. T. Hobhouse," *Victorian Studies* 16/2 (1972): 158. See his discussion of Hobhouse's views on private property and capitalism on pp. 153–56. Of special interest is a statement made by Weiler concerning Hobhouse's economic reforms which could have easily been made about Hartshorne: "The reforms he advocated would create the conditions whereby the original premise of Liberal capitalism—that individual effort will bring forth adequate reward, providing the material basis for freedom—actually worked" (p. 153).

62. C. B. MacPherson, *The Life and Times of Liberal Democracy* (Oxford: Oxford University Press, 1977), 61, 63. See also C. B. MacPherson, *Democratic Theory: Essays in Retrieval* (Oxford: Clarendon Press, 1973), Essays I, II, and III.

63. Charles Hartshorne, "Whitehead and Berdyaev: Is There Tragedy in God?" *The Journal of Religion* 37 (April 1957): 73.

64. RSP 149. Hartshorne's use of the word "private" is misleading in so far as it suggests an ultimate bifurcation between individual experience and public utility. Process social theory holds that "every action is at once a private experience and public utility . . . " (AI 39; Cf. Hobhouse, *Elements of Social Justice*, 60–61). "Narrow" or "restricted" would be a more accurate phrase. On the basis of our earlier discussion of process ethics we see that "sin" is the result of intentionally disregarding the relevance of our actions for our social environment beyond an excessively narrow area. It thus leads to forms of self-development which, while beautiful in themselves, introduce unnecessary disharmony within the wider social context: "With a larger view and a deeper analysis, some instance of the perfection of art may diminish the good otherwise inherent in some specific situation as it passes into its objective actuality for the future. Unseasonable art is analogous to an unseasonable joke, namely, good in its place, but out of place a positive evil" (AI 345).

65. Presented thus, Hartshorne's position is indistinguishable from that of Cobb who believes we should adopt a relational/communal model of human relations according to which "the growth of our good is a function not primarily of competitive advantage but of communal well-being." Such a shift will not "do away with all of the oppositions which lead to trade-off thinking" for in some instances sacrifices are unavoidable. "But we will look primarily for ways in which both desirable variables can be increased in mutually supportive fashion rather than quickly settling for the trade-off" (John B. Cobb, Jr., *Process Theology as Political Theology* [Manchester: Manchester University Press, 1982], 98, 99).

66. Hartshorne, "A Philosopher's Assessment of Christianity," 170.

67. Franklin I. Gamwell, "Happiness and the Public World: Beyond Political Liberalism," *Process Studies* 8 (Spring 1978): 22. It is this preferential

view of the good which underlies Hartshorne's claim that "[e]very legislative
act excludes things which for some are genuine values. Always someone
loses or suffers" (RSP 99).

68. Kenneth M. Dolbeare and Patricia Dolbeare, *American Ideologies*, 6.
Found in Gamwell, "Happiness and the Public World," 22.

69. Hartshorne, "A Philosopher's Assessment of Christianity," 176.

70. Ibid., 168.

71. Charles Hartshorne, "A Philosophy of Democratic Defense,"
*Science, Philosophy, and Religion: Second Symposium* (New York: Conference on
Science, Philosophy, and Religion in Their Relation to the Democratic Way of
Life, Inc., 1942), 140–41. Emphasis added.

72. Hartshorne, "A Philosopher's Assessment of Christianity," 170.

73. These two aspects of human interrelationships are also acknowledged by Hobhouse when he says: "In living together, consciously and
unconsciously we exert pressure and constraint upon one another, and
consciously and unconsciously we co-operate and draw out from each other
capacities which would otherwise lie dormant" (*Social Development*, 70). The
perfect organic harmony in which each person's development serves society
and society sustains the development of each individual's capacities, is an
ideal. But at the same time it is the criterion for determining what sort of
individual development is to be considered good.

74. Hobhouse, *Democracy and Reaction*, 227.

75. Hobhouse, *Social Evolution*, 87 n.1.

76. T. H. Green, *Prolegomena to Ethics*, ed. A. C. Bradley (Oxford:
Clarendon Press, 1890), 183. See also pp. 202, 257.

77. Ibid., 414.

78. L. T. Hobhouse, *Development and Purpose: An Essay Toward a
Philosophy of Evolution*, rev. ed. (London: Macmillan, 1927), 153.

79. John Stuart Mill, *On Liberty*, in *The Collected Works of John Stuart Mill*,
vol. 18, ed. J. M. Robson (Toronto: University of Toronto Press, 1977), 266.

80. This phrase is borrowed from Gaus, *Modern Liberal Theory*, 64.

81. Whitehead treats human civilization as a work of art. The details of
its composition "make their own claim to individuality, and yet contribute to
the whole" (AI 364). Its aim is at "fineness of feeling" and therefore a
civilization should "so arrange its social relations, and the relations of its
members to their natural environment, as to evoke into the experiences of its

members Appearances dominated by the harmonies of forceful enduring things. In other words, Art should aim at the production of individuality in the component details of its compositions" (AI 363).

82. Hartshorne, "A Philosophy of Democratic Defense," 143.

83. Ibid., 133–34.

84. Ibid., 134.

85. Ibid., 149.

86. Ibid., 150.

87. Ibid.

88. Ibid., 133.

89. Ibid., 151.

90. Ibid., 134. Is this contrast permissible on Hartshorne's own terms? In what sense is a group sympathetic at all? Groups as such do not prehend other groups or other individuals; only individuals feel other individuals. A group is as sympathetic as its constituent members and therefore to appeal to the peculiar insensitivity of groups as compared to individuals in order to establish the necessity of using coercive force contradicts a key element of his metaphysics.

91. Ibid., 136.

92. Ibid., 133.

93. Ibid., 139.

94. Ibid., 137.

95. Ibid., 138.

96. Ibid.

97. Ibid., 139.

98. Ibid., 140. Emphasis added.

99. Ibid., 140–41.

100. DR 149. Hartshorne believes that war and tyranny will best be avoided if we deliberately establish those conditions that are most likely to improve the chances of peace, that is, alter the risk-opportunity ratio so as to make peace a more likely outcome (although never certain). Far from implying a policy of unilateral disarmament and the renunciation of war,

Hartshorne concludes that "this means substantial sacrifices, in part of
luxuries for armaments, so that none may think it wise to attack us, and in
part it means sacrifices of various kinds to the end of increasing cooperation
between nations . . . " (LP 321. Cf. LP 299).

101. Hartshorne, "A Philosophy of Democratic Defense ," 151–52.

102. These criteria were specifically given for deciding under what
conditions Germany should be forcibly prevented from extending her direct
power over central and western Europe. Although Whitehead was addressing a specific problem in this article, I believe that these criteria are in keeping
with his basic ethical theory and therefore applicable to the question of
military intervention generally.

103. Jeremy Bentham, *An Introduction to the Principles of Morals and
Legislation*, ed. J. H. Burns and H. L. A. Hart (London: Methuen, 1982),
158–64.

104. Ibid., 159.

105. Ibid., 163–64.

106. Ibid., 158.

107. Ibid., 159.

108. Ibid., 158.

109. Freeden, *New Liberalism*, 172.

110. Ibid.

# CHAPTER 7

1. See PR 90(138): "Thus we arrive at the principle that every society
requires a social background, of which it is itself a part. In reference to any
given society the world of actual entities is to be conceived as forming a
background in layers of social order, the defining characteristics becoming
wider and more general as we widen the background."

2. Victor Lowe, *Alfred North Whitehead: The Man and His Work* (Baltimore: The Johns Hopkins University Press, 1985), 138.

3. John Bowle and Basil Willey, "Origins and Development of the Idea
of Progress," in *Ideas and Beliefs of the Victorians: An Historic Revaluation of the
Victorian Age* (London: Sylvan Press, 1950), 33.

4. AI 356. Whitehead is thus in agreement with Hartshorne who, as we have seen, holds that it is only as possibilities are shut out that anything can be actualized. However, unlike Hartshorne, Whitehead does not suggest that the creative process is tragic because of this. Here we must note the distinction Whitehead makes between "anaesthesia" and "aesthetic destruction." "Complete inhibition is an example of the finiteness of subjective form. It does not derogate from 'perfection.' There is then 'perfection' in its kind—that is to say, in its type of finiteness with such-and-such exclusions" (AI 329). Anaesthesia is not tragic; only aesthetic destruction, which involves the active presence of component feelings together with a feeling of mutual destructiveness, is tragic. Hence it would appear that Whitehead could support in a way that Hartshorne could not the modern liberal conception of a noncompetitive common good.

5. Gamwell rightly seeks to clarify the idea that there exists a diversity of perfections, "a notion frequently cited in discussions of Whiteheadian ethics." He continues:

> This plurality of specific teloi, each with its "seasonal relevance," should never be taken to mean that 'there is no single end toward which all change should move' in the sense that there is not general and univocal teleology in the universe. After all, highly diverse civilizations of essentially equal attainment must be essentially equal in attaining something, and diverse perfections must all be perfections, as opposed to imperfections, according to some standard or criterion.

This statement is what Whitehead meant by maximal beauty which in respect to human life is the ideal of civilization (Franklin Gamwell, "A Discussion of John B. Cobb, Jr., 'The Political Implications of Whitehead's Philosophy,' " in *Process Philosophy and Social Thought*, ed. John B. Cobb, Jr. and W. Widick Schroeder [Chicago: Center for the Scientific Study of Religion, 1981], 33).

6. MT 103. Similarly he says that importance of experience "requires adequate stability of order. Complete confusion can be equated with complete frustration" (MT 119).

7. Not every form of social order is equally suited to its task of promoting intense and harmonious experiences among its members. "There are various types of order, and some of them provide more trivial satisfaction than do others. Thus, if there is to be progress beyond limited ideals, the course of history by way of escape must venture along the borders of chaos in its substitution of higher for lower types of order" (PR 110-11[169]). Whitehead holds structured societies to be a "higher" form of order than homogeneous societies. A homogeneous society is not as conducive to the emergence of individuality among its members because such novelty is

incapable of being "canalized" by the society. Hence the "growth of a complex structured society exemplifies the general purpose pervading nature" (PR 100[153]).

8. PR 339(515). In arguing thus Whitehead adopted a position similar to that of Hobhouse. Some socialists, wrote Hobhouse, "have yet to learn that their synthesis must include all the elements of value represented by the older liberalism" (L. T. Hobhouse, "The Ethical Basis of Collectivism," *International Journal of Ethics* 8/2 [Jan. 1898]: 143). True progress is not made simply by exchanging one lopsided social system for another. "Wisdom, ethics and the higher statesmanship seek to preserve what is good in the old and fuse it with the new elements and so find the path of harmony, which is equally removed from anarchy and repression" (L. T. Hobhouse, *Development and Purpose: An Essay Toward a Philosophy of Evolution*, rev. ed. [London: Macmillan, 1927], 233-34).

9. See MT 79, AI 332-33.

10. Cobb, "The Political Implications of Whitehead's Philosophy," 21.

11. Ibid.

12. Ibid.

13. G. W. F. Hegel, *Lectures on the Philosophy of World History*, trans. H. B. Nisbet (Cambridge: Cambridge University Press, 1975), 63.

14. Charles Taylor, *Hegel* (Cambridge: Cambridge University Press, 1975), 131-33.

15. Hegel, *Philosophy of World History*, 55.

16. Ibid., 61.

17. Ibid., 32.

18. There is one difference between Hegel and Whitehead which should not go unmentioned, namely, that for Hegel a particular *Volksgeist* embodies a particular concept which spirit has of itself and once this concept is realized that people's role in history comes to an end. Spirit is rejuvenated, but in *another* people as spirit marches from East to West. While duly noting this contrast, what I believe to be important for our purposes is the basic dialectical structure of the process by which the *telos* of history is realized, a structure echoed in Whitehead's metaphysics.

19. Hegel, *Philosophy of World History*, 63.

20. Hobhouse argued that liberals and socialists were approaching the same problem of progress but from different sides. The liberal is concerned for the "unimpeded development of human faculty as the mainspring of

progress" (L. T. Hobhouse, *Democracy and Reaction*, [London: T. Fisher Unwin, 1904], 226). The socialist, or collectivist, emphasizes mutual responsibility and the solidarity of society. We have already seen how Whitehead, like the collectivists, rejects the atomistic individualism of classical liberalism in favor of an organic harmony. Now we are seeing how he links progress to the free development of individuality.

21. For an analysis of Whitehead's theory of social structure see Randall Morris, "Social Differentiation and Class Structure: Some Implications of Whitehead's Metaphysics," *Process Studies* 15/4: 256–64. Emile Durkheim speaks of earlier societies as exhibiting "mechanical solidarity" by which he means that every member conforms to a strongly defined set of values and beliefs. Where mechanical solidarity is the basis of social cohesion "there is a concomitantly low level of individuation: that is to say, since every individual is a microcosm of the collective type, only restricted opportunity is offered for each member of the society to develop specific and particular personality characteristics" (Anthony Giddens, *Emile Durkheim: Selected Writings* [Cambridge: Cambridge University Press, 1972], 6).

22. SMW 297. Hobhouse similarly held that freedom is necessary for "collective progress." To the extent that a person diverges from the "common stock" to that extent is he able to contribute something fresh to society. The proper path of progress is not the elimination of data, but "the extension of unifying conceptions over a wider field of more heterogeneous data" (L. T. Hobhouse, *The Elements of Social Justice*, [London: George Allen and Unwin, 1922], 69–70).

23. Whitehead would be sympathetic with the position taken by Marx and Hegel according to which "evil is the form in which the driving force of historical development presents itself. . . . Each new progress necessarily steps forward as a crime against something holy, as rebellion against conditions which are old, dying, yet hallowed by custom," (Quotation of Engels taken from Allen Wood, *Karl Marx* [London: Routledge and Kegan Paul, 1981], 141–42).

24. AI 330. See A. H. Johnson, " 'Truth, Beauty and Goodness' in the Philosophy of A. N. Whitehead," *Philosophy and Science* 11 (1944): 22.

25. John Stuart Mill, *A System of Logic: Ratiocinative and Inductive*, in *Collected Works of John Stuart Mill*, vol. 8, ed. J. M. Robson, (Toronto: University of Toronto Press, 1974), 927. See Graeme Duncan, *Marx and Mill: Two Views of Social Conflict and Social Harmony* (Cambridge: Cambridge University Press, 1973), 212–17.

26. John Stuart Mill, *Considerations on Representative Government*, in *The Collected Works of John Stuart Mill*, vol. 19, ed. J. M. Robson (Toronto: University of Toronto Press, 1977), 382. Here I disagree with Clark Williamson's claim that process theology, like Marxism, represents a materialist philosophy of history. Quite remarkably he concludes that for Marx, "con-

sciousness, subjectivity, ideal aims . . . are fully as important as are the persuasive agencies for Whitehead and, vice versa, for Whitehead the senseless agencies are fully as important as are the economic conditions for Marx" (Clark M. Williamson, "Whitehead as Counterrevolutionary? Toward Christian-Marxist Dialogue." *Process Studies* 4/3 [Fall 1974]: 179). A better comparison of Whitehead's theory of history to that of Marx can be found in Howard L. Parson, "History as Viewed by Marx and Whitehead," *The Christian Scholar* 50/3 (Fall 1967): 273–89.

27. L. T. Hobhouse, *Liberalism*, (Oxford: Oxford University Press, 1944[1911]), 50. The close resemblance of Hobhouse's discussion to Whitehead's theory does not stop here. Even as Whitehead speaks of the "anarchy" of speculation which must be "civilized" by reason and which is only effective through cooperation among the members of society, Hobhouse goes on to say: "[P]assion of itself is blind and its world is chaotic. To be effective men must act together, and to act together they must have a common understanding and a common object" (Ibid.).

28. Hobhouse, "The Ethical Basis of Collectivism," 139.

29. Hobhouse, *Liberalism*, 122. See *Elements of Social Justice*, 83.

30. Hobhouse, "The Ethical Basis of Collectivism," 148.

31. Hobhouse, *Democracy and Reaction*, 122–23.

32. Hobhouse, *Elements of Social Justice*, 71. Hartshorne repeatedly makes the same point. In NTT 81, for example, he asserts that the justification of evil is that the creaturely freedom from which it springs "is also an essential aspect of all goods, so that the price of a guaranteed absence of evil would be the equally guaranteed absence of good." He concludes: "Risk of evil and opportunity for good are two aspects of just one thing, multiple freedom; and that one thing is also the ground of all meaning and all existence." See also LP 202.

33. Hobhouse, *Development and Purpose*, 179.

34. Mill, *On Liberty*, *Works* 18:220. Schroeder claims that all civil communities face two dangers. "The first is the excessive differentiation and self-determination of the parts, leading to anarchy. The second is excessive centering and suppression of the parts, leading to tyranny" (W. Widick Schroeder, "Structure and Content in Process Political Theory," *Process Philosophy and Social Thought*, 69). By concentrating on political tyranny Schroeder overlooks Whitehead's general concern with the tyranny of social custom and order in all its manifestations.

35. Ibid., 18:272.

36. Ibid., 18:264.

37. Ibid., 18:265.

38. Ibid.

39. Ibid., 18:226.

40. Ibid., 18:229.

41. Ibid., 18:260-61.

42. Ibid., 18:269.

43. Ibid.

44. Ibid.

45. Ibid.

46. Michael Freeden points out that for David Ritchie the social reformer's task was to be "the pioneer and propagandist of the true consciousness, rather than merely imposing his particular opinions. By arousing individual minds to an awareness of their social nature, by providing a rational concept of society, he could elicit the ethical potential of the members of society. In the last resort ethical social reform was a question of will . . ." (Michael Freeden, "Biological and Evolutionary Roots of the New Liberalism in England," *Political Theory* 4/4 [1976]: 478-79). The reformer's ideals *compete* with other ideals in an attempt to *persuade* the general public. Similarly, Whitehead views history as "the theatre of diverse groups of idealists respectively urging ideals incompatible for conjoint realization" (AI 356-57).

47. PR 187(284).

48. Lowe, *Alfred North Whitehead*, 136-38.

49. The profession is a practical way in which Whitehead sought to avoid the extremes of a "mere unqualified demand for liberty," which might be called the tyranny of the individual, and the "equally noxious . . . antithetical cry for mere *conformation to standard pattern,*" that is, the despotism of custom (AI 71-2; emphasis added).

50. AI 77. Cf. John Stuart Mill, *Auguste Comte and Positivism,* in *Collected Works of John Stuart Mill,* vol. 10, ed. J. M. Robson (Toronto: University of Toronto Press, 1969), 313-14: "Any doctrines which come recommended by the nearly universal verdict of instructed minds will no doubt continue to be, as they have hitherto been, accepted without misgiving by the rest."

51. John Stuart Mill, "The Spirit of the Age" in *John Stuart Mill On Politics and Society,* ed. Geraint L. Williams (Glascow: Collins, 1976), 175. The problem arises in an "age of transition." In such periods the insufficiency of

ancient doctrines has become known, but no new body of doctrine has been generally accepted. Such times are dangerous because "the multitude are without a guide" (Ibid., 174).

52. Freeden, "Biological and Evolutionary Roots of the New Liberalism in England," 471–90.

53. See George R. Lucas, Jr., "Evolutionist Theories and Whitehead's Philosophy," *Process Studies* 14/4 (1985): 287–300. Lucas argues that "[n]o clearly definable doctrine of evolution is in evidence in his philosophy" (p.296). Perhaps Whitehead, like Hobhouse, felt we could "help ourselves with the organic metaphor without allowing it to dominate us" (L. T. Hobhouse, *Social Evolution and Political Theory* [Port Washington, N.Y.: Kennikat Press, 1968], 90). Victor Lowe claims that Whitehead's humanistic reflections on man were constantly colored by "the concept of evolution (not necessarily progress), biological, sociological, intellectual . . ." (*Understanding Whitehead* [Baltimore: The Johns Hopkins Press, 1959], 246).

54. James Allen Rogers, "Darwinism and Social Darwinism," *Journal of the History of Ideas* 33 (1972): 280.

55. Michael Freeden, *The New Liberalism: An Ideology of Social Reform* (Oxford: Clarendon Press, 1978), 80.

56. Ibid.

57. Hobhouse, *Democracy and Reaction*, 84–85.

58. Ibid., 115.

59. Ibid., 85. See Hobhouse, *Social Evolution*, 18–19.

60. Ibid.

61. SMW 296. Hartshorne also argued that "[b]iology teaches that aggressiveness, hostility, and self-defence are no more essential to evolutionary success than cooperation, parental tenderness, and sympathy" (LP 321). Whitehead adopts the line of argument taken by the new liberals in claiming that the exclusive reliance upon natural selection was not characteristic of Darwin's own theory (AI 44). According to Rogers, this is a more accurate reading of Darwin than that offered by the Social Darwinists. "Although Darwin emphasized the element of competition in the evolutionary process in the *Origin of Species,* he did not ignore the important aspect of cooperation. Moreover, when he came to write specifically on man and evolution he strongly emphasized the progressive role of cooperation within the human species in raising it to its present level" (Rogers, "Darwinism and Social Darwinism," 268).

62. In *Symbolism* Whitehead says that "[t]he emergence of living beings cannot be ascribed to the superior survival value either of the individuals, or

of their societies." Rather, the emergence of life "is better conceived as a bid for freedom on the part of organisms, a bid for certain independence of individuality with self-interests and activities not to be construed purely in terms of environmental obligations" (S 76–77).

63. FR 2. Hartshorne also holds to a similarly qualified acceptance of the dictum "the survival of the fittest." "[T]he Darwinian idea that adjustments are the result of competition for survival among chance variations may be in some degree true," he writes. But he goes on to say: "The 'fittest to survive' need not, so far as chance and competition are concerned, be better in any other sense, as one can see from the splendid survival of some of the lowest forms. The general trend toward more complex forms of integration can, it seems, be deduced only from purpose" (Charles Hartshorne, "Organic and Inorganic Wholes," *Philosophy and Phenomenological Research* 3/2 [1942]: 135–36).

64. L. T. Hobhouse, *Social Development: Its Nature and Conditions* (London: George Allen and Unwin, 1966[1924]), 106. As he says elsewhere, the problem with. the argument that the 'fittest' survive is that the word 'fit,' "which suggests adaptation to some desirable end, is employed without so much as an effort to determine what is desirable and what is not" (*Social Evolution*, 24).

65. Hobhouse, "The Ethical Basis of Collectivism," 147.

66. Hobhouse, *Social Evolution*, 24. In his discussion of social development Hobhouse makes a distinction between 'evolution' and 'progress' which is basically the same as that made by Whitehead between change and progress. By evolution he means any sort of growth; by social progress, "the growth of social life in respect of those qualities to which human beings attach or can rationally attach value" (*Social Evolution*, 8). The point is that not every instance of social evolution is also a form of social progress. Evolution is not identical with progress. "An evolutionary process as such consists merely in the development of one type into another, and there is no necessity that the second type should be any higher in the scale of creation than the first, if the term higher is to carry any sense of value as appreciated by human intelligence" (Hobhouse, "The Ethical Basis of Collectivism," 145).

67. Hobhouse, "The Ethical Basis of Collectivism," 150.

68. Ibid.

69. Hobhouse, *Development and Purpose*, 210.

70. Hobhouse, *Democracy and Reaction*, 126–27.

71. Hobhouse, "The Ethical Basis of Collectivism," 112. See *Development and Purpose*, 465.

72. If Whitehead, in these early writings, had taken the additional step of identifying God with the totality of the creative process his position would have been a very close approximation to the philosophy of history held by Hegel. One could identify the primordial valuation with the divine purpose, or "Concept," of this Absolute. History would then be the record of God's, rather than Creativity's, process of actualizing this Concept.

73. Hobhouse, one of the many new liberals indebted to Idealism, also viewed history as the progressive development of the Absolute. On this issue, "Hobhouse could be said to have come closer to the spirit of Hegelianism than Bradley himself. For whereas Bradley specifically denied that development or progress could be attributed to the Absolute, these themselves were ideas as centrally important for Hobhouse as they were for Hegel" (C. M. Griffin, "L. T. Hobhouse and the Idea of Harmony," *Journal of the History of Ideas* 35/4 [1974]: 650). In advancing a theory of divine self-development Whitehead adopted a position closer to Hegel, Green, and the new liberals than to Bradley.

74. T. H. Green, "Christian Dogma," in *Works*, vol. 3, ed. R. L. Nettleship (London: Longman, Green, and Co., 1891), 181.

75. See Green, *Works* 3:176, 260.

76. Green, "Faith," *Works* 3:256–57

77. Green, "The Word Is High Thee," *Works* 3:221.

78. Green, "The Conversion of Paul," *Works* 3:189, 188. Like other advocates of a positive conception of freedom, Green holds that people are free when they follow a law which is self-imposed rather than heteronomously imposed. Hence we find him claiming that since the "mind of God" is an "inward principle, not an outward restraint," we live in freedom when we live in obedience to God. See Green, "Justification by Faith," *Works* 3:197.

79. Green, "The Word Is Nigh Thee," *Works* 3:225.

80. Green, "The Incarnation," *Works* 3:219.

81. Ibid.

82. Although Green, like Hegel before him, in some sense identified God with mankind, he differs from his predecessor in holding that there can never be a full expression of God in human life. The self-realization of God in history is never a finished work; there will always be room for further development as human persons discover new potentialities for realization. Vincent and Plant argue that this is the crucial idea that Green derived from F. C. Baur and which makes Green's political philosophy more critical than that of Hegel. See Andrew Vincent and Raymond Plant, *Philosophy, Politics and Citizenship: The Life and Thought of the British Idealists* (Oxford: Basil Blackwell Publishers, 1984), 12, 13.

83. Green, "The Witness of God," *Works* 3:233.

84. Ibid. 3:234.

85. Ibid. 3:233.

86. Bernard Bosanquet, "The Kingdom of God on Earth," in *Essays and Addresses* (London: Swan Sonnenschein, 1889), 124.

87. Melvin Richter, *The Politics of Conscience: T. H. Green and His Age* (London: Weidenfeld and Nicolson, 1964), 115.

88. Green, "The Witness of God," *Works* 3:239.

89. Green, "Faith," *Works* 3:269–70.

90. Green, "The Philosophy of Aristotle," *Works* 3:73.

91. Green, "The Witness of God," *Works* 3:235.

92. Daniel Day Williams, "Deity, Monarchy, and Metaphysics: White-head's Critique of the Theological Tradition," in *The Relevance of Whitehead*, ed. Ivor Lederc (New York: Macmillan, 1961), 368.

93. Ibid., 357.

94. T. H. Green, *Prolegomena to Ethics*, ed. A. C. Bradley (Oxford: Clarendon Press, 1890), 256. Green notes that the "special features" of the object sought will vary with different ages and persons according to circumstances.

95. Ibid., 180–81.

96. Cf. Gerald F. Gaus, *The Modern Liberal Theory of Man* (London: Croom Helm, 1983), 152: "Mill, Green and Hobhouse . . . see the outcome of historical development or progress largely in terms of the fuller realisation of man's nature." Hobhouse, for instance, writes: "Thus Humanity, in the sense which the best Positive writers have given to that word, Humanity as the spirit of harmony and expanding life, shaping the best actions of the best men and women, is the highest incarnation known to us of the divine. If, indeed, we come to the conclusion that God is, and are asked what He is, we may reply that God is that of which the highest known embodiment is the distinctive spirit of Humanity" (*Development and Purpose*, 484).

97. Hegel, *Philosophy of World History*, 52.

98. G. A. Cohen, *Karl Marx's Theory of History* (Princeton: Princeton University Press, 1978), 18.

99. Charles Hartshorne, "A Philosophy of Democratic Defense," in *Science, Philosophy, and Religion: Second Symposium* (New York: Conference on Science, Philosophy and Religion in Their Relation to the Democratic Way of Life, Inc., 1942), 166.

100. Ibid., 167.

101. See John B. Cobb, Jr., *Process Theology as Political Theology* (Manchester: Manchester University Press, 1982): 111–33; Schubert M. Ogden, *Faith and Freedom* (Belfast: Christian Journals, 1979): 102–14; Charles Birch and John B. Cobb, Jr., *The Liberation of Life* (Cambridge: Cambridge University Press, 1981).

102. Green, "Faith." *Works*, 3:265.

103. Hartshorne discusses this in several places including BH 12–16, MVG 156–67, and DR 132–33.

104. PR 340(517). See Schubert M. Ogden, "The Meaning of Christian Hope," *Union Seminary Quarterly Review*, 30/2–4 (Winter-Summer, 1975): 153–64.

105. See G. W. F. Hegel, *The Philosophy of History*, trans. J. Sibree (New York: Dover Publications, 1956), 457.

106. Taylor, *Hegel*, 391.

107. Hegel, *Philosophy of World History*, 66.

108. Daniel Day Williams, "Philosophy and Faith: A Study in Hegel and Whitehead," in *Our Common History as Christians: Essays in Honor of Albert C. Outler*, ed. J. Drescher, L. T. Howe, and K. Penzel (New York: Oxford University Press, 1975), 171.

109. Georg Wilhelm Friedrich Hegel, *Lectures on the Philosophy of Religion*, vol. 3, ed. Peter C. Hodgson (Berkeley: University of California Press, 1985), 327.

110. AI 367. Hobhouse criticized Hegel on precisely these grounds. "[W]hen we are taught to think of the world which we know as a good world, to think of its injustices, wrongs and miseries as necessary elements in a perfect ideal, then, if we accept these arguments, our power of revolt is atrophied, our reason is hypnotised, our efforts to improve life and remedy wrong fade away into a passive acquiescence in things as they are; or, still worse, into a slavish adulation of the Absolute in whose hands we are mere pawns" (L. T. Hobhouse, *The Metaphysical Theory of the State* [London: George Allen and Unwin, 1918], 19).

111. Richter, *Politics of Conscience*, 132

112. I am borrowing the term 'God-consciousness' from F. Schleiermacher who used it to denote reflection upon the the feeling of absolute dependence. See Friedrich Schleiermacher, *The Christian Faith*, ed. H. R. Mackintosh and J. S. Stewart (Edinburgh: T. & T. Clark, 1968), 18.

113. The success of this conception of the final *telos* of history and the common good in the end depends upon the cogency of the process concept of God as supremely relative. The idea that the deity is able to preserve everlastingly in its own life all of the values achieved in history is generally taken for granted by process theologians. Yet as we saw in chapter three some questions have been raised concerning the coherence of this notion. The problem of human finitude is not simply the transitoriness of human life. It is also the fact that finite occasions of experience must prehend other occasions under abstraction and therefore they are unable to preserve every value in the actual world. God, on the contrary, is said to preserve every value without loss. This is the foundation of Hartshorne's claim that God alone can function as the common good. However, if there are some values that are realized in the world but that God is unable to take up into his own life, then the idea that God is our common good is undermined. Some aspects of our own good would then not be constituent elements of the common good. This in turn would imperil the function of our God-consciousness as a motivation to self-forgetful transcendence. What process philosophers must adequately defend is the idea that there is a literal identity of feeling between God and the world, that God exhaustively "feels the feeling in another." There must not be any experiences that are not also a part of the divine experience. Only in this way can process metaphysics supply modern liberal thought with a more adequate notion of God-consciousness.

# CHAPTER 8

1. Gerald F. Gaus, *The Modern Liberal Theory of Man* (London: Croom Helm, 1983), 6.

2. L. T. Hobhouse, *Liberalism* (Oxford: Oxford University Press, 1944 [1911]), 173. See L. T. Hobhouse, *Democracy and Reaction* (London: T. Fisher Unwin, 1904), 209–44.

3. Charles Hartshorne, "Politics and the Metaphysics of Freedom," in *Enquête sur la liberté, Fédération internationale des sociétés de philosophie.* Publié avec le concours de l'u.n.e.s.c.o. (Paris: Hermann, 1953), 79–85.

4. Charles Hartshorne, "A Philosophy of Democratic Defense," in *Science, Philosophy, and Religion: Second Symposium* (New York: Conference on Science, Philosophy, and Religion in Their Relation to the Democratic Way of Life, Inc., 1942): 130–72.

5. Charles Hartshorne, "A Metaphysics of Individualism," in *Innocence and Power*, ed. Gordon Mills (Austin: University of Texas Press, 1965), 131–46.

6. Hartshorne, "Philosophy of Democratic Defense," 166.

7. Lewis S. Feuer, "Recollections of Alfred North Whitehead in the Harvard Setting (1931–1937)," in *The Yale Review* (1987), 546.

8. Russell L. Kleinbach, *Marx Via Process: Whitehead's Potential Contribution to Marxian Social Theory* (Washington: University Press of America, 1982), 60.

9. John B. Cobb, Jr., "Points of Contact Between Process Theology and Liberation Theology in Matters of Faith and Justice," *Process Studies* 14/2 (Summer 1985): 125.

10. Juan L. Segundo, S.J., *Liberation of Theology*, trans. John Drury (Maryknoll, New York: Orbis Books, 1976), 25.

11. Jose Miguez Bonino, *Doing Theology in a Revolutionary Situation* (Philadelphia: Fortress Press, 1975), 90.

12. Ibid., 94.

13. Segundo, *Liberation of Theology*, 39.

14. Ibid., 13.

15. Ibid., 39.

16. Ibid., 116.

17. Bonino, *Doing Theology in a Revolutionary Situation*, 98.

18. Segundo, *Liberation of Theology*, 30.

19. Bonino, *Doing Theology in a Revolutionary Situation*, 95.

20. Johannes B. Metz, *Theology of the World*, trans. William Glen Doepel (London: Burns and Oates, 1969), 116. Emphasis deleted.

21. Ibid., 122–23.

22. Ibid., 153. Cf. Carl E. Braaten, *The Future of God: The Revolutionary Dynamics of Hope* (New York: Harper and Row, 1969), 159: "A prophetic church criticizes the present in light of the promised future of the kingdom. Its eschatological vision is the basis of its realism. The church can thus reject the temptation to *absolutize* any political or social form of life. It will *relativize* all historical realizations in light of the final goal of history—the *absolute*

*future"* (emphasis added). See Segundo's comments on the way "revolutionary" theologies seek to avoid ideological commitment by relativizing all social and political programs (Juan Luis Segundo, "Capitalism Versus Socialism: Crux Theologica," in *Frontiers of Theology in Latin America,* ed. Rosino Gibellini [London: SCM Press, 1980], 246–47).

23. Bonino, *Doing Theology in a Revolutionary Situation,* 149.

24. Ibid., 94–95. See J. Miguez Bonino, "Historical Praxis and Christian Identity," in *Frontiers of Theology in Latin America,* ed. Rosino Gibellini (London: SCM Press, 1980), 276.

25. Ibid., 150.

26. Ibid., 98. Emphasis deleted.

27. John B. Cobb, Jr. "The Political Implications of Whitehead's Philosophy," in *Process Philosophy and Social Thought,* ed. John B. Cobb, Jr. and W. Widick Schroeder (Chicago: Center for the Scientific Study of Religion, 1981), 11.

28. Ibid., 18.

29. Ibid., 18–19.

30. John B. Cobb, Jr., *Process Theology as Political Theology* (Manchester: Manchester University Press, 1982), 90.

31. See Jürgen Moltmann, *The Crucified God,* trans. R.A. Wilson and John Bowden (London: SCM Press, 1974), 329–35.

32. Not all process theologians share Cobb's enthusiasm for Moltmann's political program. For a more conservative reaction see W. Widick Schroeder, "Liberation Theology: A Critique from a Process Perspective," *Process Philosophy and Social Thought,* ed. John B. Cobb, Jr., and W. Widick Schroeder (Chicago: Center for the Scientific Study of Religion, 1981), 210–41.

33. Cobb, *Process Theology as Political Theology,* 91.

34. Ibid., 92.

35. Ibid.

36. Bonino, *Doing Theology in a Revolutionary Situation,* 149–50.

37. George V. Pixley, "Justice and Class Struggle: A Challenge for Process Theology" in *Process Studies* 4/3 (1973): 174.

38. George V. Pixley, "Perspective and Ideology in Process Theology," 6–7. An unpublished paper delivered to a conference on "Process and Praxis."

39. Ibid., 18.

40. Bonino, *Doing Theology in a Revolutionary Situation*, 12.

# Select Bibliography

## WORKS OF CHARLES HARTSHORNE

Hartshorne, Charles. "Beyond Enlightened Self-Interest: A Metaphysics of Ethics." *Ethics* 84 (1973–74): 201–16.

—— *Beyond Humanism: Essays in the Philosophy of Nature.* Gloucester, Mass.: Peter Smith, 1975.

—— "Born Equal: The Importance and Limitations of an Ideal." *Parables and Problems.* Winona, Minn.: College of St. Theresa, 1968: 59–71. Mimeographed.

—— "Causal Necessities: An Alternative to Hume." *The Philosophical Review* 63 (October 1954): 479–99.

—— "Contingency and the New Era in Metaphysics (I)." *The Journal of Philosophy* 29 (4 August 1932): 421–31.

—— "Contingency and the New Era in Metaphysics (II)." *The Journal of Philosophy* 29 (18 August 1932): 457–69.

—— *Creative Synthesis and Philosophic Method.* London: SCM Press, 1970.

—— "Creativity as a Philosophical Category." *The Journal of Philosophy* 55/22 (23 October 1958): 944–53.

—— *Creativity in American Philosophy.* Albany: State University of New York Press, 1984.

—— "The Dipolar Conception of Deity." *The Review of Metaphysics* 21/2 (December 1967): 273–89.

—— *The Divine Relativity: A Social Conception of God.* New Haven: Yale University Press, 1948.

—— "An Economic Program for Religious Liberalism." *The Christian Century* (5 June 1935): 761–62.

—— "Efficient Causality in Aristotle and St. Thomas: A Review Article." *The Journal of Religion* 25 (1945): 25–32.

—— "Equality, Freedom, and the Insufficiency of Empiricism." *The Southwestern Journal of Philosophy* 1/3 (Fall 1970): 20–27.

—— "Ethics and the Assumption of Purely Private Pleasures." *International Journal of Ethics* 40 (July 1930): 496–515.

—— "Ethics and the New Theology." *International Journal of Ethics* 45 (October 1934): 90–101.

—— "Ideal Knowledge Defines Reality: What Was True in Idealism." *Journal of Philosophy* 43/21 (10 October 1946): 573–82.

—— "Individual Differences and the Ideal of Equality." *New South* 18 (February 1963): 3–8.

—— *Insights and Oversights of Great Thinkers: An Evaluation of Western Philosophy.* Albany: State University of New York Press, 1983.

—— *The Logic of Perfection.* La Salle, Ill.: Open Court Publishing Company, 1962.

—— "Man in Nature." *Experience, Existance, and The Good: Essays in Honor of Paul Weiss.* Edited by Irwin C. Lieb. Carbondale, Ill.: Southern Illinois University Press, 1961: 89–99.

—— *Man's Vision of God and the Logic of Theism.* Hamden, Conn.: Archon Books, 1964.

—— "A Metaphysics of Individualism." *Innocence and Power: Individualism in Twentieth-Century America.* Edited by Gordon Mills. Austin: University of Texas Press, 1965.

—— *A Natural Theology for Our Time.* La Salle, Ill.: Open Court Publishing Company, 1967.

—— "A New Look at the Problem of Evil." *Current Philosophical Issues: Essays in Honor of Curt John Ducasse.* Edited by Frederick C. Dommeyer. Springfield, Ill.: Charles C. Thomas, 1966: 201–12.

—— *Omnipotence and Other Theological Mistakes.* Albany: State University of New York Press, 1984.

—— "Organic and Inorganic Wholes." *Philosophy and Phenomenological Research* 3/2 (December 1942): 127–36.

—— "A Philosopher's Assessment of Christianity." *Religion and Culture: Essays in Honor of Paul Tillich.* Edited by Walter Leibrecht. New York: Harper and Brothers, 1959: 167–80.

—— "A Philosophy of Democratic Defense." *Science, Philosophy, and Religion: Second Symposium.* New York: Conference on Science, Philosophy, and Religion in Their Relation to the Democratic Way of Life, Inc., 1942: 130–72.

—— "Politics and the Metaphysics of Freedom." *Enquête sur la liberté. Fédération internationals des sociétés de philosophie.* Publié avec le concours de l'u.n.e.s.c.o. Paris: Hermann & Cie., Editeurs, 1953: 79–85.

—— "Real Possibility." *The Journal of Philosophy* 60/21 (10 October 1963): 593–605.

—— *Reality as Social Process.* Glencoe, Ill.: The Free Press, 1953.

—— "The Social Theory of Feelings." *The Southern Journal of Philosophy* 3 (Summer 1965): 87–93.

—— "Tillich's Doctrine of God." *The Theology of Paul Tillich*. Edited by Charles W. Kegley and Robert W. Brettall. New York: The Macmillan Co., 1961: 164–95.

—— "Whitehead and Berdyaev: Is There Tragedy in God?" *The Journal of Religion* 37 (April 1957): 71–84.

—— "Whitehead's Idea of God." *The Philosophy of Alfred North Whitehead*. Edited by Paul Arthur Schilpp. Evanston Ill.: Northwestern University, 1941: 515–59.

—— "Whitehead's Novel Intuition." *Alfred North Whitehead: Essays on His Philosophy*. Edited by George L. Kline. Englewood Cliffs, N.J.: Prentice-Hall, 1963: 18–26.

—— and William L. Reese. *Philosophers Speak of God*. Chicago: The University of Chicago Press, 1953.

# WORKS OF ALFRED NORTH WHITEHEAD

Whitehead, Alfred North. *Adventures of Ideas*. New York: Macmillan Publishing Co., 1933.

—— *The Aims of Education and Other Essays*. New York: The Free Press, 1967.
—— *The Concept of Nature*. Cambridge: Cambridge University Press, 1964.
—— *Essays in Science and Philosophy*. New York: Philosophical Library, 1948.
—— "Extract from the Speech of A. N. Whitehead, Esq., Sc.D., at the Annual Meeting of the Cambridge Women's Suffrage Association, Nov. 5, 1906." Reprinted as "Liberty and the Enfranchisement of Women." *Process Studies* 7/1 (Spring 1977): 37–39.
—— *The Function of Reason*. Princeton: Princeton University Press, 1929.
—— *Modes of Thought*. New York: Macmillan Publishing Co., 1938.
—— *Process and Reality*. Corrected Edition. Edited by David R. Griffin and Donald Sherburne. New York: Free Press, 1978.
—— *Religion in the Making*. New York: Macmillan Publishing Co., 1926.
—— *Science and the Modern World*. 2nd ed. New York: Macmillan Publishing Co., 1926.
—— *Symbolism: Its Meaning and Effect*. Cambridge: Cambridge University Press, 1928.

# OTHER WORKS NOT CITED IN THE NOTES

Allan, George. "The Gods Above, the Stones Beneath: An Essay on Historical Existence." *Soundings* 51 (1968): 448–64.

Alves, Ruben A. *A Theology of Human Hope*. St. Meinrad, Ind.: Abbey Press, 1969.

Auld, John W. "The Liberal Pro-Boers." *The Journal of British Studies* 14/2 (1975): 78–99.

Avineri, Shlomo. *Hegel's Theory of the Modern State.* Cambridge: Cambridge University Press, 1972.

Belaief, Lynne. "A Whiteheadian Account of Value and Identity." *Process Studies* 5/1 (Spring 1975): 31–46.

——— "Whitehead and Private Interest Theories." *Ethics* 76 (July 1966): 277–86.

Bonino, Jose Miguez. *Toward a Christian Political Ethics.* London: SCM Press, 1983.

Brown, Delwin. "Freedom and Faithfulness in Whitehead's God." *Process Studies* 2/2 (Summer 1972): 137–46.

Cobb, John B. Jr. "A Process Christology." *Process Philosophy and Christian Thought.* Edited by D. Brown, R. James, G. Reeves. Indianapolis: Bobbs-Merrill Co., 1971: 382–98.

——— "What Is the Future? A Process Perspective." *Hope and the Future of Man.* Edited by Ewert H. Cousins. London: The Garnstone Press, 1973: 1–14.

——— and David R. Griffin. *Process Theology: An Introductory Exposition.* Belfast: Christian Journals Ltd., 1977.

Collini, Stefan. "Liberalism and the Legacy of Mill." *The Historical Journal* 20/1 (1977): 237–54.

Dumas, Andre. *Political Theology and the Life of the Church.* Translated by John Bowden. London: SCM Press, 1978.

Durkheim, Emile. *The Division of Labor in Society.* Translated by George Simpson. New York: The Free Press, 1933.

Ford, Lewis S. "Towards a Process Theology of Hope." Bibliographical details unknown. Paper found at the Center for Process Studies, Claremont, Calif.

Giddens, Anthony. *Capitalism and Modern Social Theory: An Analysis of the Writings of Marx, Durkheim and Max Weber.* Cambridge: Cambridge University Press, 1971.

Greengarten, I. M. *Thomas Hill Green and the Development of Liberal-Democratic Thought.* Toronto: University of Toronto Press, 1981.

Griffin, David R. *God, Power, and Evil: A Process Theodicy*. Philadelphia: Westminster Press, 1976.

—— "North Atlantic and Latin American Liberation Theologians." *Process Philosophy and Social Thought*. Edited by John B. Cobb, Jr., and W. Widick Schroeder. Chicago: Center for the Scientific Study of Religion, 1981: 197–210.

—— "Values, Evil, and Liberation Theology." *Process Philosophy and Social Thought*. Edited by John B. Cobb, Jr., and W. Widick Schroeder, Chicago Center for the Scientific Study of Religion, 1981: 183–96.

Gunton, Colin E. *Becoming and Being: The Doctrine of God in Charles Hartshorne and Karl Barth*. Oxford: Oxford University Press, 1978.

Gutierrez, Gustavo. *A Theology of Liberation*. Translated by Sister Caridad Inda and John Eagleson. London: SCM Press, 1974.

Hocking, Richard. "The Polarity of Dialectical History and Process Cosmology." *The Christian Scholar* 50 (Fall 1967): 177–83.

Johnson, A. H. "Truth, Beauty and Goodness' in the Philosophy of A.N. Whitehead." *Philosophy and Science* 11 (January 1944): 9–29.
—— *Whitehead and His Philosophy*. Lanham, Maryland: University Press of America, 1983.

Leclerc, Ivor. "Community, the State, and the National Society." Unpublished manuscript delivered at the International Society for Metaphysics meeting held in Nairobi on August 14–19, 1981.

—— "Metaphysics and the Theory of Society." Unpublished manuscript delivered at the International Society for Metaphysics meeting, London, 1980.

Leyden, W. von. *Hobbes and Locke: The Politics of Freedom and Obligation*. London: The Macmillan Press, 1982.

Loomer, Bernard. "Two Conceptions of Power." *Process Studies* 6/1 (Spring 1976): 5–32.

Marsh, James L., and William S. Hamrick. "Whitehead and Marx: Toward a Political Metaphysics." *Philosophy Today* 3/4 (1984): 191–202.

McWilliams, Warren. "Daniel Day William's Vulnerable and Invulnerable God." *Encounter* 44/1 (Winter 1983): 73–89.

Meeks, M. Douglas. "God's Suffering Power and Liberation." *Journal of Religious Thought* 33/2 (1976): 44–54.

Meynell, Hugo. "The Theology of Hartshorne." *The Journal of Theological Studies* N.S. 24 (1973): 143–57.

Miliband, Ralph. *Marxism and Politics.* Oxford: Oxford University Press, 1977.

Milne, A. J. M. *The Social Philosophy of English Idealism.* London: George Allen and Unwin, 1962.

Moltmann, Jürgen. *The Future of Creation.* Translated by Margaret Kohl. London: SCM Press, 1979.
—— *Hope and Planning.* Translated by Margaret Clarkson. London: SCM Press, 1971.
—— *Religion, Revolution, and the Future.* Translated by Douglas Meeks. New York: Charles Scribner's Sons, 1968.
—— *Theology of Hope.* Translated by James W. Leitch. London: SCM Press, 1967.
—— and F. Herzog, eds. *The Future of Hope.* New York: Herder and Herder, 1970.

Neville, Robert C. *The Cosmology of Freedom.* New Haven: Yale University Press, 1974.
—— *Creativity and God: A Challenge to Process Theology.* New York: The Seabury Press, 1980.

Nicholls, David. "Positive Liberty, 1880–1914." *American Political Science Review* 56 (1962): 114–28.

Nisbet, Robert A. *The Sociology of Emile Durkheim.* New York: Oxford University Press, 1974.

Ogden, Schubert M. *Faith And Freedom: Toward a Theology of Liberation.* Belfast: Christian Journals, 1979.
—— "The Metaphysics of Faith and Justice." *Process Theology* 14/2 (Summer 1985): 87–101.
—— *The Point of Christology.* London: SCM Press, 1982.

Parsons, Howard L. "History as Viewed by Marx and Whitehead." *The Christian Scholar* 50 (Fall 1967): 273–89.

Ryan, Alan. *J. S. Mill.* London: Routledge and Kegan Paul, 1974.

Shaw, William H. *Marx's Theory of History.* London: Hutchinson and Co., 1978.

Spencer, Herbert. *The Man Versus the State.* London: Williams and Norgate, 1884.

Wegener, Frank C. "Alfred N. Whitehead: An Implied Philosophy of School and Society." Bibliographical details unknown.

Whitney, Barry L. "Process Theism: Does a Persuasive God Coerce?" *Southern Journal of Philosophy* 17 (1979): 133–43.

Williams, Daniel Day. "How Does God Act?" *Process and Divinity: Philosophical Essays Presented to Charles Hartshorne.* Edited by William L. Reese and Eugene Freeman. Lasalle, Ill.: Open Court Publishing, 1964.

Woollard, A. G. B. *Progress: A Christian Doctrine?* London: SPCK, 1972.

Young, Robert M. "Malthus and the Evolutionists: The Common Context of Biological And Social Theory." *Past and Present,* 43 (May 1969): 109–45.

# Index

## A

Actual entities, 206; conditioned by environment, 25, 27–29, 43; description of, 23–24, 26, 27, 74; freedom of, 28–29, 30–33, 41–42, 229 n.14; mental pole of, 30, 40; social nature of, 28, 43

Adventure, 176–80, 181, 182, 199, 204–8

Aesthetics, 87–88, 144, 186–87, 192, 241 nn.65, 66. *See also* Beauty

Allan, George, 43, 224 n.10

Anaesthesia, 177, 192, 206, 260 n.4

Analogy, 83; Hartshorne's use of, 136–37, 212; Whitehead's use of, 43–45, 100, 117, 231 n.26

Anselm, 55

Apostles, The, 173, 174, 186

Aristocracy. *See* Monarchy

Aristotle, 174, 176

Atomism, 23, 68, 71. *See also* Individualism

## B

Beauty, 87–89, 94, 96, 97, 175, 176, 178, 192–93, 198, 204, 205, 210

Bentham, Jeremy, 80, 125, 126, 127, 168–69

Berlin, Isaiah, 150, 255 n.55

Bonino, Jose Miguez, 215, 216, 217, 218, 220

Bosanquet, Bernard, 12, 13, 130, 139, 198, 211

Bradley, F. H., 12, 70, 267 n.73

Burke, Edmond, 44

## C

Calvin, John, 248 n.46

Capitalism, 101–102, 114, 115, 140–47, 152–53, 157, 256 n.61

Causation: efficient, 24, 25, 27–29, 40, 41, 44, 63, 182; final, 24, 25, 40, 41. 63–64; Hartshorne's theory of, 48–53, 59, 137; and memory, 48–49

Chance, 134–35, 137, 141, 145

Classical economics, 140–41, 193

Classical liberalism, 60, 90, 98, 111, 113, 114, 116, 125, 155

Classical theology, 59, 100–101; political implications of, 91, 117–18, 166

Cobb, John B., Jr., 3, 19, 32, 178, 214, 215, 218–21, 256 n.65

Coercion, 114, 130, 134, 137–38, 156, 161, 163–71, 185–86, 198, 251 n.78. *See also* Force; Competition; State Intervention

Cohen, G. A., 201

Collectivism, 12, 81–82, 84, 85, 90, 201

Collini, Stefan, 12, 225 nn.25, 33, 239 n.44

Common good, 82, 83, 89–100, 101, 128, 135, 149, 155, 157–58, 197, 198, 200, 201–3, 207, 208, 242 n.69, 270 n.113

Communism, 125. *See also* Marxism; Socialism

Competition, 111–12, 115, 122–23, 124, 141, 142, 144, 145, 146, 154, 158, 189, 190, 193, 264 n.46

Concrescence, 24, 25, 30–33, 96

Love, 155, 156, 157, 165–66, 197, 201, 207

Lowe, Victor, 44, 186, 231 n.28, 265 n.53

Lucas, George R., Jr., 14, 15, 71, 72, 229 n.16, 265 n.53

# M

Macpherson, C. B., 125, 153, 236 n.4

Malthus, 173, 189, 190

Mannheim, Karl, 16–17, 216

Marx, Karl, 16, 262 n.26

Marxism, 209, 211, 213, 214, 219, 253 n.21, 262 n.26. See also Socialism

Materialism, scientific, 68–70

McTaggart, J. M. E., 12, 13

Metz, Johann Baptist, 216, 217

Mill, John Stuart, 11, 60, 125–28, 148, 150, 187, 188, 194, 211, 241 n.67, 249 n.51; and progress, 183, 184–86; and self-development, 158–59

Modern liberalism, 9, 18, 132; and capitalism, 148, 153, 256 n.61; and the common good, 89, 128, 157, 201–3; and equality, 104–105, 116; and human nature, 104–105, 127–28; and human rights, 86, 99; and idealism, 12–14, 195; and social theory, 81–84, 102; and state intervention, 111, 148, 159

Moltmann, Jürgen, 219–20

Monarchy, 119; society of actual entities as, 77, 79, 119–21

Monopoly, 59, 122–23, 141–44, 166

Moore, G. E., 49

Moral codes, 86, 92

Moskop, John C., 146

# N

Nairn, Thomas, 146

Needham, Joseph, 4

Newton, Issac, 69

Nicholls, David, 100–102, 117

Novelty, 39, 41, 138, 176, 177, 180, 181, 182, 183

# O

Ontological principle, 25, 27, 30, 32, 35

Order, 39–41, 176, 177, 180, 182, 192, 260 n.7. See also Uniformity

Organic mechanism, 70, 75–76

Organic monism, 73, 76, 90

Organic sympathy. See Sympathy

Organicism: Hartshorne's theory of, 76–78, 89, 90, 100, 124, 171, 210; principles of, 70, 74–76, 81, 83; Whitehead's theory of, 27, 73–76, 78–79, 85, 89, 94, 97–98, 99, 100, 193, 237 nn.15, 18, 21, 238 n.25

Organism: meanings of, 73–74, 76–77

# P

Pacifism, 156, 160, 163–67

Panpsychism, 48–49

Participation. See Sympathy

Peace, 204, 206–8

Persuasion, 33, 130, 138, 160, 170, 186, 198–99

Peters, Eugene, 58, 232 n.11

Phillips, D. C., 71

Pixley, George, 220, 221

Plato, 27, 35, 36, 174, 187, 193, 229 n.20

Political theology, 214, 216–19

Possibility, 51–52
Preferences, private. *See* Interest, preferential theory of
Prehension, 26–27, 87, 192, 193, 233 n.21; conceptual, 27; physical, 27, 28
Process, 24, 174, 175, 176; *See also* Concrescence; Transition
Process philosophy: and ideology, 15–19, 100–102, 114, 136, 145–47, 156–57, 211–14, 219, 245 n.100
Process theology: and political theory, 3, 4, 19, 214, 218–21
Professions, 187–88
Progress, 157–58, 174, 176–94, 200, 203; criterion of, 82, 84, 89, 191, 192, 200, 203, 257 n.73, 268 n.96; freedom necessary for, 182–84, 188, 191, 208, 262 n.22, 263 n.32
Providence, 59, 60–61, 63, 135–37, 145–46, 165, 205, 252 n.7

**R**

Raphael, D. D., 29
Relations, asymmetrical, 51, 56, 72, 73, 228 n.4, 236 n.12, 237 n.15. *See also* Internal relations; External relations
Richter, Melvin, 207
Rights: Hartshorne's theory of, 98–99, 114, 116, 137, 212; natural, 82, 85, 113, 114; relative to society, 82, 86, 99; Whitehead's theory of, 85–86, 99
Ritchie, David, 12, 150, 246 n.16, 264 n.46
Roberts, John, 95, 243 n.85
Rogers, James Allen, 265 n.61
Rousseau, J. J., 95, 96

**S**

Samuel, Herbert, 12, 151
Satisfaction, 24, 26, 27, 40, 41, 97, 192
Schroeder, W. Widick, 244 n.95, 245 n.100, 263 n.34
Segundo, Juan L., 215
Self-determination, 30–33, 59–60
Self-development, 95, 96, 110–12, 127–31, 157–60, 193, 197, 203, 256 n.64
Self-reliance, 107, 108, 111, 139, 148
Sessions, William Lad, 57
Simons, Henry, 10, 122–23, 142, 143, 144, 145, 214
Social Darwinism, 81, 188–89, 190, 193, 265 n.61
Social development. *See* Progress
Socialism, 122, 123, 141, 143, 145, 220
Society: of actual entities, 40–43, 73–74, 75, 77; instrumental value of, 88–89, 90, 92, 210, 242 n.73; organic theory of, 81–84, 154; perfection of, 93–94, 174–75, 177–78, 180–81, 182, 199, 207, 210, 260 n.5; of persons, 42, 73–74
Spencer, Herbert, 188, 189, 190
State intervention, 110–111, 112, 136–46, 148–50, 159
Sturm, Douglas, 86, 244 n.95
Subjective aim, 24, 25, 32–33, 129; as ideal, 31
Substance, 26, 47–48, 49, 70
Surrelativism, 56, 59
Sympathy, 47–49, 62, 116–17, 119, 120–21, 128, 161, 162–63, 258 n.90; limited, 107–108, 116, 117, 123–26, 141, 161, 163, 212

**T**

Taylor, Charles, 179
Theodicy, 205–6